"The astounding tale of Louis Bromfield, a rare and accomplished figure who has vanished from collective memory, despite his importance to issues ranging from organic food to the ephemeral nature of fame. An engaging and fascinating book on many levels."

—Mark Kurlansky, author of *Cod* and *Salt*

"Filled with fascinating anecdotes, thoughtful analysis and graceful writing . . . a concise, compelling biography."

—Marylynne Pitz, *Pittsburgh Post-Gazette*

"Heyman brings this champion of the organic food movement to life."

—Sophie Bushwick, *Scientific American*

"Bromfield's journey of discovery reinforces growing calls to rebuild healthy, fertile soil around the world. . . . [I]nspirational."

—David R. Montgomery, *Nature*

"Heyman shows an agility of style and deftness in handling technical subjects. He can explain important concepts in soil health and farm economics in a few, clear sentences. What's more, in Heyman's hands, these pages do not read as boring interludes between the wild story of Bromfield's life, but as an organic part of the story."

—Nathan Beacom, *Front Porch Republic*

"Louis Bromfield is the author and renaissance farmer you have never heard of but wish you had. . . . This 'Sinatra of the soil' was dismissed by many as a populist writer of potboiler novels who dabbled in gentleman farming, yet his techniques were revolutionary and are still in use today."   —Christopher Kimball, *Milk Street*

"You don't have to be someone very interested in farming or gardening to find this book engrossing."   —WOSU-Columbus NPR

"I couldn't put this book down. Few farmer-writers could fire the imagination more than Louis Bromfield. . . . In this wonderful biography, Stephen Heyman pulls the curtain back so those of us who practically idolized this bigger-than-life soil spokesman can finally understand the complicated man behind the legend."

—Joel Salatin, founder of Polyface Farm

"Bromfield drew attention to social and ecological issues that remain of critical importance, and Heyman has performed a most valuable service by producing such a lucid account of this extraordinary and appealing man."   —Philip Conford, *Agricultural History Review*

"Here is a splendid biography from which you will learn things you never suspected, a book that will renew your faith in passion and what Louis Bromfield called those peculiarly American traits: integrity and idealism. . . . It is also exactly the sort of book to read right now, when we are stuck in our homes, and, if we are lucky, watching the landscape grow greener and thinking about starting our own gardens."

—Roberta Silman, *Arts Fuse*

"Heyman marshals meticulous detail, unflinching appraisal, indelible personalities, and rich character study in a narrative that straddles worlds and eras and never flags. These elements coalesce within a fluid, remarkably propulsive writing style that keeps the pages turning. . . . An outstanding debut."   —*Kirkus Reviews*, starred review

"In this delightful and exhilarating page-turner, which takes readers from Bromfield's native ground in Ohio to Paris and back again, Heyman does an impressive job of combining all of Bromfield's interests into a cohesive narrative that captivates as both intriguing history and a significant look at early environmentalism. . . . Heyman's biography has huge crossover appeal and it is a sure bet for book groups." —*Booklist*, starred review

"Skillfully written, assiduously reported. . . . *The Planter of Modern Life* . . . makes a sturdy case that Bromfield was a pivot in the environmental movement's transition from 'the *Dust Bowl* and *The Grapes of Wrath* to Earth Day and *Silent Spring.*'"

—Nell Beram, *Shelf Awareness*, starred review

The Planter of Modern Life

HOW AN OHIO FARM BOY CONQUERED LITERARY PARIS, FED THE LOST GENERATION, AND SOWED THE SEEDS OF THE ORGANIC FOOD MOVEMENT

Stephen Heyman

W. W. NORTON & COMPANY
Independent Publishers Since 1923

Since this page cannot legibly accommodate all the copyright notices, pages 329–30
constitute an extension of the copyright page.

For information about permission to reproduce selections from this book, write to
Permissions, W. W. Norton & Company, Inc., 500 Fifth Avenue, New York, NY 10110

For information about special discounts for bulk purchases, please contact
W. W. Norton Special Sales at specialsales@wwnorton.com or 800-233-4830

Manufacturing by Lake Book Manufacturing
Book design by Michelle McMillian
Production manager: Beth Steidle

The Library of Congress has catalogued the hardcover edition of this book as follows:

Names: Heyman, Stephen, author.
Title: The planter of modern life : Louis Bromfield and the seeds
of a food revolution / Stephen Heyman.
Description: First edition. | New York : W. W. Norton & Company, [2020] |
Includes bibliographical references and index.
Identifiers: LCCN 2019044443 | ISBN 9781324001898 (hardcover) |
ISBN 9781324001904 (epub)
Subjects: LCSH: Bromfield, Louis, 1896–1956—Homes and haunts—Ohio. | Authors,
American—20th century—Biography. | Authors, American—Homes and haunts—Ohio. |
Agriculture—Ohio—History—20th century. | Farm life—Ohio—History—20th century.
| Ohio—Intellectual life—20th century. | Farmers—Ohio—Biography.
Classification: LCC PS3503.R66 Z756 2020 | DDC 813/.52 [B]—dc23
LC record available at https://lccn.loc.gov/2019044443

ISBN 978-0-393-86846-3 pbk.

W. W. Norton & Company, Inc., 500 Fifth Avenue, New York, N.Y. 10110
www.wwnorton.com

W. W. Norton & Company Ltd., 15 Carlisle Street, London W1D 3BS

1 2 3 4 5 6 7 8 9 0

For Yana,
and for her mother, Ida Litovsky,
who was also a little *teched*

He began by looking at life, and only later
did he acquire the means to express it.

—CHARLES BAUDELAIRE, "The Painter of Modern Life"

Contents

Introduction

Almost a century ago, in a market town some 30 miles north of Paris, there lived a young American who had leased an old rectory and converted it into a comfortable home for his family. He installed a giant gramophone and an ornate bar, furnished the place with antiques, painted exotic jungle scenes on the walls. *Vogue* photographed the interiors, making the house look airy and spacious, when in fact it could barely accommodate its inhabitants: the man, his wife, their three young daughters, the nanny, the cook, the secretary, the gardener, and the pet animals, which included a Scottish terrier, an Indian mongoose, and a pony named Peter.

Among ordinary people in Europe and America, the man was famous for the novels he wrote. Among famous people, however, he was known for his flowers. Every Sunday, he hosted a party in his garden, which stretched out over 2 acres along a narrow river lined with linden and poplar trees. Most of the guests were uninvited. They came from Paris, although only a few were French. They arrived in Rolls-Royces, Bugatti roadsters, and Fords from the American embassy. Each week somebody new turned up: an Indian maharani, a White Russian prince, a scattering of Rothschilds. They mingled with the regulars: foreign correspondents, fashion designers, flower breeders, art collectors, movie stars, maybe a few spies. They served themselves from a lopsided buffet, pouring Champagne and brandy, digging into potato salad, goose-liver pâté, slices of charcuterie, finishing off with coffee and cake and strawberries from the garden. Then they sat on the grass, smoking, admiring the flowers: the marigolds, the blue Himalayan poppies, the hybrid musk roses that hung in bushes from the little wooden bridge spanning the river.

A few of them took the time to study their host, and weren't quite sure what to make of him. His clothing, one French visitor noted, combined "the shirt of a gangster, the trousers of a student, and the slippers of a peanut salesman." His interests were similarly mismatched. His friend Janet Flanner, Paris correspondent for *The New Yorker*, described his conversation as a mixture of "old-fashioned French, the latest Broadway slang, dukes' and duchesses' first names, discussions on farm manures, Paris politics, Bombay palace intrigues, modern European painting, Golden Bantam corn, the operas of Richard Strauss, and the best way to cook hamburgers."

He was in his mid-thirties then. Even those who cared nothing for his two great passions—books and gardens—could tell that, in pursuit of them, he had already learned something valuable about life. He may not have been a literary genius like the newspapers claimed, but he had acquired, as one admirer put it, a "genius for living." Exactly where this genius came from was unclear to his friends, and where it would take him they certainly could not imagine as they sipped rosé or swam in the river, trading gossip and talking up the next novel they would fail to write, or the long vacation they would soon take, inhaling all the fragrant possibilities of an easy, expatriate existence that was soon to disappear forever.

—•—

If Louis Bromfield ever appears in a book today, he is shoved into parentheses or buried without ceremony in a footnote. If we remember him at all, it is only as a character in somebody else's story. As Humphrey

Bogart's best man, say, or Doris Duke's lover. As Gertrude Stein's protégé or Edith Wharton's gardening guru. As Ernest Hemingway's enemy or Eleanor Roosevelt's pain in the ass. What is surprising is not that he has his own story to tell, but that, six decades after his death, that story suddenly feels important.

Bromfield was first, if not foremost, a novelist. He belonged to Stein's "Lost Generation," the group of American artists who came of age in the 1920s, and in outline his biography conforms perfectly to type: He had the restless, middle-class, Midwestern boyhood; the unfinished Ivy League education; the adventure under fire as a World War I ambulance driver; the sojourn in Paris. There was alcohol, infidelity. There was a rapid rise, a slow, pathetic fall, and then, in his case, a precipitous drop into obscurity. Today he is little read and, outside of northeastern Ohio, hardly known. That his fame would vanish would probably not have upset him. "The most important thing in life is the pleasure you can extract from it," he told the society chronicler Lucius Beebe in 1935, while nursing a rye whiskey before his latest play opened on Broadway. "Only the young and foolish worry about posthumous reputations."

The point of this book is not to argue for a fresh evaluation of Bromfield's literary work, even though he was, at least in commercial terms, among the most successful writers of his generation. His 1926 novel, *Early Autumn*, won the Pulitzer Prize. In that decade he was regarded more highly by the literary establishment than Fitzgerald or Hemingway—a fact that would later baffle critics. Millions of his books were printed in every major language. Most of his thirty-odd works became bestsellers, and many were adapted by Hollywood, including *The Rains Came* (1939), an Orientalist fantasia set in India that won the first Academy Award for special effects.

In politics, too, Bromfield made his mark: rescuing American volunteers from the Abraham Lincoln Brigade who were trapped in prisons or hospitals at the end of the Spanish Civil War; funneling money to Free French forces during World War II; hectoring his many powerful friends in Washington—including a dismissive Eleanor Roosevelt—to do more to stop the Nazi slaughter of European Jews; and chairing committees that would help support the founding of the state of Israel.

Such political and literary exploits are the bread and butter of biographies. But this is not a story about a popular writer or a celebrity host or an influential pundit. Yes, Bromfield was all those things, but, above everything else, he was a farmer. He made his greatest impact not on the page but in the soil. He devoted his life to protecting and reviving this precious resource, a resource that was as mistreated and as misunderstood in his time as it is in our own. What Bromfield said in 1942 is perhaps even truer today: "Most of our citizens do not realize what is going on under their very feet."

—·—

Long before climate science and climate skeptics, before fracking and "Drill, Baby, Drill" and the BP Oil Spill, before food co-ops and the *Whole Earth Catalog*, before Earth Day and Rachel Carson's *Silent Spring*, there were environmental problems in this country and environmentalists who tried to fix them. They called themselves conservationists. They had seen, in their own backyards, man-made environmental disasters on par with some of the darker predictions in the latest UN Climate Report: floods, widespread soil erosion, apocalyptic dust storms, vanishing wildlife, and mass migration. By trade they were farmers and scientists, writers and bureaucrats, businessmen and social theorists. Their motivations were different, but most of them were pushed into action by the Dust Bowl and the Great Depression—the "Dirty Thirties," as these years are sometimes known. The books they wrote would go on to inspire the first modern environmentalists, the earliest self-described organic farmers, the avant-garde in the ongoing campaign for clean water, clean air, and a healthier, more sustainable food system.

For nearly two decades, from the late 1930s until his death in 1956, Louis Bromfield was this group's greatest champion. He began his work with the "foolish idea" that he could be the first of a "new race of pioneers," not the sort who "cut down the forests and burned off the prairies and raped the land" but pioneers who "created new forests and healed and restored the richness of the country"—a richness that, "from the moment the first settler landed on the Atlantic Coast, we had done our best to destroy." He wrote those words in *Pleasant Valley*, his environmental testament, which became one of the best-selling nonfiction books of 1945. At that time, the country was just exiting the cataclysm of World War II. Yet hundreds of thousands of Americans wanted to read about green manures and Jeffersonian dreams. That book gave many Americans the fantasy—or the illusion—that they, too, could find the kind of natural, self-sufficient life that Bromfield had built for himself.

Today Bromfield should be remembered because he sounded one of the earliest alarms about DDT and other harmful pesticides and began the fight for a modern agriculture that would enrich the soil and protect the planet. But perhaps more significantly, he should be remembered as one of the first figures of national prominence to both celebrate *and* problematize food, to connect it to politics and art and health and ecology. In this way, he anticipated a variety of figures from our own time, from activist farmers (like Wes Jackson and Joel Salatin) to free-range essayists (like Wendell Berry, Joan Dye Gussow, and Michael Pollan) to advocates for slow and storied food (like Alice Waters, Dan Barber, and Anthony Bourdain).

———

As much as Bromfield's story is a biography of a person, it is also a biography of a landscape—or, rather, two landscapes. The first is the garden he built in interwar France. This began its life as a literary salon of unusual distinction. But it became a kind of field laboratory, the place where he discovered—with a little help from his French peasant neighbors, and a little more from his literary gardener friends like Gertrude Stein and Edith Wharton—how to collapse the distance between literature and agriculture, how to put his love of the land on the page. The other landscape is

Malabar Farm, which he established in 1939 in Richland County, Ohio, halfway between Cleveland and Columbus. It is difficult to summarize the peculiar significance of Malabar, which the *New York Herald Tribune* described in 1955 as "the best-known farm in America, probably in the world." Today preserved as a state park, Malabar still ranks among history's more unusual pastoral experiments, where Bromfield deployed a mix of organic fertilizer and savvy PR to transform 600 barren acres into a literary-agrarian utopia—Voltaire's Ferney crossed with Old Mac-Donald's Farm.

And so, Bromfield's story is split, just like this book, between a garden and a farm, between France and Ohio. But the story is not confined to these places; instead it travels from the American heartland and Lost Generation Paris to Jazz Age New York, British India, Hollywood, and the jungles of Brazil. While the book is chiefly focused on food and farming, there are also dashes of literary drama, society gossip, and political shenanigans thrown in for good measure. Bromfield would have approved of that. He cultivated this hybrid life, which, he once joked, was divided between "nightclubs and manure piles." He began his final memoir, *From My Experience*, with a note that apologized to the reader in advance if he or she experienced whiplash after encountering so many divergent subjects in a single volume.

> It is possible that to some this book may seem lacking in organization, but this is not so. In the mind of the author at least, the materials have been put together with cunning, much as the use of bait leads an animal into a trap. Some of the chapters require hard concentration on the techniques of farming, some are concerned with philosophical reflection, and others may seem light to the point of triviality . . . In any case, life on a living farm, with its countless facets, its daily crises, its seasonal changes, resembles very closely the general pattern of this book—a record of ups and downs, which must be taken, if at all, as they come.

PART ONE

GARDEN

(1918–1938)

1

Foreign Soil

The boys had an hour to spend on shore before returning to the ship to sleep. They ran for the cafés and shops along the waterfront. His wobbliness, the fading nausea, seemed only to increase the interest he took in everything around him. The ancient houses along the harbor were made of stone and crooked black beams of wood. Some jutted out over the cobbled streets that ran perpendicular to the waterfront. One row of shadowy wooden buildings had names painted on their sides: À LA DEMI LUNE, LA BELLE DU JOUR. These were the brothels. He was far too timid, his appetites more basic. He found a cheese shop, like any other in France, to him a deep well of mystery, guarded by a full-bosomed woman in black bombazine. A tangy, almost embarrassingly intense odor filled the damp little room. He had never smelled anything like it. The only cheeses he knew were cottage cheese and cheddar—or "rat cheese," as his parents back in Ohio called it. But here there were at least thirty kinds, from the little pyramided goat cheeses to the thick Bries that lay on fresh straw. He knew none of their names. He pointed, he used his schoolboy French, and a few minutes later he had assembled a picnic: the cheese, a bottle of cold red wine, a pat of fresh butter, and a hard, fragrant ball of bread that was pillowy on the inside. Many years later, recalling that foggy night from a green-and-white farmhouse in the American Midwest, he would describe his meal in Brest as "one of the great gastronomic memories of my life."

He was twenty-one years old, six feet two inches tall, 151 pounds. The medic who gave him his army physical described his body as "hard and wiry." He had his mother's small blue eyes, sandy hair that he combed back, and big, pointy ears that gave him the guileless look of a young deer. The grin on his face was the product of shyness. His classmates mistook him for lighthearted—"the gayest of the gay" was the caption in his high school yearbook—but inside he felt twitchy, frustrated, anxious to be rid of himself, to become someone else. He was younger than his years, a virgin, whose desires and instincts were trapped by his upbringing, that double brace of Calvinist religion and Victorian manners. The only education he valued was the one he got on his grandfather's farm: how to milk cows, hunt mushrooms, plant a field of corn. But that rural life was now something to bury, as much a mark of shame as the homespun clothes his mother had forced him to wear to school. Years later, in a half-written, never-published memoir, he would refer to the young boy who had just stepped foot onto France after sixteen days at sea as nothing more than a "yokel."

Louis Bromfield was born on December 27, 1896, in Mansfield, Ohio, but in many respects his life began with his service as a volunteer ambulance driver during World War I. As soon as he landed in Brest on January 10, 1918, he felt a "strange, new vitality" sweep through him. "It was an odd feeling, a sensation of suddenly being born, if one could only remember what that was like." His war would not only be a baptism by fire but also an initiation into a world of pleasure, an experience so intense and new it scrambled the valence of things. Good or bad, whatever he encountered in France fascinated him: the smell of ripe Camembert, the stink of trench foot, a field of scarlet poppies, a line of freshly dug graves. This reaction was typical. So many Americans who came to France talked about the way the battlefields entwined the idyllic with the horrific. "The country is zig-zagged with secondary and tertiary trenches and bristles with barbed wire entanglements," wrote one ambulance driver, "but all around and in every direction the peasants are tilling the fields and the crops are growing." At Verdun, in August 1916, the philanthropist Anne Vanderbilt said that what truly astonished her "more than any of the apparatuses of war were the trailing vines and other wild flowers that covered these descents into hell as if they had been peaceful garden walks." The literary critic Malcolm Cowley, who volunteered as a French supply driver in 1917, thought it was the nearness of death that made the landscape look so alive. "The trees were green, not like ordinary trees, but like trees in the still moment before a hurricane," he wrote in *Exile's Return*. "The sky was a special and ineffable blue; the grass smelled of life itself; the image of death at twenty, the image of love, mingled together into a keen, precarious delight."

Cowley and Bromfield belonged to an extraordinarily large and talented group of American writers who served as ambulance or supply drivers in the First World War. The list includes figures who are still literary giants (Ernest Hemingway, John Dos Passos, E. E. Cummings) along with a catalog of the once-famous and now largely forgotten (Archibald MacLeish, Harry Crosby, Julien Green, William Seabrook, William Slater Brown, John Howard Lawson). They all had their reasons for volunteering: Some, like Dos Passos and Cummings, were pacifists who wanted to make a humanitarian statement. Others, like Hemingway and Bromfield, craved adventure. "I can't let a show like this go on without getting into it," Hemingway wrote his sister. "It is better to be killed," Bromfield told his mother, "than to miss the greatest experience of your generation." Different things pushed them into war but the lessons they would take out of it were practically identical. Cowley described the ambulance corps as a "college extension" program for "a whole generation of American writers." Its courses taught "courage, extravagance, fatalism, these being the virtues of men at war; they taught us to regard as vices the civilian virtues of thrift, caution and sobriety; they made us fear boredom more than death." \

Gertrude Stein and Edith Wharton—two authors diametrically opposed in style who, as it happens, would become two of Bromfield's closest friends in France after the war—both delivered aid to the front lines in their automobiles. Wharton transformed herself into a one-woman juggernaut—"the great generalissima," as her friend Henry James put it. She wrote anti-German propaganda, organized a suite of charity efforts in Paris, and delivered supplies to front-line hospitals for the French Red Cross in a giant Mercedes. The bloodshed was "unimaginable," Wharton wrote—"just one long senseless slaughter"—yet she could not help noting "the picturesqueness" of the front, and the "exquisite" feeling of getting so near to the action.

Gertrude Stein also devoted herself to her adopted homeland, where she had lived since 1903. She and her partner, Alice B. Toklas, couldn't find a car to buy in Paris, so Stein had relatives ship them a Ford Model T from America. With a bottle of white wine, they christened it "Auntie," in honor of Stein's aunt Pauline, who always "behaved admirably in emergencies and behaved fairly well most times if she was properly flattered." As volunteers for the American Fund for French Wounded, Stein and Toklas hauled food, medical supplies, and wounded men across France. They kept a copy of the Michelin Guide in Auntie's glove box and made frequent gastronomic pit stops. In Saulieu, rations included pêches flambées prepared "with delicacy and distinction," Toklas said. In Lyon, they bivouacked by a famous bistro run by Mère Fillioux, "an artist," who served them artichokes stuffed with foie gras, pike dumplings (or quenelles) in a rich crayfish sauce, and a succulent truffled chicken, slowly cooked in veal broth and white wine. Stein and Toklas might have been risking their lives for France but, like the other American volunteers, they took their pleasure wherever it came along the road.

Bromfield signed up as an ambulance driver early in the spring of 1917, abandoning his studies at Columbia Journalism School after less than a year to volunteer with the American Field Service (AFS). He lied about his age, claiming he was then not twenty but twenty-one—the minimum age to sign up without parental permission. Since 1915, the AFS had been recruiting young men on the campuses of America's best universities. The first wave of volunteers was required to pay their own way or find rich sponsors, limiting recruits to bluebloods who brought with them a certain "snobbishness." It was not uncommon for these "gentlemen volunteers" to buy bespoke uniforms from a Parisian couturier on the Rue de la Paix or to model themselves on Richard Norton, the courtly son of a Harvard art history professor who sported a monocle at the front.

After America entered the war, in April 1917, the ambulance service radically changed complexion. Now driving an ambulance on the Chemin des Dames appealed not only to dandies who had read too much Stendhal but to any man who wanted to avoid being drafted into the trenches. Although they retained their status as *ambulanciers* attached to sanitary sections of the French military, Bromfield and the other Columbia volunteers were now required to enlist in the regular US Army. Soon Bromfield's company filled with an "incredible assortment of men": dancers, newspapermen, dope peddlers, seminary students.

From the start, Bromfield saw his wartime service in France as an opportunity for self-invention and social climbing. Despite being a lowly private of modest means, he wrote letters about hobnobbing with French nobility, generals' wives, rich expatriates. He worked what tenuous connections he had. When a wealthy old American lady, a certain Mrs. Gibbons, gave the boys in his section her Paris address, most of them ignored the gesture. Bromfield stopped in for tea. "It will do me some good," he told his parents. Later, during a lull in the fighting in the summer of 1918, he claimed to have driven "a celebrated French woman," Mademoiselle Becker, who wore the rosette of the Legion of Honor. They stopped together at a chateau, where they were "entertained royally" by "Madame

Foch," the wife of the supreme Allied commander. "I have rather a good friend," he wrote in another letter to his parents, "the Marquis de Paltz, who has asked me to come to Paris."

While soon enough Bromfield would travel in a world of aristocrats and celebrities, it seems unlikely that an enlisted ambulance driver could have charmed his way into their drawing rooms in the midst of the war. Unlike the details of his military service, there are no records or photographs corroborating these visits in Bromfield's papers. Perhaps he stuffed his letters home with fancy names only to impress his friends and parents. In any case, he was looking for material, a story to tell, and a higher station from which to tell it. "I have a chance to gain something over here no matter how long I'm in the mess," he wrote to a college friend shortly after arriving in Brest. A year later—after he'd seen action at Ypres, Soissons, the Aisne, and the Marne; after he'd carried in his ambulance Germans and French, Arabs and Senegalese; after he bunked with French Legionnaires and dined at the Café de la Paix in Paris—he wrote to her in amazement: "How much more worth knowing must I be than the last time I said goodbye to you."

—•—

His first experience in battle was of retreat. By the spring of 1918, with Russia defeated, Germany was able to divert troops to the western front, achieving a slim 10 percent advantage in manpower over the Allies. This was their moment to strike before summer, when millions of Americans would be arriving to bolster the exhausted British and French troops. Aiming at the weak juncture between those two entrenched armies, the Germans threw everything they had at their enemies: storm troopers, poison gas, rolling barrages of artillery.

It was under this storm of steel that Bromfield learned his new trade. His job was split into two tasks: transporting troops far behind the lines—essentially jitney duty—and the much more dangerous front-line work of collecting the freshly wounded, which would take him as close to the fighting as terrain allowed. His ambulance, a Ford Model T, had two stretchers on the floor and another hanging down from the roof. Normally, the ambulance could fit four seated men (*assis*) or three men lying down (*couchés*). When there were too many wounded, Bromfield could collapse the top stretcher and pack more bodies inside, sometimes making use of the running boards and fenders, which increased his capacity to ten.

His wood-frame ambulance was clad in gray canvas, with a large red cross painted on both sides. Each section decorated their cars with a distinctive symbol. Bromfield's chose a raspberry, a fact he later found "significant." Light and maneuverable, with top speeds of up to 55 miles per hour, his "Katrinka"—as he nicknamed the car for some unknown reason—drove circles around the heavy Fiats used as ambulances by the French. "I can't tell you the genuine affection I have for my Ford and I would rather just drop from exhaustion than let anyone else drive it. One really fears for one's car much more than shells or gas. Nothing can be so horrible as having a motor stop in a '*mauvais coin*' when you are well loaded with wounded."

Like most American ambulance drivers, he spoke a bastard language, English spiced with French words: *pauvres blessés* for the wounded, *casque* for his helmet, *arrivés* for the incoming shells. He drank bad beer in French soldiers' bars, smoked their Algerian tobacco, wore a sheepskin coat and whipcord trousers. He ate macaroni, sardines, and canned beef known as *singe* ("monkey"). And he stained his teeth purple with half-liter rations of cheap wine, the trusty pinard, which one driver said "possessed no subtle bouquet" but was at least "heartening for the morale." He took pride in looking nothing like the American regulars, the doughboys who were just starting to arrive in large numbers. Ambulance service had a kind of gritty glamour but, as Bromfield's friend and fellow driver Larry Barretto noted, "Those who envied [us] forgot that the drivers saw nothing but the maimed, the wreckage of the conflict."

The wounds were ghastly: shrapnel tore open chests and stomachs, mustard gas caused burns and pustular white welts. One driver recalled stopping his Ford to clear a boot from the road only to discover that a foot was still inside it. Bromfield later remembered how he once opened the door of the Hôtel de Ville in Beauchamp to find "the dead literally piled in heaps." He sometimes worked eighteen-hour shifts, driving back and forth from the front-line aid stations known as *postes de secours* to the triage hospitals. In Flanders, at the Battle of the Lys in April, the fighting was so intense that thirteen of the twenty cars in his section were disabled. As the shifts grew longer, the pressure ratcheted up. "I've been so tired and nerve-worn that I almost prayed for a shell to strike me," he wrote to a friend. "It is a terrible responsibility that at times I think I shall go mad."

A break in the fighting came in May. Walking through the damp woods near Amiens, Bromfield noticed what looked like the brain of a small animal attached to a short, hollow stem on the forest floor. The thing was cream-colored and smelled just like spring: like "decaying leaf mold, the new life of ferns and wild flowers." He picked it up and brought it close to his face and was immediately transported back in time to "the thick and fragrant woods of Ohio." He had spent his boyhood hunting these "sponge mushruins" behind his grandfather's farm. He knew that when you found one, others might be nearby. The search yielded enough for a small meal. Back at quarters, the French cook in his outfit was delighted: Bromfield had found not just a mushroom but a gigantic *morille*. They could not find cream or butter, but the French cook sautéed the morels in a thin beef broth—a feast, under the circumstances—and "they turned out very well."

By early summer, the Allies had stalled the German advance. As the French regained ground, the battlefields between the Aisne and Marne Rivers became even more scarred and confusing to navigate. Sometimes, driving his ambulance, Bromfield would get lost and cross enemy lines. Once, he was briefly captured. The Germans respected his red cross and quickly released him but confiscated his uniform. In only his underwear, he snuck back to the French lines and scrounged a British tin hat, a French belt, American trousers, and Belgian boots. "I sure as hell did look international," he said. He mailed a photo of his new getup to his parents, joking about how "Fritz captured all my clothes."

The enemy struck him as less funny that June when, one night on the road into Château-Thierry, his convoy was attacked from above. "The Germans had been dropping bombs on the road ahead and behind us— one of their new tactics—and suddenly two planes swooped along side of the road firing on us with *mitrailleuses*," he wrote to his parents. "The two planes hovered between us and the moon like a vulture while every man lay flat on the ground in a field deep with clover." Bromfield returned to his vehicle unscathed, but troops farther ahead were not as lucky. On the edge of a beech forest, where one of the bombs exploded, he saw four mangled horses, pools of blood, and three dead soldiers lying on the side of the road "in a neat row in the moonlight—one without any face."

———

A massive Allied counterattack began on the eighth of August. For days, the boys in Bromfield's section had been keyed up in a "nervous state of expectation," watching guns and ammunition move to the front. Each night, they expected the attack would commence the following morning. When it finally did, at three in the afternoon, it took them by surprise. Bromfield was *en poste* when the shelling started. Within minutes, he had a load of gassed soldiers on the flatbed of his Model T and was racing toward the triage hospital.

After unloading the wounded, he drove back to the front and could see in the passing landscape snatches of what looked like completely different eras in military history. First he dodged a squadron of mounted cavalry, their "long lances glittering" as they raced down cobblestone streets on "swift little horses covered with lather." Then came the wagon-wheeled 75mm cannons, whose sound alone could blast a driver out of his seat. And finally the terribly modern, Otto Dix hellscape: machine-gun nests, thickets of barbed wire, sandbag dunes, mud, horses stranded in no-man's-land—"mute and the picture of despair."

Bromfield in the summer of 1918 in his makeshift
uniform after "Fritz captured all [his] clothes."

From the *poste*, the drivers could see the whole battlefield "spread out
before our eyes like a great map." He watched as the artillery barrage
climaxed—"a great explosion, gradually gaining intensity until the valley
roared and flashed with guns. . . . I can't describe the effects but it was

like the crescendo of a vast orchestra. . . . One could see the solid wall of flames and smoke bursting on the German trenches." The French were breaking through, the stalemate turning into a war of movement, and the ambulance corps kept pace behind the infantry. Bromfield drove "across roads ploughed by shells and mines, sometimes through fields and literally over villages" that had been wiped from the Earth, that were "simply dust." The shell craters were so large that instead of filling them, the French just bridged them with wood planks. His little Ford bounced hard over the lacerated terrain, each pothole torturing the wounded. "They cry out in spite of themselves," Bromfield wrote. "I can imagine nothing worse." By now, he was seeing all kinds of wounds—not only those made by poison gas, bullets, and shrapnel but, increasingly, bayonet wounds, dark holes that were clean "so long as the men were not left lying on the ground, otherwise corrupt with gangrene working deep into the vitals."

The danger did not dampen his curiosity. He focused on the "uncanny" sound of the German field guns (like a bedsheet tearing), the surreal sight of a truck "made in Detroit" driving down an ancient French road. It felt like the entire world was collapsing into northern France. "The innumerable nationalities bring home the immensity of the struggle," he wrote to his parents. "An American hauls Germans and French wounded to a hospital where they are unloaded by coolies from Tonkin. On the way he passes Italians mending the road and Senegalese guarding German prisoners and perhaps a patrol of Russian cavalry who have remained loyal to the cause and then gives a lift to a kiltie from the great British Empire."

But nothing interested him more than the French countryside, the pear trees trained against old stone walls, the way the "blue evening light seemed to sift down like powder among the trees of the forest." Never mind that he was discovering this magical landscape while it was being systematically devastated. In June 1918, Bromfield sent a remarkable letter home in which he placed his war experience in an almost bucolic setting. "This is really a letter from the front," it begins.

> Just over the hill are the Germans and down the road are breaking the Bosche 77 shells. I'll have to go through them in a few minutes but it won't be such bad fun. I am sitting in the back yard of a big farm against a wall in the shade of some lilacs. And in the midst of all this I am listening to the loveliest music. A French lieutenant is playing Debussy's "Clair de Lune" on a piano that has somehow escaped destruction . . . The little town must have been very beautiful but it is entirely demolished now. The garden is full of shell holes but against the wall are some glorious sweet peas—lovelier than any we have ever raised. At the end of the garden are 37 new graves—the result of an evening's skirmish.

Bromfield goes on to tell his parents about a recent visit to a chateau in the forest where he met a French countess. Her only son was killed in the first year of the war; her nephew, gassed at the front, was then "dying of slow asphyxiation." He ends the letter abruptly with a tender farewell, perhaps aware this could be the last thing he ever writes.

> I must close now. I wish you could enjoy the beauties of this country and be as content as I am. At the garden of the chateau I gathered the most gorgeous armful of roses I have ever seen. They grow wild here. Good bye and God bless you. LOUIS

Here is the pastoral idyll under heavy fire. The letter is more than an artifact of a sensitive soldier faced with the beastliness of war. It also marks the beginning of Bromfield's life as a conservationist—the first of many times when he will look out on a ruined landscape and see fertile ground.

2

Invasive Species

Every man of talent, every artist, every man worthy of the name,
every cock with brilliant plumage, spreads his wings and flies to Paris.
—HONORÉ DE BALZAC

He remembered arriving at the party with F. Scott Fitzgerald and think-ing that they did not belong there, that they were both "slummers" in this crowd. Success was the problem. Their books sold too well, their stories appeared in magazines that were too big and lowbrow—the sort Ezra Pound referred to as "Ladies' Home Urinal" and "Vanity Puke." In short, they had money, so they were able to rent grand apartments on the stuffy Right Bank. They felt more at ease on that side of the river, drink-ing cocktails at the bar of the Ritz, than in this world of self-conscious bohemianism. It wasn't the dampness and poverty of Montparnasse they minded so much as the quantity of Americans. The dollar had recently doubled in value against the franc. Hyperinflation was good when you wanted a second bottle of Champagne, but less good when you saw your countrymen swanning around Paris with 100-franc notes pasted onto their suitcases in place of steamer tickets. The Dôme and the Sélect had been invaded by tourists—or "Neanderthals," as Fitzgerald called them, "with the human value of Pekinese, bivalves, cretins, goats."

The Americans gathered in this room, however, were of a different species. Bromfield was amused by the appearance of a short, stolid woman with close-cropped gray hair who walked into the atelier like a "distinguished Roman empress" but who looked like she had just knocked off a secondhand shop. She wore old doughboy boots, gray army-issue wool socks folded over the laces, an aviator's cap made of leopard skin, a heavy pink crepe de chine dress, and a khaki sweater fastened at the throat by a sunburst brooch. Gertrude Stein knew to dress in layers because it was always freezing in Ford Madox Ford's studio, where the only heating came from a very small oil stove.

To stay warm, you drank. Ford liked to set out fancy liqueurs and French brandies next to bootleg gin brought back from a recent trip to New York. A gramophone played some old, prewar ballad like "My Melancholy Baby," but it was usually drowned out by the talk, or more specifically, by the opinions of the assembled expatriates. By now they had become famous for their opinions. They could tell you why Dada was silly and why Joyce was not, what the best brand of Cognac was and whether Prohibition would ever end—which was just another way of wondering when they would go home. Or maybe they would never go home. They had all come to Paris meaning to be writers or painters or singers, having fled "the materialism of America in order to 'grow' and express themselves," Bromfield later wrote.

Nearly all of them lived in tiny rooms or chilly apartments on the Left Bank on small allowances sent from good, solid, middle-class American families. Most of the day and a good part of the night they spent at sidewalk cafes talking about the work they meant to do. There was some free love involved, and now and then a case of adolescent alcoholism, but one had the feeling that most of them *worked* at these things, driven by the sheer determination to be bohemian. It was all rather like a game played by children, with the same gaiety and pretense—on the whole a pleasant, tinselly world—while it lasted.

The air in the two-level studio on the Rue Notre-Dame-des-Champs was dank and smoky, the atmosphere full of "hearty alcoholic laughter, horseplay and petting." Bromfield easily identified Ford: tall, tweedy, walrus-mustached and "fat in a soft, blubbery way." He was given to dancing, or at least to his own approximation of dancing, which involved prancing and gasping for air through his false teeth (the originals had been knocked out by a German shell in 1916). Ford was not surprised to discover that Bromfield came from Ohio. The Midwest, he said, was then "seething with literary impulse." Eight out of every ten manuscripts he had received as editor of the Paris-based *transatlantic review* seemed to come "from west of Altoona."

Among the many Midwestern writers at the party was a well-built twenty-six-year-old who seemed to Bromfield a bit shy around "so many spectacular people." He had a thick mustache and perfect teeth. He was in the middle of a conversation with Stein when Ford walked up behind him, placed a heavy hand on his shoulder, and "wafted him away."

"Young man," he said, pulling rank, "it is I who wish to speak to Gertrude Stein."

Ernest Hemingway could not have enjoyed being brushed aside like this. An ex-newspaperman, only recently committed to a full-time fiction career, he was still largely unknown beyond the literary journals of the Left Bank. As much as it killed him, he needed to cozy up to writers with connections, especially the ones in this room: Ford, Fitzgerald, and the new guy, Bromfield, who had just swept into Paris after publishing two successful novels, and who would soon be singled out by the *New York Times* as "the most promising of all the young American authors writing today."

—+—

Bromfield arrived in Paris after six busy years in New York City. He had been discharged from the army in the summer of 1919. Instead of finishing his studies at Columbia, he took an honorary "war degree" and set out looking for work. His mother, convinced that her son would become a famous author, had sent his wartime letters to the Mansfield, Ohio, newspapers and succeeded in getting a handful published. Bromfield used these as clips to find his first journalism job. After "vast difficulties," he was hired in 1920 at the New York City News Association, a wire service based in lower Manhattan. He began at the bottom rung as a "white collar slave," a newsboy, then a rewrite man, churning out unsigned stories from a loft on Church Street. In free moments, he read books and magazines and wrote for himself: bad poems, critical jottings, letters to the editor. He worked overnight, from eight p.m. to three a.m., and sometimes escaping the clacking of Underwoods and the clouds of cigar smoke, he walked the harbor, recording what he saw: rubbish fires "glowing in the gutters," coffee and spices "heaped up in the pier sheds that become caverns of the *Arabian Nights* when darkness falls."

His prose was wooden, but he kept whittling away at it, biting his fingernails down to stubs as he sat at his typewriter straining for the next line. He tried to write about everything: murders, subway accidents, French music, English literature. At first he affected the lofty tone of magazines like the *Atlantic Monthly*. "Sit in the corner of any club at an Eastern university," he wrote in a 1920 letter to the editor of the *Times* about indifference among college students, "and you hear discussed, not politics or sociology or economics, not even literature or art, but sports, Broadway, Babe Ruth, the price of Brooks Brothers clothing and the tyranny of Prohibition."

By 1922, his nocturnal scribbling had led to a career. He hopscotched from the Associated Press, where he was night editor, to the magazine *Musical America*, where he was the foreign editor, to *Time*, where he was a founding member of the staff, to G. P. Putnam's Sons, where he

At work in New York City in the early 1920s.

became director of publicity. "He was moving fast," recalled his secretary at Putnam, Frieda Inescort. "The starlight of destiny was in his slate-blue glance, and the thrust of his loose-knit body was unmistakably forward." Yet for all his apparent productivity, his greatest gift was *looking* busy. At Putnam, he was a notorious paper shuffler. For him to write a four-page advertising leaflet was a "major act of creation." He strolled from desk to desk with a sheaf of important-looking documents, soliciting advice, making jokes, complaining of his workload, arranging afternoon cocktails at some speakeasy, all the while his deadline approached. Gradually, each department from Editorial to Accounting to Production to Sales would become "emotionally involved in Louis's creative effort," his secretary remembered.

> The page girl in the outer office would know that Mr. Bromfield was writing a pamphlet; the file clerks, back by the fire-escapes, would know that Mr. Bromfield was extraordinarily busy. Major George Haven Putnam and Mr. Irving Putnam would sit at their

desks serene in the knowledge that young Bromfield—industrious
fellow that he was—was turning out a vast amount of work. But
the days would pass and no pamphlet would appear. . . . Finally,
when we simply had to have the pamphlet for immediate mailing,
I would firmly suggest to Louis that he had better let me finish the
job; whereupon he would agree that that was an excellent idea, and
wash his hands of the entire matter, with the air of an executive
who knew how to get things done with efficiency and dispatch.
After all, what are assistants for?

He spent the mornings in coffeehouses and the afternoons making
friends with the wits at the Algonquin Hotel. He wrote a monthly column in the *Bookman*, one of the important journals of the period. He
was a natural critic; some of his judgments read today a bit like prophe-
sies. Of Virginia Woolf: "We fancy that the novel of the coming generations will be not unlike *Mrs. Dalloway*." Of the musical genre that some
at the time called "monkey music": "Jazz will eventually become the folk
music of the United States." Of *The Great Gatsby*: It "should give satisfaction to those interested in the future of American writing." He was
a cultural omnivore, writing on avant-garde theatre, Pointillist painters,
Stravinsky's "clever but empty" debut at Carnegie Hall and the poetry
of Marianne Moore, whose arbitrary line breaks he once tried to parody:
"on a / Log / Ex- / piring frog."

Bromfield was so wrapped up in criticism and paper shuffling that
when he came out with a first novel, *The Green Bay Tree*, in 1924, and
then a five-hundred-page sequel, *Possession*, a year later, his friends were
stunned. "He had time for everything," Inescort recalled, "endless talk,
long luncheons, nightly parties, theatres, books, people of all sorts,
and—heaven knew when—time for writing novels." Journalists who met
him in the early 1920s commented on his "boundless vigor," his "aston-
ishing vitality," his "inexhaustible fund of native energy." He struck
them as "tall, nervous, volatile" with a "semi-insolent, sprawling ease."

"Somehow it impresses you that he doesn't know just how to behave when sedentary," wrote a reporter for the *Brooklyn Eagle*. "It is practically impossible for him to sit quietly in a chair and you almost feel on the verge of asking him to do so."

He carried his typewriter with him everywhere. "He even props the machine on his knees in the train and dashes off a page or two," recalled one friend. The high-society hostess Gladys Brooks, who invited him to summer at her North Shore estate in Topsfield, Massachusetts, remembered him setting up his typewriter in a meadow facing the Ipswich River. "On fair mornings . . . I could hear the tap-tap of his typewriter mingling with the note of the red-winged blackbird." Writing never seemed to tire him, and he spent the evenings afterward stretched out on the sofa—smoking, drinking, talking "on and on, halfway toward the light of morning."

Despite the pointy ears and his goofy, piano-key teeth, he was handsome in this period—slim, tall, easy-muscled. He wore smartly cut tan tweeds and blue neckties, radiated awkward charm. "The secretaries round and about," wrote another observer, "have to be chained to their desks when Mr. Bromfield appears, such a favorite is he." In the publicity department at Putnam, Bromfield spent his days goosing the biographies of young authors, and now he performed the same trick on himself, claiming in interviews that he had served as an "attaché" and "interpreter" with the French Army during the war, even allowing his publisher, Frederick A. Stokes, to say that his battlefield valor had won him the Croix de Guerre. In fact, he was an undecorated ambulance driver, a private, with a shaky command of French.

These marketing flourishes, however, cannot account for the immediate acclaim his books received. "He has entered the field," wrote Stuart Sherman, a leading critic of the day, "not as a 'promising young man' but as a maestro whose initial performance showed such finish and such virtuosity that one's only doubt was whether he would ever be able to do anything better." Other reviewers agreed, writing that Bromfield's plots were "richly imagined," his characters existed "in three, sometimes four dimensions," his style felt at once "very old-fashioned and the very last word in modernity." Even his glaring faults were turned into virtues; several reviewers saw in the shagginess of his prose the hurried grandeur of a Balzac. "His writing is frequently repetitive, often ungraceful, and sometimes ungrammatical," wrote the critic Ben Ray Redman, "but it is always powerfully alive." The *New York Evening Post* summarized the consensus: "We have added a new fixed star to the American literary firmament."

Almost every reviewer noticed a peculiar feature in his first two books: strong women. Bromfield grew up on a steady diet of English novels and always fell for the strikingly unconventional heroines: John Galsworthy's Irene Forsyte, George Eliot's Maggie Tulliver. His absolute favorite was the beautiful "adventuress" Becky Sharp from Thackeray's *Vanity Fair.* He loved her grit, her defiance, and especially how—after being given a copy of Samuel Johnson's dictionary, an indispensable reference for a proper lady—she hurled it out a carriage window. The residue of these characters congealed into the protagonists of his first two books: Lily Shane, the beautiful daughter of a gentleman farmer who flees a stultifying Ohio mill town for the freedoms of Paris; and her younger cousin, Ellen Tolliver, an ingénue who marries a traveling salesman and ruthlessly uses him as a stepping-stone to pursue her own career, as a concert pianist. Lily approaches sex in a way that feels startlingly contemporary, almost protofeminist. The first pages of *The Green Bay Tree* find her rebuffing the marriage proposal of a corrupt politician—modeled on Warren G. Harding—with whom she had an illicit affair that resulted in a pregnancy. "I couldn't give up all my life to a man because I'd given an hour of it to him," she tells her scandalized aunt.

Bromfield's conception of "the modern woman" fascinated American readers and quickly turned him into a minor authority on gender politics. Throughout the second half of the 1920s, his essays and lectures on "American womanhood" were widely discussed and debated. Journalists started describing Bromfield cheekily as "the young man who knows women." In an interview, he explained that his heroines were based on a new type, "the self-made woman," a kind of female Horatio Alger character fighting her way to the top of the big city with "unsleeping" ambition.

> Once, this sort of achievement was limited to the American boy. But in the last 25 years since women have been given their chance, the American girl is quite as likely to become a self-made success. . . . She even uses men to help her succeed, as men have always used women. She gives love and marriage the same place in her life which they occupy in the life of the average self-made man.

Such talk ruffled Bromfield's interviewer, who suggested that not only men but also their more traditional wives might feel threatened by these ambitious females. "I believe in letting women do what they want," Bromfield replied. "Not all of them want success outside the home; that's all right, too. But talent or genius should always find expression whatever its sex, both for the sake of the world and for the sake of the genius."

While Bromfield wrote about strong, modern women, he married someone who could not possibly live up to his fictional ideal. Little is known about his courtship with Mary Appleton Wood, a shy and homely socialite who descended from two venerable New England families—the Appletons and the Mathers. She had grown up in genteel poverty, her connection to old-money society more a burden than a privilege. She hated the deathly atmosphere of family functions, the way her aunts and uncles lined up and compared the children "either boastfully, to our shame, or deprecatingly, to our sorrow." The experience scarred her and as an adult she frequently felt uneasy in social situations. "The old self-consciousness and stuffiness asserts itself," she wrote. "Once again, you are plain, awkward, little Mary."

In 1920, when they met, Mary was twenty-eight—nearly five years his senior. She had already "come out" as a debutante about a decade earlier. She and Bromfield married quietly in October 1921 near the Appleton family home in Ipswich, Massachusetts. "A simple wedding without bridal attendants," the *New-York Tribune* wrote on its society page. While her family may have seen Bromfield, a penniless upstart journalist, as a last resort, Mary saw him as something else: a savior. "She had been sheltered all her life," her daughter Ellen Bromfield Geld said, "and the appearance of this gay, strong young man from the West must have been something like a fresh wind in a musty attic."

Mary admired Bromfield's progressive views, which were not shared by her family nor by most Americans of the time. We remember the 1920s selectively: flappers, speakeasies, gangsters—a burst of jazz and gin that suddenly freed America from Victorian corsetry and Protestant cant. In fact, mainstream culture of the period was regressive in the extreme. The same moralizing that led to Prohibition also resulted in campaigns against everything from jazz to the teaching of Darwinism. In Tennessee, John T. Scopes, a biology teacher who dared to bring up evolution in the classroom, was convicted under a new law that made it a criminal offense to deny "the story of the Divine creation of man as taught in the Bible." The clergy of fifteen denominations endorsed a "moral gown" for women, with elbow-length sleeves and a hem precisely seven and a half inches above the ground. The Ku Klux Klan—which began the decade as a loose confederation of a few thousand backcountry bigots—had by 1924 grown into a nationwide force with as many as 5 million members, including two US senators and the governors of Georgia and Indiana. Congress passed laws restricting immigration, adding new quotas based on national origin that were designed to exclude "undesirables." "America," President Calvin Coolidge said, "must be kept American." A New York University sociologist wrote a popular book titled *The Melting-Pot Mistake*, while the *Saturday Evening Post*—which published Fitzgerald's stories—warned that immigrant hordes would soon turn Americans into "a hybrid race as worthless and futile as the good-for-nothing mongrels of Central America and Southeastern Europe."

Bromfield marveled at the cultural chasm that separated Broadway from Main Street. Joyce's *Ulysses* had been banned in the United States in 1921; the Post Office burned copies of the book found in the mail. The Paris *Tribune* speculated that Sylvia Beach—the young American who was publishing the novel out of her Paris bookstore, Shakespeare & Company—might never be allowed to return to America. In 1925, a day after Bromfield lectured on Woolf, Aldous Huxley, and E. M. Forster in a small New England town, he was astonished to discover the subject of his talk described by the local newspaper as "the lunatic fringe of contemporary literature." It was easy to find a reason to flee American provincialism, to follow in the flowery footsteps of Henry James and become an expatriate. James had already observed, at the turn of the century, how swift ocean liners, sophisticated railway networks, and the telephone made it feel as though the world was shrinking "to the size of an orange that can be played with."

No place seemed to capture the modern moment like Paris. The French capital was many things in the 1920s—permissive, cosmopolitan, overflowing with fine food and wine—but above all it was cheap. A Champagne cocktail at the Ritz bar cost only 28 cents (or $4 in today's money). A picturesque Left Bank apartment above a sawmill? About $17 per month (or $100 today). Even a writer with a tiny American income could live luxuriously in Paris. Bromfield booked a crossing for November 1925. The *New Yorker*, which had been following his career, put him in its gallery of "Heroes of the Week": After writing an "excellent first novel," and an "even better second novel," Bromfield had "been smiled upon by the Lord and allowed to go and live in Paris."

—⋅—

He romanticized everything about his return to France, even the bad weather—an icy rain—which became, in his unfinished memoir, snow that "fell softly in feathering whirls about the street lights of the Rue Saint-Jacques." It had been six years since he left the Gare Montparnasse in his army uniform, bound for Brest and the boat home. Now he was twenty-nine, with a one-year-old daughter, Anne. He was grateful that it was dark in the taxi because he did not want Mary to see him crying. These were not "simply the sentimental tears" of a tourist returning to the sidewalk cafés and chestnut trees. "They were caused by something far more personal, by the memory of the France I already knew and by the intuition of the France which still lay before me."

He rented the top floor of a modernized Haussmannian apartment building on the Boulevard Flandrin, at the very western edge of Paris. The New York critic Henry Albert Phillips described visiting him there, being admitted by "a typical French maid" into a grand apartment with ornate wooden panels and expensive antique furniture. The whole side wall of an "enormous" room was given up to windows that framed the lakes, bridle paths and wooded islands of the Bois de Boulogne. Phillips sat down to a lavish luncheon "prepared by a French cook at half-hour's notice." Then he and Bromfield withdrew to the *salon*, where they sat before a wood fire and drank a "hundred-year-old" cordial. "And what," he asked, "do you think Mr. Bromfield has to pay for all of this? I really haven't the heart to tell you!"

Bromfield loved playing the Parisian (or what he thought was Parisian). He began to carry a large white wooden walking stick and to wear a beret. He rose late, breakfasted on brioche and café au lait, took up oil painting, filled his shelves with books bought from the green wooden stalls along the Seine, and feasted in restaurants where one ate "better than anywhere else in the world." He thought the delights of Paris were "inexhaustible."

His wife had a different picture of the city, slightly darker and sadder, in line with her general outlook on life. Mary spent the first months adjusting to the fact that the gray sky and dampness were "permanent," that central heating seemed to work only in the warm weather, that the elevators "even in the most luxurious apartments" were out of order half the time. Eventually, she adapted, taking the city on its own terms. "The

After moving to Paris in 1925, Bromfield often
painted landscapes in the Bois de Boulogne. He said
the delights of the city were "inexhaustible."

temptation to walk in the soft gray air is irresistible," she wrote in one
of her occasional travel pieces for *Vogue*. "Shop windows tempt you. . . .
You wish you had the kind of dark, piquant French face that can wear the
new hats at their most extreme backwards tilt." She was, if not beautiful,
at least fashionable. Cecil Beaton once photographed her in Paris in a
drooping V-neck Deco dress, with her chestnut hair curled into a wavy

bob and her face turned away from the camera so you could only see the outline of her profile.

Mary's Paris life was old-fashioned, wifely, consisting of shopping, mothering, planning the menu, handling Bromfield's social dates, distributing the canapés. "At least," she would say, "no one can say I am not a good hostess." Their favorite meals as a couple were "informal, arranged almost at the spur of the moment." Some of the most uncomfortable evenings were spent in the company of Scott and Zelda Fitzgerald, who lived one neighborhood over and of whom they saw "a great deal."

The Bromfields and Fitzgeralds were a study in contrasts: the first couple stable and thriving, the second wild, beautiful, but falling apart. Zelda, twenty-five, already showing signs of the mental illness that would overwhelm her, was then fantasizing about a career as a ballerina. Scott, thirty, had recently published *The Great Gatsby* to strong reviews but was crushed by the novel's weak sales. "Is Gatsby dead?" he wrote to his editor, Maxwell Perkins, in December 1925. "You don't mention it."

The Fitzgeralds' large flat on Rue de Tilsitt, near the Arc de Triomphe, was in many ways a bad imitation of the Bromfields' apartment. Mary and Louis were house-proud and crafty: they furnished the place with tapestries from the decorator Ernest Boiceau and antiques from Paris flea markets. Their salon was filled with fresh flowers and fancy children's toys. They built a phonograph collection and hung paintings by themselves and friends. The Fitzgeralds' apartment, by contrast, struck Bromfield as "characterless and almost sordid": dull striped wallpaper, imitation Louis XVI furniture that came straight out of Galeries Lafayette. "It was rather like a furniture shop window," Bromfield thought. "I always had the impression that the Fitzgeralds were camping out there between two worlds," as if they yearned for a stable adult existence but couldn't quite figure out what that was made of.

Bromfield witnessed their descent, and much later wrote up his observations in a letter to Fitzgerald's first biographer, Arthur Mizener. A big problem was alcohol. The Bromfields drank with relish—gin and whiskey, Champagne and light French wines like Rosé d'Anjou, which they served to guests in quantity. But they kept themselves in check, at least during these years. Not so with Scott and Zelda. "They had promised each other to give up drinking," Bromfield remembered. "But it was no good. Scott would drink and then Zelda would join in out of what seemed to be a kind of despair." Bromfield described Fitzgerald as a lightweight. "One cocktail and he was off," he said. "It seemed to affect him as much as five or six drinks affected Hemingway and myself." Bromfield preferred Zelda, who not only "drank better," but also had a "stronger character."

At one point early in 1926, Fitzgerald called Bromfield long after midnight. Bromfield was in his pajamas, but Fitzgerald said it was urgent: Could he come over? When Bromfield arrived, Fitzgerald was "pacing up and down the furniture shop window looking haggard and miserable." Zelda was lying in bed; a doctor had just left after administering a "hypodermic to quiet her." "I have the idea that when he called he may have wanted to discuss his problems but by the time I arrived he had turned reticent, and beyond telling me about Zelda's condition apparently had nothing to say . . . He had these spells of being frightened of being left alone." It was clear to Bromfield that, as much as Paris helped some Americans find themselves, others discovered there only how lost they were.

———

In his letters, Fitzgerald expressed a casual contempt for Bromfield's work, but there was nothing casual about Ernest Hemingway's feelings for Bromfield, which over the decade would bubble into a toxic stew of envy and scorn. At first, Hemingway only poked fun at Bromfield, giving him derisive nicknames like "Bloomfield" or "Brommy" and spoofing the Victorian sagas he wrote, which were set in stodgy New England mansions or the gilt-edged *salons* of the Faubourg Saint-Germain. "Bloomfield's next book is about a preacher," Hemingway wrote to Fitzgerald in 1927.

> Bloomfield will probably make him a decayed old new england preacher named Cabot Cabot Cabot and naturally he talks only with God—to rhyme with Cod. But sooner or later I can see that the decayed French aristocracy will come into the book and they will all be named the Marquis Deidre de Chanel and will be people whom Louis Bromfield [—] the most brilliant and utterly master of his craft of all the younger generation of decayed French aristocracy novelists [—] will have studied first-hand himself at the Ritz . . .

Bromfield thought Hemingway was his friend. The two men met late in 1925, probably at one of Ford's parties. After they dined together at Bromfield's apartment, Hemingway asked if he could come back with his wife Hadley—she was "wild to see" the place. "She doesn't believe it can be as wonderful as I say." Hemingway may have genuinely admired Bromfield's apartment, but that is certainly not the impression he later gave to Fitzgerald. "I went out there to dinner one night and they had a lot of *vin ordinaire* and cats kept jumping on the table and running off with what little fish there was and then shitting on the floor. Bloomfield, in the effort to make me feel at home, did everything but put his feet on the table. I thought to show I felt at home perhaps I had better piss in the finger bowls."

Around this time, Hemingway was hard at work on his first novel, *The Sun Also Rises*. He thought the book was a triumph and had no intention of giving it to his current publisher, Horace Liveright, who had failed to promote his story collection, *In Our Time*, which was a commercial flop. Bromfield, always generous with new friends, used his New York literary connections to find Hemingway a new publisher. He brokered a deal in which Alfred Harcourt, of Harcourt & Brace, would buy the unfinished novel sight-unseen. "We shall try to do the young man as much credit as he'll do us, and that's considerable," Bromfield quoted Harcourt as saying in a letter he wrote to Hemingway in December 1925.

Hemingway probably never intended to take the deal that Bromfield put together for him, but he shrewdly used it as leverage with Maxwell Perkins at Scribner, who—aware of the competition—offered Hemingway a large advance and a 15 percent royalty rate. On a trip to New York in January 1926, he signed with Scribner and later sent Bromfield a six-page letter justifying his decision. The letter was larded with flattery; Hemingway seemed to want to make sure Bromfield didn't feel used. He complimented Bromfield's literary stature: "You and Ford seem the most genuinely admired novelists in N.Y." He built up their very brief friendship, telling him that "Hadley sends her love" and that they were looking forward to "seeing a lot of you both" in the spring. In a letter to Fitzgerald, Hemingway said that Bromfield had been "damned decent."

These are the last generous words that Hemingway wrote about Bromfield. The rest of their relationship is a portrait in one-sided resentment, inflamed by Bromfield's growing success. Bromfield's third novel, *Early Autumn*, and Hemingway's first were published one week apart from each other in October 1926. Hemingway's book initially received mixed reviews, but *Early Autumn*—a harsh portrait of New England's Puritan upper class based on Mary's family—rocketed up the bestseller charts and delighted most mainstream critics. "He is, of all the young American novelists," John Carter wrote later in the *New York Times*, "pre-eminently the best and most vital." Such reviews must have irritated Hemingway, whose own hometown paper, the *Chicago Tribune*, dismissed *The Sun Also Rises* as a "bushel of sensationalism and triviality." He vented his frustrations to Perkins, saying that the critics had misunderstood his book. He didn't mean for it to be "a hollow or bitter satire but a damn tragedy." He had purposely avoided trite literary devices knowing full well that this was what the critics expected. "I cut out 40,000 words of the stuff that would have made them happy" from an earlier draft. "It would have made them happy, but it would have rung as false 10 years from now as Bromfield."

Incidentally, Bromfield and his wife wrote Hemingway separate letters praising *Sun*. "Jesus Christ," Bromfield told him, "You've written a swell book." Mary told him to forget the bad press. "What rubbish people write." She again invited Hemingway to dine with them. Despite his quibbles about the wine and cat shit, he accepted: "It will be great to see you again." But Hemingway's personal life was falling apart. He had been carrying on with another woman for months and, in December, his wife Hadley finally filed for a divorce. By March of 1927, he was "broke," having given her all his *Sun* royalties.

As Hemingway fell on hard times, Bromfield's luck only improved. In May, *Early Autumn* won the Pulitzer Prize. The Paris papers photographed the thirty-year-old author in his opulent apartment looking like a cartoonish fop—hair slicked back, wearing a paint-splattered smock, typing with a cigarette in his mouth in one picture, a cat on his lap in another. It wasn't just the Pulitzer: A play based on Bromfield's first book was to premiere on Broadway, and his fourth novel (*A Good Woman*) had climbed to the top of the bestseller list. "It never rains but it pours," he told the papers. Bromfield's reputation as the "young man who knows women" led to a high-paid lecture tour on the subject of "American womanhood" across the Midwest. Hemingway peevishly wrote to Perkins suggesting he and Scott Fitzgerald launch a competing lecture tour. "Maybe you would come too and we could all lecture on Am. Womanhood. Maybe Flo Ziegfeld would loan some specimens of Am. Womanhood and it could be an illustrated Lecture."*

By the fall of 1927, Hemingway could hardly pick up an American newspaper without seeing Bromfield's name. He might have thought there would be some respite in the pages of *The Boulevardier,* a sophisti-

---

* The Broadway impresario Florenz Ziegfeld Jr. (1867–1932) was known for his "Ziegfeld Follies," a series of theatrical revues featuring beautiful, skimpily clad chorus girls.

Bromfield, age thirty, in his Paris apartment after winning
the 1927 Pulitzer Prize for his third novel, *Early Autumn*.

cated new humor journal for the American colony, but here too was an
article by Bromfield. The essay, "The Real French," was meant to lampoon pretentious expats who spoke a try-hard "gargling French" and
scoured the country in search of paragons of "authentic" Gallic culture.
But Bromfield used the piece mostly as an excuse to extol his own experience with the "real French": how he had been their attaché in the war
(false), how he had shacked up in "dugouts," "dunghills," and "chateaux" with every sort of Frenchman from "Montmartre *maquereaux*"
(or pimps) to "princes of ancient blood." He concluded by suggesting that the "realest of real French" might be his own domestic staff:
"my cook Yvonne from Normandy, my chamber-maid Helene from
the Nièvre and my chauffeur Lucien whom [*sic*] comes from Villette."

Hemingway had enough. He wrote to the editor of the *Boulevardier* saying he would offer a column in the next issue as a response to
Bromfield's pomposities. The result, "The Real Spaniard," published in

October 1927, was a stereophonic parody, skewering Bromfield while also flavoring the prose with an absurd, Dadaist tang:

> I spent the European war in Spain it is true as an *attaché* to the Spanish army, sleeping often enough in dunghills and chateaux and the like, but to me the Spanish never seemed real. Somehow they didn't. They seemed like cathedrals. . . . I must say that I felt discouraged and was on the point of hiring me a parlor maid, a cook and a chauffeur named Pilar, Concepcion and Isidoro respectively, to see if they would be the real thing like good old Brommy found, when, picking up the *Heraldo de Madrid*, I glanced over the *Telefonos y Telegrafos* and saw that thirty six people had been drowned by falling into the sea [from] an autobus in Extremadura. Something told me they were the real Spaniards and they were all dead.

This public teasing of "old Brommy" concealed a more tortured private animus. After reading another rave about Bromfield's latest book in the *Chicago Tribune*, Hemingway wrote Fitzgerald in a fury. "Did you see how Fanny Butcher the woman with the Veal Brains called Brommy the American Fielding? Jesus Christ," he fumed. "There isn't and won't be any American Fielding but I am resolved that son of a bitch"—he stopped himself mid-sentence: "Oh, hell . . ."

While his resentments cooled as the decade faded, Hemingway would never forget his old Paris punching bag. In the 1930s, after Gertrude Stein singled out Bromfield as a favorite American novelist, Hemingway said that she "lost all sense of taste when she had the menopause." In 1949, Hemingway mocked Bromfield for abandoning serious literature in favor of the "Secretariat of Agriculture." That Bromfield's farm memoirs and potboilers remained popular only proved to him that most American readers were philistines. He once complained to the *New Yorker* writer Lillian Ross about the "bloody bores" who stopped him on the street in Cuba. "I just wanted to tell you, Mr. Hemingway," they would gush, "I think you are our greatest writer. You and Louis Bromfield." Ross said that line "made me laugh out loud." She was not the only one who thought it was a joke that these two writers had *ever* been placed in the same company. "Do you remember," wrote an astonished Malcolm Cowley in 1945, "when Hemingway *and* Louis Bromfield were coupled by the critics as the two giants of a new generation?" The comparison was by then so ridiculous, Cowley said, that even "little children" could tell the artist from the hack.

———

Bromfield was ignorant of Hemingway's feelings in the 1920s, and even if he had been made aware of them, he was probably having too much fun to care. He fell in with the society set in Paris, aristocrats whose real names—the Duchesse de Mouchy, Princess Scherbatoff—sound almost as silly as the fake ones Fitzgerald made up for the guest list of some Swiss grand hotel in *Tender Is the Night*: Geneveva de Momus, Mme. Bonneasse. "Well, what nationality are these people?" Fitzgerald's character asks. Bromfield would later paint this world of "international white trash" in garish colors, dismissing the Riviera as the "Côte d'Ordure" (garbage coast). But for the moment he was dazzled by the fading light of the beau monde. He went to dinner dances in Neuilly with the grande duchesse Maria Pavlovna of Russia, drank cocktails with Élisabeth de Gramont, the duchesse of Clermont-Tonnerre, on the Champs-Élysées. It was not only aristocrats and literary celebrities on his dance card; so many different types of people called at his Paris apartment that it reminded him of "the lower level of the Grand Central."

His exploits on the Continent were widely covered in the American press. "Those who cherish the future of American literature watch every move he makes with jealous apprehension," Brooks Atkinson wrote in the *Times*. He wintered in Swiss resorts like Caux, where he skied down the Alps and skated across lakes wearing a waistcoat, bow tie, and skinny wool trousers that ballooned out above the knee. "You should see the flying Bromfields on the ice," he wrote to a literary columnist. He summered in the Basque Country, renting a house on a cliff in a humble fishing village outside the resort town of Saint-Jean-de-Luz. There he wrote each morning in an abandoned seventeenth-century fort overlooking the ocean before running outside: to sunbathe or play *boules* or buy langoustines for dinner. He crossed into Spain, visiting Pamplona for the bullfights, which Hemingway glorified in *The Sun Also Rises*. "Very poor sport," Bromfield said. "Rather shabby altogether." The glitziest evenings were spent at La Réserve de Ciboure, a restaurant perched on the purple-black rocks above the Bay of Biscay, where, Mary wrote in another dispatch for *Vogue*, one dances "in the open air with the sound of the sea in one's ears and only the feathery tamarisks overhead." Spanish hours were the fashion; no one ate before ten; and jewels glittered "against the tan skins of the women," who ranged from the queen of Spain to the "the latest little *cocotte à la mode*."

The writer Edna Ferber joined the Bromfields in the Basque Country twice in the late 1920s. A friendship blossomed and, a few years later, Ferber wrote that she never met anyone else who had Bromfield's "capacity for enjoying life and his gift for communicating that enjoyment to others." She remembered how he spoke back then, the way the sun and sea got into his voice: "You're coming to our house to dinner tonight. . . . I've taught the cook to do Ohio food, she gives it a French slant and it's wonderful. . . . Mary's found a little dressmaker in Biarritz who copies all the Paris models for practically nothing. . . . I'm doing a novel too, but you've got to knock off at noon the way I do and get in the sun and bathe. The violet rays here are magic."

At the time, Bromfield might be forgiven for thinking that Europe belonged to Americans like him. His country had emerged from World War I economically ascendant and culturally assertive. The American abroad—Bromfield wrote in an essay in the *Saturday Review of Literature*—now moved across the Continent feeling "the power of an

The writer Edna Ferber, who vacationed with Bromfield in the Basque
Country in the late 1920s, marveled at his "capacity for enjoying
life and his gift for communicating that enjoyment to others."

immense and wealthy nation at his elbow." It was his people who were
"setting bankrupt nations on their feet, providing *all* the music for cab-
arets and music halls, plastering the sides of ancient bridges with signs
advertising Veedol and Atlantic gasoline, placing automatic filling stations on quiet village streets." No longer did the New World need to
apologize to the Old for its lack of cultivation. The American abroad who
had interested Henry James—typified by the hapless Daisy Miller, who
sets upon the Continent in search of sophisticated society only to contract malaria in Rome—had become as "extinct as the dodo." Replacing
her was a "steel-clad Diana," freed of "the ambitious and vulgar mother"
and tossing off a cocktail to mark the beginning of her day. "She [is] quite
on her own, clad in a minimum of clothing, all cut in the most beautiful
style by Chanel or Vionnet or Lanvin, with shingled hair and an air of
independence and *savoir-faire.*"

But steel-clad Dianas were not the only Americans in Europe. Back in Paris, the flood of tourists and expats were upsetting the natives by flaunting their wealth and trampling over local custom. A few Americans even lodged a formal complaint with their ambassador, convinced that the customary closure of retail stores in Paris from noon to two p.m. was "some kind of anti-American plot." So much English could be heard on the boulevards that a sarcastic shopkeeper put a sign in his window: "French Spoken Here." There were reports of Americans who threw their depreciated francs on the street and chuckled "as French passers-by scurried after them." Tensions were rising; Americans thought they were being overcharged for everything. Fistfights broke out between taxi drivers and tourists over fares. Students in the Latin Quarter boycotted American goods. In July 1926, a mob of Frenchmen shouting anti-American epithets attacked holiday-makers boarding charabancs for "Paris by Night" tours.

The French and Americans reconciled the following spring. On the night of May 21, a single-engine plane was spotted off the coast of Cherbourg. Only a week earlier, a pair of French fliers had attempted to make history by crossing the Atlantic in the reverse direction. They were never heard from again. Now it seemed that a lone American, another Midwesterner, Charles Lindbergh, had done it: flying more than thirty-three hours from Washington, DC, and arriving in France ahead of schedule. As soon as his plane was sighted, word spread quickly to Paris. Louis and Mary Bromfield were among the estimated 150,000 people who gathered at the airfield of Le Bourget north of the city to see the *Spirit of St. Louis* slip out of the night sky.

A sea of revelers washed over the small plane as soon as it landed at 10:22 p.m. Lindbergh—cleft chin, brilliant smile, wisps of hair peeking out of his leather helmet—made a move to jump down from the cockpit but twenty hands immediately reached for him and "lifted him out as if he were a baby." Bromfield had not seen such an outpouring of emotion since the Armistice. "It was a beautiful night brilliant with stars," he wrote in a letter to a novelist friend, Henry Fuller, "and I found the moment when the sound of the motor came vaguely out of the darkness from the direction of Cherbourg one of the greatest experiences I've ever had."

The "spectacular enthusiasm" crossed borders, races, and classes. It was "a profound and unconscious sense," Bromfield wrote, "of the simple dignity of Man." But this universalism coexisted with the feeling that there was something uniquely American in Lindbergh's mild-mannered idealism, in the innocence and audacity of his ambition. A few people in the crowd wondered aloud whether the young man might be "awed into idiocy" by this hero's welcome.

"No, he's not likely to be," Mary said. "He comes from the Middle West." Bromfield agreed. He wrote that Lindbergh's "whole performance was a perfect fulfillment of the ideal type which the American democracy is supposed to produce."

The coming years would complicate, if not entirely invalidate, this judgment, but on that night all the excitement of the decade seemed to condense for Bromfield into one pretty picture. *Paris in the 1920s*: Was there ever a better time and place to be American? Their money went far, their world seemed at once big and small, and they were still young enough to think they were free. Mary had her doubts, though. She saw life flowing along "easily, pleasantly, and rather mistily," but she could dimly perceive that something in it was missing, that Paris was just "a beautiful empty shell," a place in which "you do not belong, in which you have no root."

3

Hothouse

SENLIS, 1929

In interwar France, the medieval city of Senlis was a popular weekend getaway from Paris, especially for members of the American colony. "Let's go to Senlis," Jake Barnes suggests to his expat friend Robert Cohn in the first few pages of *The Sun Also Rises*. "Senlis is a good place and we can stay at the Grand Cerf and take a hike in the woods and come home." From the train station, it took only five minutes to walk to the town's most delightful attraction—its central marketplace—which was housed in a lacy thirteenth-century Gothic church.

On Tuesdays and Fridays, all of Senlis bought here. Rich families sent their *cordon bleu*, or home cook, to do the shopping but the mistress of the town's most impressive chateau did not trust her cook to buy economically. So she went herself, an elegantly dressed lady haggling alongside poor old women muffled in black wool who only left their houses for market and Mass. Senlis was also home to a garrison of Spahis, French cavalry soldiers from Algeria, whose turbaned orderlies streamed through the church in brilliant red-and-white uniforms, giving the provincial tableau a dash of the souk.

Each section of the Marché Saint-Pierre belonged to a different type of produce. The whitewashed nave was mottled in shades of green: let-tuce, leeks, artichokes, endives and small peas. The light shining through stained glass warmed the apricots and berries, making them fragrant. Potted flowers were sold beneath the curves of the Gothic groining. The meat was sectioned off in the cool apse of the church. Some animals were still alive, like Madame Goujoun's pink-eyed rabbits, which she would gladly club on the head with a wooden stick and skin for you on the spot. One transept was filled with mountains of sweets: delicate macarons, sablés, and cakes. The other transept belonged to Madame Veuve Legendre and her cheese. Her specialty was Roquefort, pungent blue-green wheels of sheep's-milk cheese. Even a small taste would stay on your tongue all afternoon. The last stop was the cloisters, the coldest part of the church, which contained the fish market. If you had money, you bought spiny lobsters. If you were on a budget, maybe you asked for skate wings, which, despite their slimy appearance, were delicious once capered and swimming in a slick of Madame Legendre's butter.

Every week in summer artists set up their easels in front of the church to try to capture the scene, which spilled out of the arched doorways onto the cobbled square. An accordion player hawked sheet music while a suspender salesman sling-shot his wares into the sky so they hung from the lampposts. Everyone stopped in front of the corset vendor, Gaspard, who, rather than extol the virtues of his cheap panties and ecru-bordered lingerie, simply slipped them on over his street clothes and began to dance. Saint-Pierre was not the only place of worship in Senlis that found a secular second life. The city had once been a religious power center, but over the centuries its stock of convents, monasteries, and episcopal palaces were slowly converted into movie theaters, barracks, a carpenter's workshop, apartments, even a barn. "This old town," the 1919 Michelin Guide noted, "is so rich in relics of the past that it puts its ancient religious monuments to quite profane uses."

—•—

What if we moved here? How many Americans, visiting a village in France—overwhelmed by the abundance of such a marketplace, by the grandeur of the architecture, by the low prices in the window of some realtor's office—have asked themselves versions of that question, seriously or not. Mary and Louis Bromfield asked it in 1929. By then, leaving Paris had become the thing to do for many of the exiles in their circle. Gerald and Sara Murphy—the rich and glamorous couple who would inspire Fitzgerald's *Tender Is the Night*—first moved to a rosy brick house in the Paris suburb of Saint-Cloud in 1924, before creating their famous Art Deco "Villa America" near Antibes a year later. Gertrude Stein and Alice B. Toklas found a country house near Aix-les-Bains in the late 1920s, and for over a decade would spend summers there growing their own salads and herbs, an experience that made Toklas feel "like a mother about her baby—how could anything so beautiful be mine." Many other Americans built gardens closer to Paris. Harry and Caresse Crosby, the founders of the Black Sun Press—which published early editions of Hemingway and Henry Miller—settled into a medieval mill near Senlis in Ermenonville in 1928, where they kept a menagerie that included rare birds, donkeys, even a cheetah. Other expatriates moved to Chantilly, Fontainebleau, Rambouillet, and Versailles. Leaving Paris for the countryside became their version of settling down in the suburbs, a way of adapting to changing circumstances—getting older, wanting more space, having children—without pulling the plug on the whole adventure.

Many other expats—including Pound, Hemingway, Fitzgerald—had already left France or would do so soon. Economics played a part. On October 29, 1929, the stock market crashed—$14 billion, gone in a single day. A few bankers blew their brains out, everyone else tightened their belts. The Depression would not hit France for a couple more years, but the exchange rate that had fueled so much expatriate extravagance began to tilt against the dollar. It was no longer so easy to live so well in

France, which meant if you stayed, you already had roots, or you wanted to plant them.

A whole colony of American bons vivants settled in Senlis, in the Oise department 30 miles north of Paris. They liked that the town was romantic, that it was small (with a population of around 7,000), and that it was practical: less than an hour from the boulevards of the capital, twenty minutes from the airport at Le Bourget, and ten minutes from the main line of the Chemins de Fer du Nord, which led to Brussels and London. It had a great hotel-restaurant, Le Grand Cerf, run by a pupil of Escoffier. Some of its American residents were prominent: polished businessmen like Bernard Carter, who led the Paris branch of JP Morgan and lived in a mansion by the old Roman arena, or celebrated libertines like Carl Erickson, whose drinking parties in his mansard house on the Rue de la Chancellerie were almost as well known as his drawings of Chanel and Schiaparelli fashions in *Vogue*.

But when Bromfield settled in Senlis, he instantly became the town's most famous resident. At first, this was because he was a best-selling author, but, eventually, it was because of his garden, set along a lazy river on the outskirts of town. Janet Flanner called it "the finest flower garden of any American in the Île de France." Francis Rose, an artist protégé of Gertrude Stein who often painted Bromfield's garden, compared it to "a ripe and rich Monet." The horticulturalist Russell Page remembered the rarities that Bromfield cultivated there. "It was the only garden in France," he said, "where the hybrid musk roses grew. They were allowed to grow into large loosely trimmed bushes hanging over the river, loveliest with their clusters of cream and white and rose-pink flowers just as the light began to fade. Planted near them, *Lilium regale*, tobacco flowers and night-scented stocks filled the evening air with scent."*

---

* Often called the royal or king's lily, *Lilium regale* is a white, trumpet-shaped flower with a striking yellow throat.

———·———

Before there could be a garden, however, there had to be a house. Flush with book royalties and undeterred by the economic crisis, the Bromfields began shopping for one in Senlis in 1929. They visited a real-estate agent, who tacked photographs of farms and "manoirs" on a board like picture postcards. Choosing one seemed "too easy," Mary said, until they discovered that, curiously, none of those pictured was actually available. They had all been sold or rented. The agent politely inquired if Madame and Monsieur would like to see something of the same *genre*. But the houses he took them to were of a completely different *genre*. One was a villa (described as "*très coquette*") that Mary said was "monstrously" renovated; another was on a small dark street, "damp and unwholesome," with a tiny paved court that the agent generously called "*le jardin*"; the last was an old mill that resembled "a box with windows poked through" and could have worked nicely as "an institution for the mad."

They were disappointed. But then Mary learned an important lesson about life in France: You never get what you want by going directly to the source. "If you want a good cook, you will hear about her from the veterinarian. If you want to buy a horse, the person who knows just the horse you want is the baker. If you want a house, the antique dealer will find it for you." They "bribed" Madame Brisset, the cheery, feather boa-wearing proprietress of the antique shop Au Bon Vieux Temps. She would get a finder's fee—not to mention a promising client—if she could only secure them a house, in particular one house that they had spied from the road on the outskirts of town. It was a few minutes' walk downhill from the center, between the sixteenth-century ramparts and the forest. Here was a different Senlis, patchworked with communal gardens and light woods: a gently rolling landscape of hedge, heath, and orchards. The only sounds piercing the provincial stillness were the swishing of the River Nonette (the Little Nun) and the distant shouts of schoolboys playing soccer in the courtyard of a Jesuit school. "I wanted that particular house and none other in all France," Bromfield wrote later. "It was small, but it was conveniently placed on the edge of the town, with a lovely view across communal gardens, marsh and forest. But above all, it had water—a little, crystal-clear, trout-filled river . . . which flowed through the garden and against the very wall of the house." He imagined himself sitting in a renovated salon, fishing through the tall windows, a crystal chandelier the only thing that could entangle his line.

To realize this fantasy, the Bromfields had to solve a series of problems. The house, which had been built in the eighteenth century, had the grand name of Presbytère de Saint-Etienne. It had once housed a Capuchin priest but, by the time the Bromfields found it, had deteriorated into a shabby, undistinguished pile of limestone functioning primarily as a laundry. The garden was a mess, the river obscured by sheds and washhouses. On an adjacent property was an overgrown kitchen garden and the ruins of a thirteenth-century red-roofed chapel, covered in ivy branches as thick as a man's arm. A widow by the name of Jarry lived in the house, but it was owned by three spinster sisters, Les Mancherons, all above seventy. These women belonged in the previous century: They had never ridden in automobiles, they secluded themselves in an ancient mansion in the center of Senlis, and regarded anything new and foreign with suspicion. They had been born in the Presbytère and considered the place the *berceau*, or cradle, of their family. Bromfield offered them twice, even three times, what the house was worth. They refused: "What would we do with the money?" The Mancherons didn't trust stocks or bonds; to them, Bromfield said, land was "the only thing."

They would, however, lease the property under certain circumstances. "Few peace conferences," Bromfield said, "have entailed more diplomacy, more papers, more threats and false moves." He negotiated with the middle sister, a seemingly gentle woman who revealed herself to be "a born manipulator," deploying her lawyer and notary "as stooges when she wanted to put over hard provisions in the contract about who was to pay

In 1930, Bromfield began renovations on the Presbytère de Saint-
Etienne, an eighteenth-century rectory he had leased in the
medieval town of Senlis. There he would build a celebrated garden
along a "crystal-clear, trout-filled river" called the Nonette.

for repairs to the roof or the cutting of the weeds," and so on. "In the end
I paid for everything, being just what she thought I was, an easy-come,
easy-go American who, when he wanted something, was willing to go to
any lengths to have it."

Bromfield spared no expense on renovations—never mind that he was renovating a house he didn't himself own. The work took over a year and was still not finished when the Bromfields arrived in Senlis, early in the spring of 1931. Progress had been made, however: Modern heating and plumbing were installed, the washhouses were removed from the garden, and a stable had been converted into a garage. But the house was still in disarray: the floors muddy, the plaster and paint unfinished. You would open a door to a room and find a half dozen workmen "each stepping on each other's toes." The Bromfields decided to rent a room at the Grand Cerf so they could supervise construction. Bit by bit, they disentangled the men, delegated their responsibilities, demanded shortcuts, and exchanged an "enormous" quantity of "French abuse." On June 10, they finally moved in.

Now, Mary said, came the "fun" part: decorating. "Exuberant" might be the most charitable way to describe the interior of the Presbytère. From Madame Brisset, they bought antiques of every period, Louis XIII through Second Empire: crystal chandeliers, gilt chairs, a Directoire dining-room table, frilly wooden beds. They had Ernest Boiceau design them a circular rug for the salon, with a lemon-yellow background and a modern pattern of big white flowers. Their curtains were white glazed chintz with big lemon grosgrain ruffles and tie-backs. They bought a huge "1830 mirror," which they hung opposite the garden, "so as you walk from the outdoors you could see the whole garden reflected in its gaudy outlines." They hid a large, "hideous" gramophone behind a floral screen that Bromfield painted himself. The walls were white and above the Louis XV mantelpiece they hung a frameless plain glass mirror. "The effect was marvelous," Mary said. "The 1931 mirror and the 1830 mirror look at each other in surprise." It was a house that captured them perfectly: bright, flowery, tacky, fun, indiscriminately in love with France.

—•—

Bromfield could afford to build this extravagant house because he was making more money than ever before. His last story collection, *Awake and Rehearse*, was a bestseller. *Cosmopolitan* offered him a lucrative five-year contract to serialize his new novels, beginning with *Twenty-Four Hours* (1930), an ambitious attempt at replicating the daylong narrative structure used in *Mrs. Dalloway* and *Ulysses*. The book received uneven reviews—*The Nation* called it "shoddy and even slovenly"—but it still became a bestseller, confirming Bromfield's mass appeal. By this point he had written seven books, and was regarded as one of the most important American literary voices. He breezed into New York once or twice a year, raising a flag at the Algonquin for a long stream of parties and literary teas. Gossip columnists swarmed, and none of them wrote more entertainingly of Bromfield's visits than Lucius Beebe, whose society column in the *New York Herald Tribune*, "This New York," was syndicated across the country. Beebe called Bromfield, the future dirt farmer, "one of the most glittering and opulent of the Paris-Manhattan commuters."

> His comings and goings are heralded by loud outcries and the popping of double Magnums. Every year the Bromfields establish their winter palace at the Algonquin, and Frank Case, the manager, assigns a special engineer to keep the revolving door from overheating its bearings, so vast is the concourse of visitors coming and going. All late evening arrivals with dented opera hats who are unable to identify themselves are shown to the Bromfield flat and it is reported that the hot and cold water spigots in the washrooms are replaced by gold and enamel faucets marked "brut" and "extra sec" to indicate the type of champagne that is on tap.

Such a reputation began to attract the attention of Hollywood. In 1929, the movie mogul Sam Goldwyn had offered Bromfield a contract job writing screenplays in Los Angeles. This was the moment when the talkies were turning the movie business into a massive industry and studios had the capital to bribe "highbrow" talent—from Pulitzer Prize–winning authors to Mitteleuropean composers—who had previously "scorned the silent screen." Bromfield arrived in Los Angeles in January 1930. His plan was to "spend time on the studio lot, learning about production before writing a line." Instead, he played bridge and tennis, went to parties, and befriended a struggling young actor named Humphrey Bogart. All the while he drew from Goldwyn a weekly salary of $2,500 (roughly $37,000 in today's money). He did write one movie treatment (for the Evelyn Laye vehicle *One Heavenly Night*) and punched up the script of *Dracula* starring Bela Lugosi. But Goldwyn didn't think much of his efforts. "That fellow Bromfield came out to Hollywood but he didn't do any work," he told the New York *Daily News*. "His main business here seemed to be taking sunbaths, chattering and drinking tea. He is a great chatterer and a champion tea drinker." For his part, Bromfield felt like Goldwyn had ignored him. "Why did you hire me?" he demanded of the Warsaw-born studio executive, who was famous for his conversational errors. "For your name, Mr. Bronstein," Goldwyn said. "For your name." In the end, Bromfield paid to get out of his contract and wrote off Hollywood as "colossally unsatisfactory" for a writer—"a provincial little town"—and returned to France via Italy and Switzerland at the end of the year.

The one thing Bromfield did take out of his American sojourn was a new assistant. In her memoir, his daughter Ellen tells how they met, in the fall of 1929, when Bromfield was briefly in New York, struggling to meet several deadlines ahead of his trip to Hollywood.

> Holed up in his room at the Hotel Algonquin, cursing noisily at the clutter of work around him and staring with gloomy longing at the crisp New York autumn day beyond his window, his thoughts were suddenly interrupted by a knock at the door. Opening it with some impatience, he found himself looking down at a swarthy, mustached figure, nattily dressed in a plaid sports coat, silk scarf and golfer's hat, a portable typewriter dangling from his right hand.

"I hear you're up to your ass in paper work," came the forth-
right greeting.

"Jesus Christ." My father gave an abject groan.

"Not quite." The little man's hat seemed to rise up on horns as
he grinned. "But I think I can take care of this mess. My name's
Hawkins."

George Hawkins came from Long Island and sounded like it. He was
plump and bald and wore a curious *W*-shaped mustache. He was first
hired to run interference between Bromfield and his studio bosses in
Hollywood. Then, when Bromfield was about to leave for France, Hawkins offered to go with him. Bromfield was uncertain. Yes, he was flush
at that moment, and could certainly use a hand with paperwork, but the
Depression was on and who knew when his luck might run out. "I'm
perfectly capable of sustaining myself in a state of pauperism," Hawkins
replied. "Money's no object. There's only one thing I will not tolerate and
that's taking orders. I like to do my work when and where I goddamn
please." Bromfield agreed, and Hawkins moved into the house in Senlis.
In no time he made himself indispensable, not only as a secretary but
also as Bromfield's editor, majordomo, garden helper, living-room jester,
and drinking partner. Hawkins was gay, closeted in a careless way, and
living in Bromfield's large and permissive household allowed him to
entertain "his friends," as Bromfield called them, and to "lead a life apart
for days at a time."

Hawkins joined Bromfield at a moment when his family was growing.
A second daughter, Hope, had been born in 1927; Ellen, the third, would
arrive in 1932. Bromfield's three girls were cared for by a middle-aged
nanny, Jean White, whom Ellen remembered as "a Scottish foretaste of
hell's fire and brimstone." She and Bromfield frequently got into fights
over the girls' diet. She thought the food Bromfield fed his daughters—
buttery omelets, onion soup, quiche made with foraged mushrooms—
would lead to "boils and rickets." Nanny preferred a regimen in which

In the early 1930s, the Bromfield ménage expanded
to include a mischievous secretary, George
Hawkins, and a Scottish nanny, Jean White.

all food was "boiled, measured, strained and fortified." "Good God,"
Bromfield would say, after seeing on his children's plates Nanny's latest
dietetic sludge. "Must everything be pre-digested? Just imagine the spectacle when I introduce them to society and they're obliged to refuse *le
poulet au vin* because it hasn't been passed through a sieve!"

———

The construction workers treated the garden of the Presbytère as a dumpster. The old plumbing was wrenched out and thrown through windows, joining a trash heap of cinders, old plaster, broken bottles, and rusted bicycle parts. The only living things were those that grew of their own accord: a double row of old linden trees and a scraggly, semicircular hedge of lilacs. To Mary, building a garden here looked "hopeless."

Bromfield knew how to grow flowers and vegetables from working on his grandfather's farm. But the gardens he remembered from Ohio were slapdash affairs: "spare, sickly, ill-tended and yellow." He later recognized them as vestiges of a "frontier agriculture," in which the pioneers plowed and fit "any kind of ground" and planted seeds "with extravagance so that no matter how poor the soil or the care of the garden there will be *some* return of some kind." Quality was never important: "No one talked about what is good food and bad, what food has taste and what has not."

France seemed to him the opposite of Ohio, a place where the land was sacred, and where necessity and tradition had turned the garden into a "work of art," free of weeds and empty spaces and made to produce the maximum in yield and flavor. Bromfield closely watched how his neighbors worked the land. One of them—a sporadically employed machine-tool worker named Bosquet—fascinated him. Later, in his farm books, he would turn Bosquet into an emblem of Gallic self-sufficiency. On his 2 acres beside the Nonette, he raised enough to feed himself, his wife, and three children. He grew all kinds of vegetables, even artichokes, which could be seen as "wasteful" because they take up a lot of space. "But Bosquet liked artichokes and wanted them when he wanted them, without spending hard-earned money to buy them." He also had pears, plums, quinces and apples—grown "mostly on dwarf trees which yielded prodigious crops." His paths were lined by strawberry plants. He kept hens for laying and capons for eating, a dozen ducks and a hatchful of fat Belgian hares. He had a pig that lived off vegetable tops and two she-

The Bromfields, circa 1934. From left: Anne, Hope
(on Peter the pony), Louis, Mary, and Ellen.

goats that got their forage from the roadside. His livestock made manure, which he gathered along with all sorts of kitchen scraps in a constantly ripening compost heap. A year later that compost was returned to the soil in the form of rich humus full of benevolent bacteria and fungi—all the elements that make for healthy soil.

Bosquet lived in a small, tightly packed world, allied with nature, reliant on little else. He was a poor man whose life seemed rich. Bromfield enjoyed seeing him working in the garden or sitting in his cottage behind his house, where he drank wine and talked politics with his friends, sometimes singing with them to the accompaniment of a rusty concertina. Bromfield envied Bosquet's sense of rootedness—and he wanted to experience that life for himself. He had had enough of Paris and New York, enough of the Ritz bar, the parties in Biarritz, the literary cliques in Montparnasse. In Senlis, he wanted to spend his days with the sun on his back and the earth between his fingers. "I've reached my second childhood," he told his friend, the critic Harry Hansen, "and returned to the life of my youth, spreading manure and enjoying myself thoroughly in the country. I have half a suspicion that I shall end up a horticulturalist rather than a novelist."

Bromfield's literary friends were surprised by his new passion. "Louis has gone back to nature, gardens furiously in blue denim overalls," reported one correspondent, who speculated that soon Bromfield would be speaking only "horticultural Latin" and sleeping upon a "mattress stuffed with seed catalogs."

The man who taught Bromfield how to garden the French way was named Victor Picquet. He was a strong, ruddy peasant who, regardless of the season, wrapped his belly in yards of flannel ("*contre la grippe*"). "He was not very bright," Bromfield said, "but he had a wonderful way with flowers, vegetables and animals." Picquet was born in the Pas-de-Calais, spoke an "ugly, half-Flemish" patois, and had never been to high school. Before he became Bromfield's full-time gardener, he worked as a day laborer on the renovation of the Presbytère. But he had gardened since he was a boy and he knew all "the tricks handed down from generations of peasants who had raised half of the food they consumed in small confined plots." He had only one foible. "If I did not watch him, he would put down half the garden in leeks, that backbone of all good French soups."

When the ground thawed in March, Picquet and Bromfield dug in. They trucked out the cinders and broken bottles and trucked in topsoil. They arranged a series of small terraces leading up from the river to the highest level of the garden. They built trellises to support climbing plants. Next they began transplanting the first flowers: delphiniums, phlox, perennial poppies. They trained roses and wisteria against the ancient walls. They converted the red-roofed chapel into a garden shed. In its old well, they kept a brew of water and chicken manure that "ripened like wine" under Picquet's supervision.

Beside the chapel, Bromfield wanted to plant a *potager*, a kitchen garden that would supply his family with fresh herbs and vegetables. He had only just started digging in this ground when his shovel uncovered something strange: fragments of some kind—pale, hard, but too porous to be rock. Bromfield realized he was digging in the chapel's graveyard. He did not hesitate, just worked the human bones he found back into the earth with a bit of chicken manure. "He felt no qualms about thus treating consecrated ground," Ellen wrote. "How could he? For nothing was nearer to his conception of God than the cycle in nature which begins with birth and ends with rebirth."

They divided the *potager* into six neat small squares, separated with paths bordered by strawberry plants, just like in Bosquet's garden. Bromfield chose to plant a mix of two strawberries: a "luscious" larger variety and the small, perfumed *fraises des bois*. Inside the squares he planted vegetables: beets, carrots, eggplant, cabbage, and snowy heads of cauliflower that his children loved to eat roasted with melted butter and breadcrumbs. By the river, where the ground grew moist, they put in celery, leeks, and, farthest down, a green mat of watercress. Bromfield was learning things from Picquet. He learned how to train peach trees in espaliers, so they grew in a straight line flush against the ancient stone wall, which, when warmed by the sun, helped to ripen the fruits. He learned how to stretch his garden's productivity into winter, growing escarole and endives under big glass bells called *cloches*, so he could have fresh salads year-round. He learned the basics of intercropping: alternating cabbages and leeks with rows of asters or marigolds, to their mutual benefit. In exchange, he showed Picquet a few things about American horticulture, introducing him to Bantam corn, Hubbard squash, and the Ponderosa tomato, whose vines quickly grew up the 10-foot stone wall and down the opposite side to the ground. Everything they put down flourished. It was shocking—the trash heap, once cleared, concealed a land bristling with fertility.

Bromfield did not need to dig up those old French bones to know that the banks of these rivers had been inhabited for centuries. He imagined previous generations of his neighbors, listening out for the *clop-clop* of hooves, which would send them "quickly to the door with broom and dustpan in case the passing horse had left behind the precious manure." His neighbors' gardens had been cultivated intensively for perhaps a thousand years, yet somehow they were more fertile than ever before. Why was this the case in France, he wondered, while in America a farmer could exhaust rich virgin soil in the space of one or two generations?

While the *potager* reflected Bromfield's respect for French technique and tradition, the neighboring flower garden was brash and showy, raising eyebrows in conservative Senlis. The six color photographs that survive offer clues about the palette, which was extremely varied: hot pink and crimson red from the Godetia and poppies; faded pink and deep purple from the flat-petaled cottage flowers like Viscaria and phlox, towers of phosphorescent blue from lupine, larkspur, and delphinium. Marigolds and calendulas radiated orange (and a strong scent that kept away pests). In the showier section, Bromfield planted rare dahlia cultivars and *Nigella damascena* (or love-in-a-mist), with its spiky blue flowers encircling a Medusa-like seed-head. He grew Canterbury bells that looked like dainty teacups and Nemesia that looked like small butterflies. Then there were the roses: voluptuous musk roses and rambling varieties like the American pillar, with its floppy petals and golden stamens that blossom in dense clusters of carmine pink. Most precious to him were the hybrid tea roses. Bromfield preferred two in particular: Mrs. Aaron Ward (pale pink, fragrant, looking like a ball of ruched taffeta) and the appropriately melancholy Souvenir de Claudius Pernet (a drooping yellow rose named for its creator's son, who died in World War I). By early fall, Bromfield said his garden had become "voracious," consuming "all my time," making it impossible to sit still by a window and write when there was so much work to be done outside. "It is really indescribably beautiful at the moment . . . I look at it in wonder that a year ago there was nothing here but waste land."

———

It did not take long for the garden, visible from one of the main roads into Senlis, to attract attention, which Bromfield cultivated almost as carefully as his roses. Farm families in their black Sunday clothes began to gather on the bridge overlooking the Nonette to gaze at the flowers that crowded the narrow brook. The artist and food writer Samuel Chamberlain, who lived a few blocks away from Bromfield on the Rue du Temple, remembered motorists stopping to "gape in ecstasy." * Soon French newspapers started sending correspondents to interview the green-fingered American author. After meeting Bromfield, one journalist, from the weekly magazine *Marianne*, described him as a walking contradiction. His suntanned, leathery skin lent him the air of a "Danish sailor," but he drank his old *fine* like the best French connoisseur. He earned a fabulous living as a writer, but he claimed that he was "born to be a gardener" and spoke of his dahlias "with more emotion than one of his books."

Bromfield liked to be seen mixing with earthy peasants like Bosquet and Picquet, but while he craved the simplicity of their existence, his attempts at achieving it for himself amounted to little more than rustic pretensions. He never cut himself off from the swirl of Paris, from the "chi-chi and whoopee" as he called it. Instead he simply imported these things into the countryside. By the fall of 1931, the society set in Paris—especially its American expatriate subsection—knew to reserve Sundays for Senlis. It was "exciting," Gertrude Stein said, a place where anyone might show up, where each time "something will happen." Bromfield's entertaining philosophy, described in a letter to his friend, the British polymath Edward Marsh, was simple: "make no effort at being host beyond providing plenty of good food and wine, and let nature take

---

* Chamberlain (1895–1975) would draw on his culinary adventures in Senlis in the 1940s, when he introduced a whole generation of Americans to French cuisine in the pages of a revolutionary new magazine called *Gourmet*.

its course." The buffet was cold and constantly replenished. The liquor flowed like wine, the wine flowed like the Nonette. As if there were not enough flowers in the garden, Bromfield filled each table with a vase of stems arranged, Janet Flanner said, like "perfect imitations of the flower paintings by the sixteenth-century painter Brueghel." (The Paris-based fashion designer Mainbocher was so impressed with Bromfield's bouquets that he asked him to do the arrangements for his runway show.)

Bromfield invited everyone, and anyone, to Senlis, aiming for a group of people that was "startling in its variety." "He liked to mix people like cocktails and see how they'd react to each other," his daughter Hope said. There were fiercely intellectual writers like Rebecca West and hopelessly romantic ones like Michael Arlen. The fashion designer Elsa Schiaparelli came in a little black suit and tiny boater hat, wearing junk jewelry that she managed to make chic. The Maharani of the Indian state of Cooch Behar arrived in a flowing silk sari and emeralds. Occasionally, a movie star dropped in: Douglas Fairbanks, Myrna Loy, Ina Claire. They mixed with foreign correspondents, like Walter Duranty, the pro-Stalin shill who ran the Moscow bureau of the *New York Times*; professional athletes, like Helen Wills, who won Wimbledon eight times in an eyebrow-raising knee-length skirt; and socialites like the six-foot-tall Lady Juliet Duff, who might arrive with fresh parliamentary gossip obtained during her weekly piquet game with Winston Churchill.

The guests were socialists and monarchists, Jews and anti-Semites, gay and straight, rich, very rich, and broke—if not for their rich friends. They were headed for scandal, insanity, obscurity. Some would be dead within a decade, blown out of the sky by the Luftwaffe like the actor Leslie Howard. Others would ruin themselves through drink or a string of ugly divorces. But for the moment they seemed content to admire the poppies and have another glass of wine. Bromfield took their photographs, and Mary carefully pasted each one into scrapbooks. Janet Flanner once said that Bromfield "collected people (and noted their value) the way some men do stamps." The pictures show them sitting on the

The fashion designer Elsa Schiaparelli and the decorator Van
Day Truex (with cigarette) were some of the creative types who
flocked each weekend to Bromfield's garden outside Paris.

grass in three-piece suits or belted floral dresses, accessorized to death:
foulards, folded handkerchiefs, boutonnières, pendant necklaces, veils,
fussy tilt hats that are useless in the bright sun. They let their hair down,
take their shirts off, wrap towels like turbans about their heads. They
drink Champagne from shallow crystal coupes, they drink coffee out
of demitasses. Soon enough everything shaped like a cup becomes an
ashtray. Their eyes get glossy behind funny owl-eyed sunglasses. They let
their feet dangle in the river.

On Sundays, every member of the Bromfield household had a role to
play. Mary made the introductions. Picquet waited on tables. George Hawkins fixed drinks, before repairing to his hammock and falling asleep. The
girls shelled peas into a big wicker basket. The cook, Marguerite, kept the
buffet supplied: charcuterie and olives, potato salad, deviled eggs, lemonade, strawberry shortcake. Bromfield, as host, was also the entertainment.

He liked to dress in monochromes, sometimes all black, which made him look like a Left Bank poet, sometimes all white, which made him look like a Basque pelota player. One reporter assigned to profile him said he told "such funny stories that he practically disabled me for the rest of the interview." He walked around the garden with a long stick, pointing out his flowers while dropping references to aristocrats and manure in the same sentence, a habit that annoyed his friend Edna Ferber. "For godsakes, Louis," she once told him, "brush the caviar off your blue jeans!" Flanner had more patience with Bromfield's earthy side. "He's a country man," she once wrote, "who happens to plow with his pen."

—◦—

Gertrude Stein was a fixture at Bromfield's garden parties. When he lived in Paris, Stein had hosted him on a few occasions for tea or a glass of port at her apartment on the Rue de Fleurus. But it wasn't until Bromfield moved to Senlis that Stein became excited about the possibility of a true friendship. "Why?" asked Toklas, after Stein accepted an invitation to Sunday lunch. "Because," Stein replied, "he knows all about gardens."

Stein's first visit to Senlis, in the fall of 1931, was complicated by the presence of her dog. Basket, a standard white poodle, was a celebrity—both Man Ray and Cecil Beaton would eventually take his portrait. He was trimmed and tonsured by the best dog groomer in Paris and Stein gave him regular sulfur-water baths to keep his coat gleaming white. Arriving at the Presbytère, Stein made the tragic error of bringing Basket into the garden, which was the domain of Dash, Bromfield's dog. A grizzled, pugnacious old Scotty, Dash could not compete with Basket in terms of fame, but he was well known throughout Senlis as "a tramp and a Don Juan." He would fight—or mate with—dogs of any size and disposition. Whenever a dog in Senlis had puppies, Bromfield said, odds were its owner would claim that Dash was the father. Dash's greatest conquest was a huge German police dog named Marquise, who gave

Gertrude Stein and Alice B. Toklas in the Presbytère's "Jungle
Room," whose murals were painted by Louis and Mary.

birth to "half-pint police dogs with smooth black coats, Scotty heads and
magnificent sweeping black tails arching over their backs."

Dash had "never seen anything like a poodle before," Mary said, "and
was disgusted with his fancy and fastidious person." He attacked. Basket
howled. Two tables in the garden were overturned, one guest was accidentally kicked in the shins by another, and two others were bitten before
Basket was rescued, "his beautiful marcelled white coat streaked with
blood." Stein, Mary said, "was horrified and intervened rather helplessly

and got a bite for her pains." As for Basket, he had to be "nursed and comforted for the remainder of the day."

Bromfield later sent Stein a postcard—the first item in an extensive correspondence—in which he expressed hope that "Basket didn't suffer" too much. If upset, Stein did not hold a grudge. "The girls," as Mary called Stein and Toklas, soon became "regular customers" at the Sunday lunches. They talked about literature, politics, art, gossip—but mostly they talked about gardening. "We are going to plant morning glories, we are going to plant everything," Stein wrote to Bromfield before inviting him down to their country house to spruce up the vegetable patch. "Alice," she said, "has a million questions to ask you."

4

"Teched"

Gertrude Stein liked to brag about her achievements in the garden: her "strange vegetables" and "wonderful English pansies." But she was not a natural. She complained to Bromfield about meager harvests (nothing but "rocks and trees and hay") and she did not like the rain even when her flowers badly needed it. "I at heart am only 1/3 gardener," she once confessed. Bromfield always encouraged Stein's efforts, but he met his horticultural match in another expatriate writer of even greater renown: Edith Wharton.

Bromfield and Wharton were so obsessed by gardening that their other shared occupation—literature—seemed almost incidental to their friendship. "We seldom discussed our writing," he said, "but we talked frequently and at great length of our dahlias and petunias, our green peas and lettuces." They shared cuttings and seeds, visited flower breeders, lunched with garden designers, and engaged in playful competition. By the early 1930s, their hobby had brought them close enough that Bromfield sounded bashful when he admitted to Wharton that he had "found another literary gardener in the person of Gertrude Stein." But, he reas-

Edith Wharton was Bromfield's close friend and fellow
gardener. "We seldom discussed our writing," he said,
"but we talked frequently and at great length of our
dahlias and petunias, our green peas and lettuces."

sured her, Stein's approach was "far more intellectual and less passionate
than our own."

Wharton knew Stein only by reputation. Although both women had
resided in or around Paris since the early 1900s, in terms of literary and
personal style, they inhabited distant planets. Wharton thought Stein's

lesbianism was perverse, her prose baffling. As a rule, she disliked anything that smelled too strongly of Modernism, once describing *Ulysses* as a "turgid welter of schoolboy pornography." Practically the only thing she and Stein shared was a friendship with Bromfield. Both women frequently visited Senlis, although only Stein would come to the parties. Wharton preferred private luncheons with Louis and Mary on the terrace, after which they would go over the flower borders together. Once Wharton wandered by accident into one of the Bromfields' Sunday free-for-alls, having stopped by the Presbytère on her way home to pick up a bottle of apple brandy, a gift that Bromfield had brought her from Normandy. Wharton took one look at the crowd, shuddered, and turned the other way. "Perceiving that everyone who was not at Longchamps was lunching with you," she wrote to him later, "I gave up the attempt to force my way through the serried ranks of motors at your door and snatched the precious Calvados from your kind cook."

Wharton lived in a grand country manor, the Pavillon Colombe, only a short drive away from Senlis in Saint-Brice-sous-Fôret. Although she and Bromfield were both Pulitzer Prize–winning expatriate novelists, in other respects they had little in common. She was thirty-four years his senior, a product of Washington Square and Newport, a friend of Henry James and Theodore Roosevelt, who was fluent in four languages and had spent most of her life in Europe. She easily could have written him off as a bumpkin or an arriviste, and she poked fun at the mixed company he kept. "I've been at the Crillon," she wrote to him in 1933, "but did not call you up because I was sure you'd be smothered in Maharajas and race meetings and ducal cocktail parties—at such moments when the garden could spare you." She looked askance at other hard-drinking writers in his set, including Scott Fitzgerald, whom she had met during a disastrous tea in 1925. He had showed up to Saint-Brice with his friend Teddy Chanler and seemed either "overawed by Mrs. Wharton's formal manner," Chanler said, or drunk from the cocktails he had to fortify himself on the ride up from Paris. After introductions, the conversation stalled and Fitzgerald launched into a bawdy anecdote about a young American couple—perhaps Zelda and himself?—who had taken up residence for two weeks in a brothel that they mistook for a hotel. Wharton was not amused. In her diary, she described the meeting with one word: "Horrible."

—·—

Though it lasted only six years, Bromfield thought his friendship with Wharton was "as close in many senses as I have ever known." He wrote those words shortly after her death, in 1937, in an unpublished memoir in which he insisted that, contrary to her haughty reputation, Wharton was a "passionate woman," so unlike the "snobbish, vulgar society which she satirized and detested." What defined her, Bromfield thought, was a consuming love of nature that few people understood. "For her a drouth was a kind of illness from which she suffered physically, and the persistent cold rain which ruined the roses and damaged the prospects of a magnificent flowering was a kind of personal agony." Bromfield could recognize this quality in Wharton because he felt it in himself. The trait they shared was extremely rare, something he always sought but seldom found in others, something that was first explained to him when he was just a boy by another woman with a mysterious connection to the earth.

Her name was Phoebe Wise. According to Bromfield, she was a vague relative: his great-great-grandfather and her grandfather were brothers. She was born in the 1840s and spent her entire life in a tiny gabled house on the outskirts of Mansfield, Ohio. Local newspapers described her as a "woman-hermit." She lived with feral animals in an atmosphere of grand decay: her cottage seeming at once creepy, squalid, and alluring—like an Ohio frontier analogue of Miss Havisham's ruined mansion.

The historical record yields only a few hard facts about Phoebe's early life. Her parents came from Boston. Her father was a county surveyor and later a minister. Her mother taught school. As a young woman, Phoebe also worked for a time as a schoolteacher but was not seen much in Mansfield, except when she would ride the streetcars into town to buy cheap

Bromfield's eccentric cousin Phoebe Wise possessed
a deep and mysterious connection with nature
that she called being "*teched*." It was a trait she
also recognized in the young Bromfield.

jewelry or ribbon from the general store. Many in Mansfield thought she
was adopted and that her birth parents were Delaware Indian, perhaps
because of her copper skin and her hair, which, Bromfield wrote, was "as
black as a crow's wing."

She had always kept her distance from people, especially those in
positions of power. "She was immensely selective—in her own way, a
snob," Bromfield wrote. "She had no time for the conservative or the

conventional whom she held in contempt as limpets clinging to the rock of conformity." Despite her striking beauty, she never married. "I don't like men," she once told a reporter. "They're not truthful, and not satisfied with one woman . . . I don't look to humans for my happiness—people are too treacherous." Phoebe preferred animals. Visitors to her house described kittens playing in her lap, and birds and little chicks jumping up on the arms of her chair to coax for crumbs. Phoebe spoke to her curly-haired black dog "with all the seriousness of chatting with another human being," and her white Arabian horse, Scotty, occasionally walked up behind her and nuzzled her cheek.

Bromfield was entranced by Phoebe. All his life, he could not stop writing about her. She was the subject of at least two of his short stories and also became a major character in his 1933 autobiographical novel, *The Farm.* By the time he wrote about her under her real name, in his 1945 memoir *Pleasant Valley,* he feared he had exhausted "the subject, like an etching plate which has grown old and worn from use. Yet I cannot stop myself even now, for I think I have never met any individual who left upon me so profound an impression."

The last time Bromfield had seen her, while visiting Mansfield in 1917 before shipping off to France, she was in her seventies and wearing a yellow taffeta dress, "very long with a slight train which she did not lift but permitted to drag grandly behind her," collecting dust and leaves. She wore black lace mittens and a "rusty black picture hat" to which she pinned wild asters picked from the roadside. If his description made her sound like a "dowdy scarecrow," Bromfield said, the impression she gave off was the opposite, one of a *chic* woman who carried herself with "an air of immense dignity, even majesty."

Throughout Phoebe's life, her isolation, extravagant spinsterhood, and eccentric appearance made her the subject of rumors, the most persistent of which was that she had squirreled away her parents' fortune somewhere in her cottage north of town on the Olivesburg Road. Those rumors sometimes attracted the wrong kind of attention.

A few days before Christmas 1891, Phoebe, then in her late forties, was at home when she heard a strange noise in the sitting room. Three armed men wearing red bandanas had broken the lock of her door with a crowbar and barged into her house. One grabbed Phoebe by the throat. They bound her hands and feet and demanded to know where her treasure was hidden. She told them truthfully she had no treasure, but they did not believe her. One man brought a torch to the bottom of her feet and burnt her soles. She screamed, but her story did not change. The men ransacked Phoebe's house, tearing up carpets, bedding, even the floorboards, discovering what few valuables she had: a diamond ring, a gold watch, and a chain. Upon leaving, according to the account in the *Mansfield News*, the burglars noticed a freshly baked pie in the kitchen and, in a strangely discordant instance of courtesy, asked Phoebe for permission to help themselves. Then they left without untying her.

Phoebe eventually freed herself and summoned the police from a nearby telegraph station. Accounts of her bravery appeared in newspapers near and far. She received not only fan mail but "seven or eight" marriage proposals. One admirer tried to endear himself to her by offering "a sure cure recipe for burned feet." Another told Phoebe patronizingly that "there ought to be a man about the place and there would be less danger of robbers."

Among Phoebe's admirers was a young immigrant, variously described as Polish or Hungarian, by the name of Jacob Kastanowitz, whose infatuation with the brave woman apparently grew into an obsession. Once he hid in the basement of her home, other times he peeked into her open windows or used a metal wire to push aside her curtains and look in. In July of 1892, he sent Phoebe a letter requesting they meet. Enclosed in the envelope was an "obscene drawing"—"lewd in the utmost degree"— made with colored crayon and "other obscene matter of an unmentionable character." Kastanowitz was eventually arrested and confined to an asylum for a time, but Phoebe's "pestiferous persecutor," as one paper called him, never relented. Finally, on the night of May 22, 1898, Kastanowitz showed up in a hysterical state at Phoebe's door. "Marry me or shoot me!" he screamed. Phoebe fired a single shot from her .32 caliber Winchester rifle through a window in the direction of the noise and heard nothing more from Kastanowitz. In the morning, she found his corpse on her front porch.

An inquest was held, and hundreds of townsfolk, mostly women, attended in Phoebe's defense. "I'm not guilty" she said firmly, and declined to make a further statement, even refusing to give her age. Ruling that it was a case of "justifiable homicide," the prosecutor did not press charges. As the verdict was read, the Mansfield women in the audience burst into applause. A newspaper headline put the case in terms of frontier justice: "PHOEBE WISE RIDS HERSELF OF AN INTOLERABLE NUISANCE." From this point, the legend of Phoebe Wise only grew. She became a local celebrity, her opinion sought out on everything from financial management to women's suffrage. "Would I vote if I was given a chance? Well now, you just watch me once and see!" she told one interviewer in 1914. "I haven't spent the past twenty-five years of my life wrestling with crooked politicians and scheming lawyers without seeing the urgent need of a few good, clean-minded women in the field of public affairs."

—·—

Bromfield first met Phoebe when he was a small boy of maybe ten. Her house was almost suffocated in vegetation, its fretwork mangled by "thrusting shoots of wisteria and trumpet vine." The garden had become "jungly," full of old-fashioned blooms like mock orange and daylilies. Bromfield had arrived in a horse-drawn buggy with his father, Charley, a real-estate speculator with political ambitions who had spent the day canvassing nearby. While Charley went inside to talk to Phoebe, Bromfield explored the overgrown garden, "making friends with the animals, both wild and tame." He stopped at a spring pond and busied himself building little boats out of twigs and sailing them on the surface. Scotty, Phoebe's white horse, who was then just a colt, approached. Bromfield began to play with him, laughing when Scotty dipped his muzzle into the pond and tossed the cold water over Bromfield's head.

Phoebe had by now come out of the house with his father and began to watch Bromfield with an intense interest. "Cousin Charley," she said, "that boy is *teched*." Bromfield did not know what this word meant, and in his confusion he looked up at Phoebe. He wrote that he felt something when he looked into her "burning black eyes," some "strange current of sympathy and knowledge, which bound us together forever afterward." Later, heading home in the buggy with his father, Bromfield asked what exactly Phoebe had meant by *teched*, which she had pronounced with a soft "ch" sound, like "fetched."

He laughed and replied, "She means a little crazy, like herself." And then after a little time he added with a sigh, "A lot of people think Phoebe is crazy, but I don't. I think she's awful smart."

"*Teched*" is a rural idiomatic version of "touched," which the Oxford English Dictionary defines as "mentally deranged to a slight degree." But that was not quite the way Phoebe meant it, nor the way Bromfield later construed it. To them, being *teched* was something beautiful if strange, an uncanny ability to blend into the pattern of life—to connect in some profound yet humbling way with the natural world. Plenty of others have embodied this feeling: Saint Francis of Assisi preaching to the birds, Johnny Appleseed refusing to graft his apple trees because he did not want to cause them pain, Henry David Thoreau seeing in the elliptical flight of hen hawks above Walden Pond traces of his own thoughts. Bromfield called *teched* an "inner sense of mystical feeling which makes people one with Nature and with animals and birds." He recognized that quality in himself and, despite her sophisticated, urbane veneer, he recognized it intensely in Edith Wharton.

Although she never used the term, Wharton knew she was *teched*. Her favorite fairy tale as a child was the story of the "boy who could talk with the birds and hear what the grasses said." Wharton wrote in her memoir that she felt "akin to that happy child." And one day, when she was five or six and walking with her uncles and cousins through the woods around Mamaroneck, she felt "something in me quite incommunicable to others that was tremblingly and inarticulately awake to every detail of wind-warped fern and wide-eyed briar rose." She wasn't merely sensitive to the superficial beauty of these plants but to "a unifying magic beneath the diversities of the visible scene—a power with which I was in deep and solitary communion whenever I was alone with nature."

—•—

Wharton acquired the Pavillon Colombe, her neoclassical country home in Saint-Brice, at the end of World War I, when much of northern France was depopulated and many of its storied estates all but abandoned. After moving in, she transformed the neglected 7-acre property into a remarkable series of gardens as she had done at the Mount, her country house in Lenox, Massachusetts, and would later do at the Castel Sainte-Claire, her villa in Hyères, in the south of France. Her design was arranged in stages. Stone steps led down to a long graveled terrace dotted with flowerpots and simple lawn furniture. Dwarf orange trees grew out of green wooden boxes. The first smell to hit you was that of jasmine, then lavender, a thick row of which separated the terrace from a more formal section of parterres. The overall impression at Saint-Brice was one of severe splendor: a hedge of clipped boxwood, an archway made of trained lime trees, orchards arranged by season. A flower border, made up of peonies, delphinium, and a wall of lilac, concealed a "big sunny" *potager,* from which she supplied her cook with fresh vegetables and sold the surplus to her neighbors. The high stone walls were filled with climbing roses, red lashes of begonia, clematis, and trumpet vines.

Wharton's close friend, the American expatriate banker John Hugh Smith, said she once told him that she thought "her gardens were better than her books." Nowhere was she happier than standing amid her flow-

Louis and Mary often visited Wharton's formal
gardens at the Pavillon Colombe in Saint-Brice-
sous-Fôret, a short drive from Senlis.

ers in her wide-brimmed straw hat, armed with a basket and pruning
shears. She walked through, admiring this, correcting that, before lin-
gering over her stone pool filled with water lilies and "fat old goldfish,"
which she would feed out of a little embroidered bag. A pair of toy dogs
followed behind her. "Wherever you first caught sight of her, active and

occupied, in this picture of her creation" one friend recalled, "she seemed to be settling down to peace in the world with the happiest assurance that everything around her, all for which she need answer, was right."

In their many letters, Wharton and Bromfield discussed their gardens in minute detail, obsessing over the weather and suggesting special varieties that might thrive in northern France. "When are you coming north?" he wrote to her in the spring of 1932, when she was at her winter home in Hyères.

> Everything has leapt forward so that now the borders look green and ready to burst into bloom. The *Meconopsis baileyi*—the blue Himalayan poppy—which seems to be the great sensation in England, and which I got as plants from Suttons (given it takes a year to germinate) are thriving, much to my delight.* And so far I can see we lost nothing by the minor frost of a month ago save a few arrivals about which I was never very optimistic. What fun it is to go over the borders, plant by plant and find everyone successful beyond your dreams! All my prized Canterbury Bells and campanulas are ready to burst into splendor. And the forests now are turning yellow with daffodils. This house is full of them.

To this horticultural report, she replied in kind.

> You make me envious with your spring flowers, & I wish I could make you envious with some of mine *here!* You must (if you haven't already) plant some of the marvellous hybrid "Iris de Jardine" . . . Mine are a perfect glory now, & I imagine that they are

---

* Suttons, the horticultural supplier now based in Devon, England, provided Bromfield with many of his exotic flowers.

mostly hardy[.] My species irises are enchanting too—& even the
shy "Pavonia" has produced one exquisite flower. But this is not
"Country Life" & I must stop. (But, *oh*, my peonies!!) . . .

Wharton always asked Bromfield to visit. "Come & see my Primulinuses!!"* she would write. Or: "If you cd see my peonies & California irises here now, you'd drown yourself in the Nonette!" Or: "I want
to swank about the roses to you & Mary before long, for they've got
their second wind now. Couldn't you two come to lunch some day this
week—say on Wednesday or Saturday?"

As Wharton's health declined and political news in Europe dark-
ened, both writers would seek refuge in their gardens. Bromfield told
Wharton he thought cultivating flowers was "the best insurance against
the complications and depressions" of the moment. In 1936, when general strikes paralyzed France and the Right and Left were on the brink
of open warfare, he remarked to her that "Nature continues to take no
notice of the imbecilities of mankind and despite even the bad weather
the garden is lovely and the roses have never been so fine." Wharton
agreed. "Yes; the garden is the last moral life-preserver left," she said. "I
pity those who haven't it."

—┼—

Bromfield and Wharton were easily the most accomplished gardeners
among the literary expatriates, but they were by no means the only
Americans in France for whom the garden was a passion and a sanctu-
ary. A decade before Wharton began revamping the gardens at Saint-

---

* *Pavonia* is a likely reference to *Iris pavonia*, an old name for the peacock iris (*Moraea
aristata*). *Country Life* is a popular English gardening magazine, published from 1897
by Edward Hudson. "Primulinuses" possibly refers to the *Gladiolus primulinus*, a type
of gladiola.

Brice, the Ohio-born poet and heiress Natalie Clifford Barney moved
into a sixteenth-century mansion on the Rue Jacob, in Paris. A wil-
lowy beauty, Barney was openly, even ostentatiously, gay; she opposed
monogamy and wanted to revive the spirit of Lesbos in her leafy garden
shaded by a giant chestnut tree. It was here, in the glow of Japanese lan-
terns, that Barney united a community of female lovers and artists for
regular Friday salons. They recited poetry, drank liqueurs, ate cucumber
sandwiches. Friendship was their religion: In the corner of the garden
was a small temple with Doric columns and the words À L'AMITIÉ—
to friendship—chiseled over its entrance. Men were welcome: James
Joyce, T. S. Eliot, and Jean Cocteau all visited. Many years later, so did
a young Truman Capote. But the majority of guests were gay women,
according to Sylvia Beach, who came there with her longtime companion and fellow bookseller Adrienne Monnier. At Miss Barney's, "one met

A group of lesbian expatriate artists and writers—sometimes
called "*amazones*"—often visited the Presbytère, including
(from left, after Mary Bromfield) Esther Murphy, Janet
Flanner, Noël Haskins Murphy, and Solita Solano.

lesbians, Paris ones and those only passing through town," Beach said. Those ladies, who normally wore "high collars and monocles," sometimes changed into Grecian robes, held hands, and ring-danced in the garden.

One of these women was Noël Haskins Murphy. She was a singer, a good friend of the Bromfields who frequently came to their Sunday garden parties in Senlis. Murphy would return the favor by inviting the Bromfields to her own garden in Orgeval, west of Paris, where she owned a two-story stone farmhouse. Murphy was dramatically beautiful, a mix of Garbo and Dietrich, "with high cheekbones and hay-colored hair." She seemed to embody a type—the "careless, flamboyant Amazone in shorts and skirts." Flanner fell in love with her. Hemingway, as ever enthralled and terrified by a liberated woman, claimed she made him "nervous the way cats do some people."

Unlike many of her bohemian friends, Murphy did not originally come to France in search of artistic or sexual freedom. She bought the house in Orgeval mostly so she could be close to the gravesite of her husband, Fred Murphy, who had died of wounds suffered during World War I. Slowly at first, she began to remake her life. She launched a career as a lieder singer. She turned her house into a kind of countryside bed-and-breakfast, charging friends (like the novelist Djuna Barnes, who sunbathed nude in the garden) 10 francs a day if they insisted on paying for food and drink. She grew herbs, vegetables, asters, dahlias, Madonna lilies, zinnias, and lavender, which she hung in the bedrooms. As with Natalie Clifford Barney, her garden became a protected place, a world apart, a controlled space where she could begin a new life on her own terms.

Noël's brother-in-law was Gerald Murphy. He and his wife, Sara, moved to Paris in 1921 and quickly became the most celebrated escapists of their generation. The Murphys somehow embodied all the romance and excitement of American expatriate life between the wars. They threw legendary parties, they painted sets for Diaghilev's Ballets Russes, they went on vacation with Picasso and Stein. Scott Fitzgerald famously fell in love with both of them, and used them as models for the characters of Dick and Nicole Diver in his anguished masterpiece *Tender Is the Night*. Years later, in 1962, Calvin Tomkins profiled the Murphys in an article in *The New Yorker*, in which he wrote that the one thing Gerald and Sara "wanted above all was a garden." For them it was an essential part of life. "Outside of a man and a woman, and children and a house and a garden," Gerald said, "there's nothing much." When the Murphys settled in a "small and unpretentious chalet" in Cap d'Antibes, in 1925, their dream finally came true.

Whatever happened in and around that garden of the Villa America seemed exciting, considered, planned—even the outbursts and drunken rows at their parties were calibrated to make just the right kind of splash. The food, the conversation, the company had a set-designed perfection. "I could stand it for about four days," Dos Passos said. "It was like trying to live in heaven. I had to get back down to earth." There were pepper, fig, and olive trees, white-leafed Arabian maples, eucalyptus, mimosa, heliotrope, and a huge linden overshadowing the terrace. In *Tender*, Fitzgerald spends some of the novel's first pages describing that garden in language that is at once precise and slippery. The path is filled with "an intangible mist of bloom," the peonies are "massed in pink clouds," the roses are "transparent like sugar flowers in a confectioner's window." There is a feeling that it cannot last, that it may suddenly disappear—as it did when the Murphys lost two of their young children to illness in the 1930s.

Bromfield may not have experienced the kind of family trauma that marked the lives of Gerald and Sara Murphy. He may not have needed the garden to create a safe space for the sexual freedom that Noël Murphy and Natalie Clifford Barney craved. But he would seek there a respite from his own looming battles with depression and longing, with impotence and dread. Like so many other Lost Generation figures, he would draw strength from having a patch of earth whose shape he could control and order, especially when the rest of the world started spinning out of control. "The well-being which came to him in the garden was perhaps the only real peace my father ever knew," Ellen Bromfield Geld wrote. "Watching him from a distance as he worked among his flowers in the chapel or beside the Nonette, one could almost see the calm come over him. Sometimes he simply stretched out on the grass and fell asleep."

5

Tangled Roots

SENLIS, 1932

Some day, there will come a reckoning. The country will discover that
farmers are more necessary than traveling salesmen, that no nation
can exist or have any solidity which ignores the land. But it will cost
the country dear. There'll be hell to pay before they find out.

—LOUIS BROMFIELD, *THE FARM*

Bromfield and Wharton gardened in a sleepy part of France, a flat plain
of soft grass that spreads out like a picnic blanket between the Seine and
the Oise Rivers above Paris. The landscape here has been cultivated intensively for so long that it can sometimes be difficult to tell where nature
ends and design begins: country lanes are bordered by bolt-straight rows
of poplar trees, beech forests are carpeted with wildflowers, old farms
seem to be growing out of the earth. When Sherwood Anderson came
here, in the early 1920s, he was struck by the intimacy of the agriculture,
how the peasants and market gardeners fussed over the smallest patches
of land, working the soil with spade and sickles instead of horse- and gas-
powered machines. "It is as though every grain of dust in all France," he
wrote in his journal, "had been run through the fingers of some peasant's
hands." Wharton also noticed this, the way French farmers managed to
exploit the land "to its utmost clod" without losing "its freshness and

naturalness," as if agriculture had somehow "mated with poetry instead of banishing it."

The American expatriate's conception of French agriculture, however idealized, recognized an important fact: farming was sacred in France in a way that it was not in America. French schoolchildren were made to memorize the words of Maximilien de Béthune, a minister in the court of Henry IV, who wrote that "plowing and grazing are the two breasts from which France is fed." Many French intellectuals romanticized the peasants. Jean-Jacques Rousseau said, "It is the rural people who make the nation." The historian Jules Michelet claimed that farming was "the holy work of France." Agriculture was so important to the French revolutionaries that, in 1793, they replaced the Gregorian calendar with an entirely new system devoted to its most granular details. Months corresponded to important events in the farming season—like the wine harvest or the germination of crops—while days were named for different plants, animals, and farming implements (July 28, for instance, is the Day of the Watering Can). Farming remains a symbolically vital part of French culture. A major event in any French presidential campaign is the visit by candidates to the Salon International de l'Agriculture to pet cows. The ancient concept of *terroir* is today enshrined in a complicated "appellation" system, which validates the uniqueness of many French agricultural products, from wine to the caviar-like lentils of the Puy valley to the blue-footed Bresse chickens that, by law, must each have ten square meters to forage on as many escargots as they fancy.

The glories of the country's agriculture, however, often concealed the drudgery and poverty endured by most French farm laborers. Karl Marx famously described French peasants as "potatoes in a sack." He criticized the way they were isolated from one another, often failed to pool their talents and divide their labor, and earned their livelihoods "more through exchange with nature than in intercourse with society." Yet Bromfield viewed the peasant's self-sufficiency—regardless of the hardships that brought it about—as a quality to admire and emulate. He knew that, for centuries, some sections of rural France functioned as autarkies: economically independent communities where, besides certain essentials like iron and salt, farmers could grow or trade everything they needed to survive. Even into the late nineteenth century, there were some remote hamlets in France where, according to the historian Eugen Weber, "money was almost unknown." Bromfield saw the inheritance of that self-sufficiency in men like Picquet and Bosquet, who raised much of what they ate, treasured their small plots, and would refuse any offers to sell so they could pass their security on to their children. "Any French peasant," Bromfield wrote, "had more permanence, more solidity, more security" than the average American. The French *paysan* seemed to him a romantic figure, bound to his *terroir*. If he was a cliché, he was not an unattractive one. His American counterpart, the dirt farmer, had become by 1932 something else: a cautionary tale.

———

At the same moment when Bromfield and Wharton were taking tea in their French gardens, an economic catastrophe was hollowing out the American heartland. By the end of 1932, the national unemployment rate had climbed to nearly 25 percent. In Bromfield's native state of Ohio, jobless numbers would soon be far worse: 50 percent in Cleveland, 60 percent in Akron, 80 percent in Toledo. Some city-dwellers fainted in the streets from hunger while farmers a few miles away burned their worthless wheat for fuel. Bromfield correctly speculated that this Great Depression was caused not only by bad stock-market bets and the domino-set structure of international debt. It also had an agricultural origin, rooted in some of American farmers' earliest mistakes—mistakes for which the country was finally paying a terrible price.

America's original agricultural sin was treating the land like an inexhaustible resource. Thomas Jefferson understood this temptation. The Virginia planter's romantic vision for America as a nation of virtuous farmers masked the very real hardships he had earning a living from his corn and tobacco fields (even with the help of slave labor). Perpetually in debt, he struggled with maintaining fertility from one growing season to the next, and once suggested in a letter to George Washington that maybe he should not even bother, since in America "we can buy an acre of new land cheaper than we can manure an old one." Washington bemoaned this fact in a letter from 1797: "We ruin the lands that are already cleared and either cut down more wood, if we have it, or emigrate into the Western country. . . . A half, a third, or even a fourth of what land we mangle, well wrought and properly dressed, would produce more than the whole under our system of management; yet such is the force of habit, that we cannot depart from it."

This was a habit that successive generations of farmers could not break. Rather than conserving the health of their soil by rotating or diversifying their crops and carefully deploying available fertilizers, they essentially *mined* their fields until the land grew sickly and yields declined to zero. Then, they just moved their crops and herds westward. That migration left a trail of destruction. Forests were cut down, prairies were plowed under, millions of acres of the best mixed-legume grass in the world were overgrazed, overtilled, or burned. The result was "rampant erosion, sour soils, mounting floods from runoff and . . . vanishing wildlife."

Though reckless and inefficient, agriculture remained America's economic backbone through the turn of the twentieth century. In 1900, 40 percent of the population still lived on farms and another 10 percent were somehow involved in the business of agriculture. The onset of World War I came, initially, as a gift to this group. As Europe's grain fields turned into battlefields, the global demand for American crops spiked. From 1913 to 1917, the price of farm commodities increased by more than 80 percent. The government—using slogans like "Food Will Win the War"—encouraged farmers to ramp up production, expand acreage, adopt the latest scientific practices and buy heavy gas-powered machinery. To pay for it, farmers were urged to take on debt. After all, crop prices were still climbing. In 1918, they edged up yet another 25 percent. Many farmers began to abandon "general farms," or self-sustaining family operations—which typically grew a little bit of everything, and which produced their own fertilizer in the form of manure from livestock—to work in huge single-crop farms, or monocultures, that required more chemicals and larger machines: potatoes in northern Maine and Idaho, cotton or peanuts in the South, corn in the Midwest, fruits and vegetables in California. Some of the greatest agricultural expansion occurred in the Great Plains, where farmers began to push wheat and corn into the semi-arid belt around Kansas and the Texas Panhandle.

Then, in 1920, far quicker than it inflated, the bubble burst. The causes were various: increased competition from new markets like Argentina, the revival of European agriculture, and the passage of Prohibition (which hurt rye and barley farmers). The result was "the most terrible toboggan slide in all American agricultural history," wrote one economist. In 1920, the price of wheat, which had been selling for $2.50 a bushel, fell to under $1. Corn prices dropped by 75 percent. Farmers sought out new tools to help them weather the failing market: machines, fertilizers, pesticides, and hybrid seeds that doubled or even tripled their crop yields. But these innovations, meant to help the farmer, had the paradoxical result of making his problems even worse. Over the decade, as the market for agricultural goods collapsed, farmers took 13 million acres out of production. The fact that so much less land was under cultivation had no effect on prices, however. The new chemical fertilizers and seeds had by then made farming so much more productive that, even though the total acreage plummeted during the 1920s, overall farm output still *increased* by another 9 percent. The crisis became chronic. Land values collapsed, rural bank failures tripled, and nearly a million farmers lost their homesteads to foreclosure—yet there was still more food than ever before.

By Black Friday, in 1929, much of rural America had been in its own Great Depression for nearly a decade. At first farmers did not panic over the stock-market crash, thinking crop prices had nowhere to go but up. But to their horror, prices dropped even further. Corn fell from about a dollar a bushel in late 1929 to less than a quarter by the middle of 1932; hog prices lost an additional 50 percent. There were more foreclosures, along with a rash of suicides and crime. Those best positioned to help the farmers were slow to recognize the problem. After visiting Depression-era Kentucky, Dr. William DeKleine of the Red Cross wrote: "There is a feeling among the better farmers in Boyd County that the drought is providential; that God intended the dumb ones should be wiped out; and that it is a mistake to feed them." The socialist writer Oscar Ameringer crossed the country in 1932 and described a nation rife with agricultural waste: bushels of wheat left in the fields of Montana, apples rotting in Oregon orchards; a sheep farmer who had to slaughter three thousand sheep and throw them down a canyon because they cost more to ship than they were worth—and he didn't want to let them starve. Newspapers wrote about California citrus growers spraying carloads of oranges with kerosene to keep away foragers and Wisconsin dairymen protesting federal farm policy by dumping 40,000 pounds of milk onto the highway. To those suffering from the Depression, reading about the wholesale destruction of food while standing on a breadline became an unbearable irony—"the paradox of want amid plenty" in the words of journalist Walter Lippmann.

Nowhere was it so bad as in "the Dust Bowl"—the name an Associated Press reporter later gave to an area of western Kansas, southern Oklahoma, and the Texas Panhandle. Throughout the early 1900s, farmers had driven their steel moldboard plows through 1 million acres of virgin prairie, planting wheat, which earned them $1.25 a bushel in 1927 but only 33 cents in 1931. By the following year, a severe drought had set in. The overplowing and the lack of water had turned the prairie into a dry cake mix, which the strong winds of the plains kicked up into massive storms that blackened the sky, blinded cattle, and suffocated gardens. More than seven thousand people died of "dust pneumonia."

The American social reformer Morris L. Cooke compared the soil crisis to a national case of cancer. "America is doomed agriculturally," he wrote, "unless the problems of drought, dust storms, floods, and worst of all, erosion are taken seriously."

—†—

Sitting in his lush garden outside Paris, Bromfield was overwhelmed by the suffering and waste caused by this man-made crisis. The news fed into his own sense of ennui, his personal depression. His shimmering arrival on the literary scene—the Pulitzer Prize, the breathless comparisons to Fielding and Balzac—was now all behind him. His latest books were trifles, droll stories of expatriate life, halfhearted genre experiments. Each became a bestseller, each earned a few critical plaudits, each satisfied nearly everyone but himself. His sojourn in Hollywood in 1930 left him disgusted by the hollowness of American culture. Herbert Hoover's heartless, ham-fisted response to the economic crisis depressed him further. Paris and the fashionable ski resorts had lost their glamour, the literary cafés had lost their lure. He stayed at home in Senlis, relishing only his garden. In an essay, he took stock of his position. He had retreated from an America "blatantly represented" by Wall Street into "the greater quiet of Europe." Yet his mind, "depressed and searching," had become "one long query. A great *why*? A great *what is it all about?*"

To answer these questions, Bromfield began to write a book that was entirely unlike his earlier novels. It would be a family history, written as a lament. It would track the true story of the rise and fall of the Bromfield family farm in Ohio but, he told Cass Canfield, his new editor at Harper, it would also tell a larger story, about how industry replaced agriculture as the linchpin of American society. Bromfield believed that this development explained the cultural defect at the heart of the Great Depression. He saw his family's farm—and the proud rural culture it represented—as the embodiment of Jefferson's agrarian vision for America, in which freedom and democracy flourished in a society composed of self-sufficient yeoman farmers. This version of America had lost out to the merchant-based plutocracy of Alexander Hamilton, who had opened the door to big banks and speculative schemes that had now driven the country to the brink of financial ruin. Bromfield wanted to weave this political parable into his family's story, to write not only a nostalgic paean to a vanished agrarian world but a polemic, railing against the pollution and rapaciousness of big business; the priggish, small-minded townsfolk he grew up with; the flavorless conveniences they celebrated as "progress."

Bromfield opened the book with a long dedication, addressed to his three children, the eldest of whom, Anne, was then just eight. It explained that this story was not only a record of the self-sufficient pastoral world that his grandparents built but also a call to recapture it.

> "The Farm" is the story of a way of living which has largely gone out of fashion, save in a few half-forgotten corners and in a few families which stuck to it with an admirable stubbornness in spite of everything . . . It has in it two fundamentals which were once and may be again intensely American characteristics. These are integrity and idealism. Jefferson has been dead more than a hundred years and there is no longer any frontier, but the things which both represent are immortal. They are tough qualities needed in times of crisis.

The book is called a novel but structurally it barely satisfies the demands of the form. The narrative is just description; the closest thing we get to a protagonist is Johnny, the stand-in for Bromfield, whose story is told in a sloppy mix of the first and third person. There is practically no dialogue and very little action. It is as though someone sat you down in the front parlor, gave you a cup of cider, pulled out the dusty albums and daguerreotypes, and took you down every branch of a giant and sometimes spooky family tree.

Critics loved the book anyway. The reviewer for the Minneapolis *Star* said Bromfield's embroidered autobiography would win him a second Pulitzer: "It teems with life, smells of reality, is swollen with a motley variety of character and incident." Even those critics who found the story a slog still praised parts of it. A reviewer for the *Nation* complained of "the detail—the tedious detail!" Yet he believed there was a beautiful ribbon buried in all that yarn, "the work of a writer who moves us as only a few novelists in America have the power to do." In commercial terms, the book was immensely popular: it sold two thousand copies a day, reaching the top of the bestseller lists by September 1933. As usual, that commercial success rankled Bromfield's literary peers. While Scott Fitzgerald was agonizing over the bad reviews of *Tender*, his wife, Zelda, soothed his ego by deriding Bromfield's achievement. "Let Bromfield feed their chaotic minds on the poppy-seed of farm youth tragedies," she wrote, calling his book one of the "isolated epics" that attracted impressionable readers but lacked "any quality save reverence."

—⁜—

The Farm spans some 350 pages and covers the history of the Bromfield clan from its arrival in the Ohio frontier country in the early nineteenth century to Bromfield's departure for World War I. It begins with Johnny's (read: Bromfield's) first memory of the family farm. It's Christmastime and he is a boy of maybe five, sitting on his mother's lap in a horse-drawn sleigh. He hears sleigh bells, sees the "fat rumps of the horses" and the steam rising off their wet coats in the winter air, and he smells "the odd musty odor which the worn old buffalo robe gave off when it was wet." The sleigh stops at a white picket gate. The snow that seemed so violent as they raced across the country lanes now comes down softly, "like feathers," and the bells give out only an occasional tinkle when one of the horses shakes himself. A door opens: there is music, followed by the appearance of a "tiny old lady," Johnny's grandmother, and a scattering of "enormous" relatives who sweep the boy up in "a hubbub of greetings and

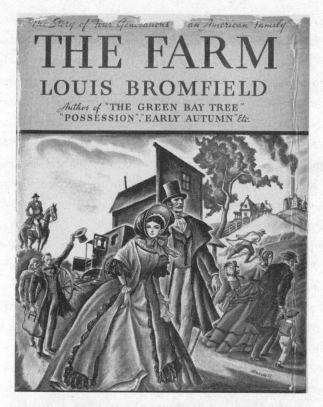

The cover of Bromfield's best-selling 1933 novel, *The Farm*,
which romanticized his family's agrarian past.

noisy kissing." He is in a kitchen that smells incredible, a mix of "coffee
and sausages, roast turkey and mince pie." His grandmother brings him
a sugar cookie and sits him down in an old walnut ladder-backed chair
to remove his muffler and leggings.

The chair originally came from Scotland, like Bromfield's long-dead
great-grandfather, who is called the "Colonel" in the novel. Bromfield
imagines him, a half-century earlier, seated in this same spot, dressed in a
robe and slippers. He is a pipe-smoking, port-drinking Renaissance man,
fluent in French, conversant in philosophy and naturalism, an heir to
the Enlightenment, with a large fortune, who fought in the War of 1812

and was the "last man out of Washington the day the British burned the White House." He had owned a grand plantation in Maryland but was sick of "the politicians and the bankers" and "the meanness of civilization and of man himself." He gave his slaves their freedom, sending them "into the world with new clothes and money in their pockets." And then he set out west, riding a mare named Belle at the front of an ox-cart caravan across the Allegheny Mountains into the young state of Ohio. Like many pioneers, he sought to carve a new world out of the wilderness. His dream was borrowed from Jefferson: to live in an agricultural commonwealth, where the leaders were "natural aristocrats" whose power, wealth, and dignity came out of the earth.

The portrait of the Colonel, like much of *The Farm*, is a mix of historical fact and romantic flourish. It is based on Bromfield's real great-grandfather, Jacob Barr, who did in fact hail from Maryland and who owned a farm across from Antietam Creek. He had served unremarkably in the War of 1812 as a captain, not a colonel, and owned five slaves, according to the 1810 census. In 1823, after the death of his first wife, Frances, and ten-year-old son, Samuel, Barr sold off his land and property and moved west. Perhaps he did espouse the universal rights of the Enlightenment, but it is unlikely that he could have afforded to free (instead of sell) his slaves. A court record noted that, contrary to the "fortune" Bromfield said he had, Barr was actually "insolvent" when he showed up in Mansfield. He was fifty-one years old, a dignified, soberly dressed man—according to a surviving oil portrait—with a white beard and small, beady blue eyes that he passed on to Bromfield's mother and to Bromfield himself. He remarried a woman named Elizabeth and settled on a farm 3 miles west of Mansfield, on which he raised five daughters, all of whom eventually left the farm to marry except the second youngest, Susan Adelaide, known as Addie, a wisp of a woman, serious in manner, with a kind and sensitive face.

She eventually wed Robert M. Coulter, a migrant farmhand also of Scottish extraction, and together they inherited Barr's farm. While the character of "the Colonel" was heavily embroidered, a way of projecting Jefferson or Voltaire into Bromfield's family tree, the portrait of Coulter, Bromfield's maternal grandfather—who is called "Old Jamie" in the novel—hews closer to the historical record. Born in 1831, he had grown up on a farm, a broad-chested, big-bearded Scot, whose lack of formal learning would be a lifelong source of shame. Bromfield writes that Jamie was routinely abused by his father—a Presbyterian of the masochist variety who loved only self-punishing work and fire-and-brimstone sermons. One day, when Jamie could no longer take his father's beatings, he struck back, "not once but many times, until the older man, bloody and beaten, gave way in defeat before a son who he found was no longer a little boy." Jamie ran inside the farmhouse, kissed his mother goodbye, took a mule and whatever possessions he could carry, and set off for California. "He went, like all the others, to dig for gold in the mountains and pan for it in the flooding streams." But he was disgusted by the greed of the miners and overwhelmed by the frenzied life of the frontier and the big western farm country with its 1,000-acre orchards and vineyards that extended to the horizon.

> He wanted well-ordered fields with brooks which ran clear and cool unmuddied by torrents in spring. He wanted gardens and a fine dairy and a half-dozen good horses. His dream was of a farm which could survive, cut off from all the rest of the earth, which was in itself a small world complete and above all else independent.

So Jamie returned to the Midwest, riding halfway across the country into Mansfield, which is called "The Town" in the book. He asked for work in the tavern and was directed 3 miles west to the Colonel's farm. He rode through two small valleys before he caught sight of a white rambling house, a big gray barn, tall corn, fine cattle, an avenue of trees—the sort of farm "of which he had dreamed." He nervously introduced himself to the elegantly dressed colonel, whose long gray hair was tied up in a bow. In less than ten minutes, "they had made their bargain." Jamie was then surprised to be invited to join the family for a noontime dinner. At the Colonel's table, he was overwhelmed by the finery, the silver and linen and delicate china, which made him feel "twice his great size. All his fingers were thumbs. When he spoke he blushed and mumbled his words." In a short time, Jamie married one of the colonel's last eligible daughters and the couple skipped their honeymoon "for it was midsummer and already the hay stood ready to be cut and the wheat was turning yellow in the broad fields below the house."

These two men—Captain Barr and Robert Coulter, idealized as "the Colonel" and "Old Jamie"—became two sides of Bromfield's model agrarian. The first is a philosopher, a gentleman-squire, a utopian carving a new world out of the wilderness; the second is a dirt farmer, passionate, instinctive, maybe a little *teched*. "Jamie, in the mere necessity for physical activity, could never, like his father-in-law, have remained apart, surrounded by books and specimens, simply supervising the work. For his temperament it was necessary that he should take part, helping with the ploughing and the threshing, the harvest and the milking. He had to have the feel of the earth on his big freckled hands."

—·—

Before Bromfield's great-grandfather died, in 1855, he may have thought his dream of an agrarian democracy was actually coming true. Bromfield writes that Mansfield on the eve of the Civil War, before it became a fume-belching industrial center, was just a marketplace for the neighboring farms. There were no absentee landlords, no half-starved tenants, and no tariffs to protect businessmen at the farmer's expense. "Each farm was in itself a world as nearly complete and self-sustaining as it is possible for such a small unit ever to be." Even the farmhands were relatively well off, living in "a patriarchal pastoral world where the dignity of labor was understood." The farm laborer's food, his bed, his amusements were "roughly the same as those of the man who hired him." But the serenity of this—clearly idealized—rural society was disturbed by the "wheezing of the wood-burning locomotives," which betokened other machine-made noises: that of factories, and rolling mills and blast furnaces.

As Mansfield industrialized, the farm economy changed. Farmers no longer milled the flour from their own wheat. They sold the wheat and bought their flour in town, and "in the vast difference in the price which they received for their wheat and paid for their flour lay the roots of one aspect of their constantly increasing troubles." Immigrant laborers from Europe moved into the Flats along the railroad tracks, and Bromfield does not resist ugly caricature in describing them, with their "ferocious black mustachios" and smoke-blackened faces, eating from stinking communal soup tureens in overcrowded boardinghouses. "They were the first peasants to come into that world, but they no longer tilled the earth; they worked in the swarming factories and mills." In this "atmosphere of soot and carbon dioxide," the shade trees died, sewage was dumped into the open gutters, and leaked out of town and began to pollute the fishing streams.

The wealthiest parts of the industrializing town were also, in their way, repellent. Unlike the Colonel's farmhouse, "which had an air of belonging to the earth itself," the new homes built by the emerging elite in Mansfield were "boastful houses conceived by childish minds and executed in children's blocks." Merchants, manufacturers, speculators, and coal and railroad magnates transformed the city. The industries they built began to attract the children of the farmers from the nearby countryside who were dazzled by the rich men's motor cars and antique furniture and "pictures bought from shrewd dealers." They could not see that there was "no core to that spurious aristocracy, but only the trappings which make a shabby enough disguise."

———

While the Mansfield area was becoming less hospitable to agriculture, the Coulter family farm still thrived. On their 100 acres they had pigs, sheep, beef cattle, dairy cows, all manner of poultry, and a large team of horses. They grew corn, oats, wheat. They had thick pastures and orchards of peaches, apples, and damson plums. They had a massive garden—the delight of Bromfield's grandmother—with muskmelons and cantaloupes, beets, carrots, celery, cucumbers, Hubbard squash, and a half-acre of strawberries. They had a fruit cellar heaped with apples and root vegetables and a dry, cold attic with rows of hams and flitches of bacon. Bromfield's grandparents also raised children on this farm—three daughters and five sons—although none appeared to have any interest in continuing the family tradition. Each of the Coulter girls married and left the farm. The last to escape was Bromfield's mother, Annette Coulter, born in 1862, a full-faced, ever-scowling woman with a man's nose, small blue eyes, and dusty hair.

She chose for a husband a handsome man who proved a poor agent for her ambition. Charley Brumfield was a bank cashier and, later, a real-estate speculator. He had light-blue eyes, an extravagant handlebar mustache, and a delicate, almost beautiful face. They married in October of 1885 and settled in Mansfield in a slate-gray house on West Fourth Street, perched between the Flats and the pretentious wealthy houses—a nice symbol of the family's precarious financial position. Annette gave birth to a daughter, Marie, in 1886 and a son, Lewis, ten years later. (Sometime during his military service, Bromfield would change his name from Lewis Brumfield to the nobler-sounding Louis Bromfield. After he became a prominent author, his parents also adopted the stylized surname.)

Nettie decided even before her children were born that they would be successful and sophisticated. She wanted, as she once put it in a letter to Bromfield, to have bred them "to some purpose." She subscribed to a voguish philosophy called "prenatal influence," whereby a mother could shape the future of a child while the baby was still in utero. She decided her firstborn would become a pianist and bought a piano while pregnant and taught herself to play to imbue the fetus with musical ability. Her daughter, Marie, began formal piano lessons at age six. If she sulked or cried instead of practicing, Nettie would lock her in her room. Bromfield's literary education began around the same age as Marie's musical one. Nettie had decided he would become a great writer, and spent what little extra money the family had on books that she force-fed to him: Tolstoy, Dickens, Thackeray. She wanted the books to teach Bromfield not only how to write by example but also to infect him with a hunger for the world beyond sooty Mansfield and the rolling fields that surrounded it. The worst thing he could ever do, she said, was "waste your life on a farm."

Nettie succeeded in transmitting wanderlust and ambition to Bromfield, but these things coexisted—and conflicted—with the desire he inherited from his grandfather to till the earth. As a small child, Bromfield wrote, he attached himself to his grandparents' farm "with a strange tenacity, as if the Farm, instead of the house in the town where his parents lived, was really his home." For a child, the farm was a place of constant excitement. "Always, it seemed, there was something new. Sometimes it was a calf or a litter of puppies, sometimes a rat-hunt with the big sheepdogs among the standing shocks of corn, sometimes it was maple-sugarmaking." In March, he followed his grandfather to a pond in the forest at the end of the farm, where stood a tiny wooden-shack: the sugar-house, where sap from the maple trees would be boiled down into syrup. It was a whole-night affair. Bromfield and his younger brother Charles Jr., born in 1899, sat beneath blankets watching their grandfather tend the fires beneath big iron tanks.

> You went to sleep only when you could no longer keep your eyes open, and sometimes in the night the hooting of an owl wakened you, terrified, to find that you were safe and warm, with your grandfather sitting in a big easy chair by the table, reading farm reports by the light of the kerosene-lamp. And in your nostrils was the scent of burning hickory logs and of maple sap boiling in the vats.

When the sap finally rendered down into a thick syrup, his grandfather tossed a ladleful of it outside on a snow bank, where it hardened into a "thick toothsome candy" that the boys could eat.

Such lyrical, shamelessly romantic recollections of rural life are the best parts of *The Farm*. In a similar tone, Bromfield described following his frail grandmother into the center of the farmhouse, where there was a big dark cupboard called the "buttery." This was the place where she secreted away the cakes, pies, cookie jars, bottles of cider, vats of butter, and stone crocks of buttermilk. Sometimes, Bromfield wrote of his cousins, "there was a whole procession of greedy little monsters who clung to her full skirts while she opened the door. And the small mouths watered at the complicated perfume of cider and pies and cookies and apples which swept over them as the door was opened. It was an aroma which Johnny never smelled again for the rest of his life, an odor which has disappeared in a world where foods come in tins or wrapped in sanitary paper."

The sanitary paper, the mass production of food, the trappings of technology and industry—these things that others might term "conveniences"—Bromfield viewed as denuding and desensitizing. He wanted his book to be an emotional accounting of what they actually cost. He did this in a hundred different ways, taking up some seemingly banal feature of the rural Ohio landscape—like fence posts—and showing how a wild and beautiful world was being supplanted with a cookie-cutter, soulless one. In the countryside during his boyhood, "straight bare fences of galvanized wire" were replacing the undulating pickets that had once almost carelessly sectioned off one farmer's land from another's. The fencerows had been, for children, a place of excitement and mystery, where rabbits hid and thrushes built their nests. In summer, they "stood half-hidden by the growth of blackberries and bracken, hazel bushes and hawthorn." They provided elderberries for wine, nuts for the cellar, and wild berries for jam. They had an ecological value, sheltering coveys of quail and pheasants which destroyed the insects of the cornfield. And they were beautiful, especially in fall when they turned "crimson and gold and purple and the little husks of the hazelnuts began to burst open."

But as Bromfield grew up, the old fences began to disappear, the farmhouses began to fall apart, the young people, the next generation, those who should have tended the land, vanished into factories and offices in Mansfield and other cities. And their parents, the farmers, seeing the cost of their equipment rise and the price of their produce fall, began to take out their frustration on the land itself, robbing the soil of its fertility just as it seemed to be robbing them of their livelihoods.

—·—

As Bromfield's grandfather Robert Coulter approached his eightieth birthday, he was no longer able, physically or financially, to maintain the farm by himself. He began sharing it with a series of tenants who were mostly poor, uneducated, and harried. Under their care, the gardens grew grubby and brown, the orchards became unkempt, the soil filled with gullies. Bromfield's grandfather had to watch the farm to which he had given his life become sick and feeble, like himself. He clung to his peach orchard, where he picked the peaches himself, handling them tenderly so "that their bloom should not be bruised." In 1909, when Bromfield was thirteen, Coulter took a fall from his haymow. His injuries were serious. Shortly thereafter, he moved into town to live with his daughter and her family. He spent his days puttering in the Bromfields' small garden behind the house, digging among the flowers and pruning the trees. Bromfield recalled that there was something "infinitely pathetic" in his gardening:

> When he had finished digging over a flower-bed there remained not a single lump; the earth had been worked to powder. His big muscular figure seemed hopelessly out of proportion to the narrow limits of the town lot. He was like Hercules working at a piece of needlepoint.

As the family farm slipped away, Bromfield's father, Charley, imagined another route to plenty: speculating on exhausted farmland. He would buy overlooked plots, restore them to marginal fertility, and sell them or rent them to tenants at a small profit. He began to advertise his farms in the newspaper as "Brumfield's Bargains." He should have instead invested in outlying districts of Mansfield, where old farmland was being bought at a premium by the expanding mills and factories. But instead he focused on "romantic farms hidden away in remote valleys, for which there was no market at all." Bromfield later described his father's efforts as "primitive." He cleared away the brush and reseeded with clover; he filled gullies with cut vegetation and rolls of rusted fence wire. But the soil barely responded. It is not clear why Charley kept making bad bets on old farms, or why the fearsome Nettie permitted him to do so, but as time wore on the family pushed itself closer and closer to "economic disaster." They knew the life of the small farmer was dying out. Yet something—habit, destiny, stupidity—kept drawing the family back to the land.

The next scheme involved cattle, which Charley began to raise on all those worthless pastures that he could not find buyers for. He would take his son out of school for the day and go through the county searching for shaggy, half-wild breeds of cow that could perhaps flourish on the poor land. The young Bromfield was insensitive to the economic pressure associated with these missions. He loved driving the cattle along pollen-covered country lanes in warm weather, watching as the cows scented water and plunged happily into the nearest stream. The cattle adventure ended like the farm-flipping one: in failure. The family financial situation grew more desperate. Nettie was furious that Charley had gambled away their stability. Bromfield thought his father's problem was a lack of education. If only he could learn how to become a *scientific* farmer, then he could reverse the family's fortunes. So he broke his mother's heart by enrolling in Cornell University in the fall of 1914 to study agriculture, not literature. For reasons that are unclear, he left this brief college chapter entirely out of *The Farm*.

In Ithaca, Bromfield blossomed. He escorted pretty girls around campus, lunched regularly with the chair of the English Department, and became friends with two Russian émigrés, who introduced him to the famous ballerina Anna Pavlova when she performed at the college in November 1914. "This is the life," he told his parents. But while Bromfield flourished personally at Cornell, he was preoccupied with the family finances. Whatever useful agricultural information he learned in the classroom he sent to his father. He and Charley began an excited correspondence about how to modernize a family farm: new gardens, new equipment, improved livestock. Bromfield was amazed by Cornell's farm buildings and greenhouses. The vegetables and flowers he saw there "caused tears to come to my eyes . . . Oh, I was filled with wonder." At one point, Charley wrote to Bromfield about a new property in Lexington, 7 miles southwest of Mansfield, that looked like an ideal site. Bromfield could not contain his excitement. "Just think if we could all live at the Lexington farm. I could raise carnations, roses and chrysanthemums for wholesale market as well as winter vegetables. . . . Papa could farm and take care of a first class Guernsey herd."

But the Lexington deal fell apart. Charley, drowning in mortgage debt, went bust and had to sell off all of "Brumfield's Bargains" at cut rates to raise cash. Eventually, the family was left with only two properties: the old Coulter farm and their house in Mansfield, where Bromfield and his siblings grew up. Bromfield was adamant that they should sell the house without delay. "It was either that or the farm," he said after, "and I would never think of giving up the farm." Unable to pay spring-semester tuition, he dropped out of school and returned home in December with just $2 in his pocket. His plan was to use whatever he learned during his brief stay at Cornell to turn the farm around. Maybe, he told his mother, he would even have enough free time to try his hand at a novel. "Just think, Mamma, if I could write and live on the farm at the same time. Wouldn't that be heaven?" No, Nettie said, it would not be heaven. His mother found the idea of Bromfield returning to the land "revolting." She knew that farming, at least in her father's day, might provide a good life, but success was never guaranteed even under the best conditions: "Cholera might wipe out the hogs, or the prize cow might choke herself on an apple, or the hoof-and-mouth disease might suddenly reduce the whole of a fine dairy to a heap of charred carcasses."

No letters exist detailing Bromfield's yearlong attempt at reviving his family farm, but he wrote about the experience bitterly in the final pages of his novel. It felt, he said, like his family had entrenched itself "in the last remaining fragment of a world which scarcely existed any longer." Bromfield threw himself into that world with all his heart. He loved the feeling of leaving a field of corn with each furrow neatly cultivated and every weed buried. He took "keen pleasure" in the sight of wet timothy falling beneath the knives of the mowing machine and the smell of the earth stirred by the plow. But from the farmhouse, his mother seethed as she watched him haul manure. It was an "indignity which she was determined to crush." Nettie had "all the force of economics" on her side. Bromfield, even with the few tricks he learned at Cornell, could not make the math of the farm work.

What good was it to pack apples carefully wrapped in paper, to ship to the big markets of the East, when shipping and the middlemen left nothing for the farmers, and often enough the middlemen took precious dollars off the price because the apples arrived bruised and damaged, a charge which the farmer could never know was true? What good was it to raise wheat for a price which made it sounder economics to feed to the hogs than send it to market? Why have a fine dairy when it showed no profit at the end of the year while the men who owned the canned milk plant grew rich and built fine houses? Why grow potatoes for a dubious profit of a few dollars a field? Why? Why? Why?

He felt himself going round and round as if "on a treadmill, sweating to arrive nowhere." Often he would be seized by an "insane restlessness," a desire to run away forever. He saw that the future of farming was technological. His grandfather's farm was bordered on one side by a vanity farm, built by a Mansfield rubber manufacturer, who "poured into it many thousands of dollars a year." In describing this operation, Bromfield eerily anticipates, in 1933, many of the signatures of industrial agriculture. It looked less like a farm and "rather more like a factory." The cows became "machines which never browsed like normal cows but were fed upon artificial foods" and "never left their stalls save when they went to the bull (a necessity with which no machine was yet able to cope). Calves no longer played and romped in pastures but were kept shut in corrals where food was carried to them. . . . In the pastures there were no longer any trees, since there was no need to provide shade for cows which never left the stables, and trees cut down the productivity of every field."

The last straw came one morning in October 1915, when Bromfield took a horse-drawn wagon into the woods to fetch a load of firewood. When he pulled on the reins to stop the horses, and the "chocking and creaking" of the wagon ceased, "there was another sound which seemed to fill the air." The noise came from a new factory on the edge of Mansfield, pounding out shells to be shipped to France for the war. He felt "a sudden sickness" and knew that the farm was finished. When he returned with the wood, Bromfield saw his mother standing in the kitchen door. "She was silent for a moment, and then said, 'Listen.' It was all she said, but she knew she had won."

The farm was sold. Bromfield, finally assenting to the destiny his mother had willed for him, enrolled in Columbia Journalism School to become a writer. His beloved grandfather died in 1917 while Bromfield was making ready to sail for France. In the book's final scene, he describes what it was like to see the family farm again a decade later, when he stopped in Mansfield in 1927 while on his "American womanhood" speaking tour. He arrived in a "shiny motor," looking "prosperous," dressed in "fine clothes." He knocked on the door of the farmhouse. The woman who answered wore a cotton kerchief wrapped around her head. She spoke only Polish. She could not understand who he was or why he came. For a moment, he thought of moving the graves of his great-grandparents, who were buried on the farm, into the town cemetery where Phoebe Wise and Robert Coulter and the rest of his family were interred. "But what was there to move?" By then they had become, "like the arrowheads and the glacial boulders," just another feature of the Ohio landscape. He left the graves, and today they are broken in pieces but still there, behind the ruins of Captain Barr's original farmhouse, which is now flanked by a state and federal highway.

The Farm changed Bromfield profoundly. He began to reevaluate his exile in France: Now, he said, it wasn't about diversion or pleasure or the advantageous economics or about France at all. It was about recapturing a lifestyle and set of values. "I moved my family to France so we could live a genuinely American life," he told a reporter after the book's publication. "During the days of mad finance in the United States, the principles on which the strength of our country was built vanished from our national life. But on my little farm, beside a river, though it is in France, I can raise my children on those homespun and democratic ideals which I believe will soon again be called American." In Franklin Roosevelt, who took office early in 1933, Bromfield saw, however imperfectly, a modern Jeffersonian Democrat who could return fairness and heart to America. He also started to see the Depression as a kind of a cleanse, a harsh purgative that might, with the help of Roosevelt's New Deal, actually restore the country. "The Depression," he said during a guest appearance on NBC Radio in April 1933, "has created a new America."

Gertrude Stein, for one, thought much of his book. "Speaking technically, you have gone a long way in unmuddling yourself," she told him.

The Farm struck her "in some subtl[e] and gentle way" as a breakthrough, the work of a "genius," a way of flipping the heroic archetype of the American pioneer—that of James Fenimore Cooper or Hamlin Garlin—on its head. Bromfield, she thought, was the first to capture the plight of the descendants of those pioneers, those "wandering Americans" who were now frontierless and uprooted from the land their ancestors had cleared from the wilderness. "The important thing is that you have done something entirely new," she told him. Later that year, when Bromfield's life story and her own, *The Autobiography of Alice B. Toklas*, were both flying off bookstore shelves, she wrote to him: "I adore our being best-sellers together."

Bromfield gave Wharton an inscribed copy of *The Farm* but no record survives of what she thought about it. The two writers may have shared a love of cultivating flowers and vegetables, but Wharton had little interest in the rough exigencies of agriculture. And when Bromfield started talking, later in the year, of actually buying a farm in the United States, possibly in Maryland, Wharton could not conceal her horror. "What a thunderbolt!" she wrote. "I wish that writing a book called 'The Farm' wouldn't immediately make you decide to buy one! If action always follows so rapidly on thought you will have an agitated existence—and so will Mary!"

6

Blight

Edith Wharton's health was failing. She had survived a stroke a year earlier. Now seventy-four, she felt dizzy and tired all the time, beset by one ailment after another: stomach problems, angina, deteriorating eyesight, repeated bouts of flu. "I'm an incorrigible life-lover & life wonderer & adventurer," she told one of her friends around this time. "But bodily suffering strikes at the roots of all these joys." Her maladies did not keep her from visiting Bromfield, however. One day in August, she came to the Presbytère for lunch. She looked exhausted but brightened when Bromfield told her about a flower breeder named Hureau who ran a nursery in a neighboring village where he grew the most exquisite dahlias.

Bromfield remembered Hureau as a "strange, wild character," almost "like something which had escaped from the forest," with a "fierce" mustache and bright blue eyes. A photograph from the 1930s shows Hureau standing proudly amid his shoulder-high blooms, a bit more polished than Bromfield let on, his gray hair carefully coiffed, his workwear (a broad-collared short-sleeve shirt and fitted suspenders) appearing rather fashionable to modern eyes. Hureau "wanted desperately that the world

Bromfield can be seen in the mirror photographing
one of his dahlia arrangements.

should be a fine and beautiful place," and he contributed to this end
by breeding dahlias, creating mesmerizing new cultivars that received
awards at the flower salons in Paris. One of them—a "scarlet wonder"—
was named for Henri Barbusse, the communist author of *Le Feu*, who
was Hureau's neighbor. Bromfield liked to joke that his namesake dahlia
wasn't quite "red enough."

Hureau was also a Communist—"not in a dull doctrinaire way,"

Bromfield said, but "in a primitive, fundamental fashion." Wharton thought Hureau's politics were dangerous nonsense. "She had read a great deal of Marx," Bromfield said, but "the nature of communism in practice shocked her, and when I attempted, from the point of view of my own generation, to explain what I believed it to be, she would shudder a little and say, 'I cannot see it. I do not believe that anything will come of it. It is not workable.'" Wharton was willing to overlook Hureau's communism, however, in order to get her hands on his dahlias. It was late summer, the perfect moment to see the blooms, but also hot and humid and Wharton was still recovering from her latest flu. Never mind all that, she told Bromfield, they should go at once.

They drove northwest from Senlis through the beech and oak forest of Halatte, which was filled with wildflowers, to the nearby village of Aumont. At the nursery, Bromfield introduced Wharton to Hureau. She regarded him suspiciously, at first. But as she followed him through the fields, moving from dahlia to dahlia, listening to him discuss his breeding experiments, telling him about the soil at Saint-Brice, she began to loosen up. For an hour and a half, they "swanked" about flowers, before Wharton ordered 1,000 francs' worth of dahlia tubers that she would never live to see in bloom. While they spoke, Bromfield witnessed something "wonderful" develop between Wharton, the famous "friend of Henry James, who dined in the most beautiful homes in the world," and this "half-wild communist peasant." They became "like brother and sister," laughing and trading jokes. "I think," Bromfield continued,

> it is always thus that I will remember her, dressed in the dignified old-fashioned clothes made for her by the little dress-maker in Hyères, moving among the glorious dahlias . . . She walked slowly, savouring the beauty of each flower, her parasol held high so that she should not bruise one fragile petal, my friend Hureau's old hunting dog sniffing in a friendly way at her heels.

After tea, Wharton climbed into her old-fangled Panhard for the ride back to Saint-Brice. Hureau, charmed by the attention paid to his creations by this distinguished lady, cut dozens and dozens of dahlias for her as gifts to take home. Bromfield helped load the flowers, filling the floorboards and seat around Wharton until her car looked like a decked-out hearse. Wharton couldn't help but laugh: "I look," she said in French, "like a first-class funeral."

Bromfield saw her only once more, when he visited Saint-Brice at her suggestion, to admire the garden. She was too sick then to receive him, but in a gesture that seems almost too literary to be real, Bromfield said that Wharton appeared in her bedroom window, and the two writers gazed portentously at each other. It was like "seeing a ghost"—she looked pallid, reconciled to death, yet somehow he felt they had "communicated." He described the moment as "one of the strongest impressions of my life," saying "on that day we talked to each other, in the way people talk to each other who have a passion and an understanding for the earth and the plants born of its fertility."

A mutual friend, the art historian Louis Gillet, saw Wharton on the day she died. "You can't imagine what this face looked like in death," he wrote.

> She had her familiar regal air. Not the slack, unwilling look which the dead often have, nor the appearance of struggle and fight, but rather a prodigious air of indifference and scorn, as if she were saying: "So? What does it matter to me? Do you think I'm going to give in and abase myself just because you are the stronger?" That's what her expression seemed to say, and her silence appeared to be an expression of pride. It was not very Christian, but it was magnificent.

Edith Wharton was buried on Saturday, August 14, 1937, at the Protestant cemetery in Versailles. At her funeral, there was neither music nor a eulogy but her gardener, Émile Gaillet, brought flowers from Saint-Brice, and her friends threw handfuls of the soft earth of the Île-de-France on her grave. Her literary agent described the event as "a simple funeral full of dignity," in which Wharton was surrounded by the two things she loved most: "friends and flowers." Some of these friends might have thought later that it was good that Wharton died when she did. If she had lived only a few more years, she would have had to watch the Europe she loved destroy itself.

The German military had a year earlier occupied the Rhineland, in violation of the Treaty of Versailles, which was supposed to guarantee a demilitarized buffer zone to protect France from its perennial enemy. This should have meant war, but the divided, economically depressed country responded with only a shrug. Defeatism was in the air, mingling with anti-Semitism. By 1937, the French writer Jean Giono announced that, in the event of a new Franco-German conflict, he'd rather be a living German than a dead Frenchman. Céline went further, writing in a pamphlet that a global alliance of Jews was leading Europe toward catastrophe. "I don't want to go to war for Hitler, I insist, but I don't want to wage war against him for the Jews." Meanwhile, in Germany, Goebbels's Degenerate "Art" Exhibition (with "art" written in scare quotes) attracted over 2 million visitors by vilifying the works of painters like Marc Chagall, Wassily Kandinsky and Paul Klee. In Spain, the Republicans were in retreat. Franco had shocked the world by bombing the Basque market town of Guernica in April, but France and Britain and the United States had all officially taken a noninterventionist position. The Spanish Civil War became a battle fought along ideological lines between leftists of all stripes, backed by Soviet Russia, and the Fascist bulwark of Franco, Hitler, and Mussolini. By winter, a Nationalist army supported by the Luftwaffe had taken control of the north of Spain. A Franco victory, it was clear to Bromfield, was only a matter of time.

Bromfield's own politics had grown more engaged over the decade. In 1934, he served on a committee that helped end the fourteen-year exile of the left-wing radical Emma Goldman. He described himself then as an unapologetic internationalist—"I detest nationalism"—and looked at the rise of fascism with visceral horror, writing that the world is passing through one of "the most debilitating periods" in history. "Nobody really knows where we are and that applies to me." Aping Gertrude Stein, he began lamenting "the Saxon element," or the influence of Germany and pro-German rhetoric in Europe and the United States. One of his broadsides, published in the London *Daily Herald* in August 1936, warned Britain in dire and prophetic terms about making appeasing gestures toward an increasingly "predatory" Germany.

> Every slight encouragement given by the British government to Hitler brings a little nearer to the British Empire the horror of war, the collapse of Europe and the possible dismemberment of the Empire itself . . . Europe, it seems to me, has reached that point where Democracy must defend itself and advance or retire to destruction.

The threat of war did not spoil Bromfield's appetite for parties and high society. If anything, his social activity only increased at this time, as if he were trying to grab hold of something that was slipping away. He had intimate lunches in Paris with film stars like Miriam Hopkins. He stood in the front row, smoking a cigarette next to Salvador Dalí, at Elsa Schiaparelli's August 1936 fashion show. More parties at the Ritz, more Sunday bacchanals in Senlis. That winter he spent in Saint Moritz. The Rodgers & Hart tune "There's a Small Hotel" was playing everywhere then, with its romantic message for couples to get away, just the two of them, to some small hotel in a "make-believe land" with "not a sign of people." But Bromfield had no interest in a romantic getaway with Mary: He picked the biggest and grandest hotel he could find,

Badrutt's Palace, a gingerbread colossus framed by a huge lake and fluffy ski slopes. A strange feeling hung in the Alpine air. He spoke to people for the first and last time: like Winston Churchill's wife, Clementine, and Erich Maria Remarque and the actress Peggy Joyce. The resort was filled with "nice British boys there for the skiing and bobsled races, and a fine assortment of very expensive trollops and not a few spies." They drank too much Champagne; the gaiety seemed to him "hysterical."

The escape was only temporary. By spring of 1937, Bromfield's state of mind had become agitated. He could see Europe was hurtling toward disaster but there was not yet a clear side for him to take. He loathed fascism, he wasn't a Communist, and he was disgusted by the spineless dithering of the French and British governments. "During the last few years before the end of Europe, the feeling of frontiers, hostility and peril became increasingly acute," Bromfield wrote later. "I think no intelligent American, no foreign correspondent, living abroad during those years between the wars, wholly escaped the European sickness, a malady compounded of anxiety and dread, difficult to define, tinctured by the knowledge that some horrifying experience lay inevitably ahead for all the human race. Toward the end the malady became an almost tangible thing, which you could touch and feel."

His politics may have become more engaged at this time, but privately Bromfield began to talk more and more about leaving Europe and buying a farm somewhere in America—perhaps even back in his native state of Ohio. He would fall asleep after one too many scotches in front of an open fire in the Presbytère and find himself dreaming of the mint-scented pastures in the glacial valleys near Mansfield or the orchards on his grandfather's farm. "It was as if all the while my spirit were tugging to return there, as if I was under a compulsion."

—·—

Christmas Eve came on a Friday in 1937. Bromfield remembered there was snow falling in his garden. The coziness of his house seemed to mock him. One room was covered in autographed photographs of his famous friends. In another there were jungle scenes on the walls that he and Mary had painted in imitation of Henri Rousseau and a tiger rug where in winter his portly secretary George Hawkins would sit naked under a sun lamp. This was his home. He did not want to leave it. The children had strung up Christmas decorations: long chains of gold paper, silver stars, holly, and bunches of mistletoe cut from the poplars at the end of the garden. The cook, Marguerite, was preparing a massive Christmas dinner in the kitchen. She asked Bromfield to buy some last-minute provisions, maybe a wheel of cheese, or oysters, or a few more bricks of foie gras. Bromfield went to the market in the church of Saint-Pierre. The soft snow made the cobbled streets slippery and blurred the outlines of the half-timbered houses and the spire of the cathedral in the distance.

Bromfield saw a version of his own anxiety in the faces of the vendors. They knew, he wrote in an essay two years later, that "they had no leaders but only politicians," that whatever was coming they could do nothing about it. There was at least some solidarity in that shared knowledge. Bromfield chatted with the mayor, "an old-fashioned socialist who wrote verse and only wished well to all," and with Alcide, whose white, flea-bitten horse, Flodrop, drew a small omnibus around town. "I wished them Merry Christmas and Happy New Year before the end of the world. Although I left out the latter phrase, my heart spoke it."

That night, after dinner, the Bromfields went to the ancient cathedral of Senlis for midnight Mass. In attendance were all those whom Bromfield had seen at the market and many more—his neighbors. He picked their faces out of the candlelight one by one as the voices of the choir singing "Adeste Fideles" echoed through the vaulted roof. The Bromfields stood up with the rest of congregation and followed the white-haired archpriest and the choirboys with their cross and censers out into the Place de la Cathèdrale. Bromfield pictured himself moving in this solemn crowd. He felt that the men and women beside him were "my fellow countrymen." He looked skyward: the stars were shining, the snow had stopped. Mary and the children had broken off in the direction of the Presbytère. Bromfield lingered behind, watching Hope and Ellen as they laughed and made snowballs. He knew this was their last Christmas in Senlis. "The long-awaited nightmare was closing in," he wrote. "And after it had passed the pleasant world of this old town would never be the same again."

———

By the spring of 1938, Bromfield found Paris eerily empty. His admiring stateside chronicler Lucius Beebe noted that he was now "the last of the old regulars stemming from the 1920s to be found still picking up his morning mail at the Ritz bar." At Mainbocher's fashion house, Mary ran into Wallis Simpson, the now infamous American divorcée and fashion plate. Her new husband, formerly King Edward VIII of England, had a year earlier given up his crown to marry Simpson against the wishes of the Anglican Church and the British prime minister. Now the couple, rebranded as the Duke and Duchess of Windsor, were living in plush exile in France. The Bromfields had been friendly with Simpson in England and had supported the couple during the abdication crisis. But Bromfield was alarmed by recent overtures that the duke (known as David to his friends) was making toward Hitler, including a much-publicized tour of Nazi Germany that he and Wallis took in the fall of 1937. Nevertheless, the Bromfields accepted Wallis's invitation to join them for dinner at their rented house in Versailles. It was a bad night, Mary recalled in a 1943 article for *Town & Country*.

> We were received by dozens of footmen and lackeys in white wigs, red jackets and knee breeches . . . We stood in line for quite a while feeling like asses—at least I did—and then the Duchess came in and went from one to the other briskly and cheerily. Following her was a little figure with pouchy eyes and dressed in kilts, and this

was the Duke. Louis whispered to me, "Little old lady passing by," entirely ruining my curtsy . . .

The food was "delicious" but the dinner went on too long, and David spoke "peevishly" to the powdered lackeys in "abominable" French, confiding in Mary that French servants were all "badly trained." After dinner, Mary and the other ladies "withdrew," leaving Bromfield and the duke to chat privately about politics. Only ten minutes elapsed before the former king of England came running for his wife, entering the anteroom "with a flutter of his kilts and a hunted look in his eye." Later Mary discovered what had happened. The duke told Bromfield that his beloved French would never "stand up" to the "cold steel" of Hitler's Wehrmacht, and Mary wrote that "an argument of great violence ensued, wherein Mr. Bromfield hurled respect to monarchy to the four winds of heaven, frightening the little fellow nearly out of his wits."

It was not only the Windsors who suddenly struck them as corrupt. The whole glittering society set in which they had mingled so happily for over a decade now seemed as ridiculous as David's kilt. Its last gasp came in July: the decorator Elsie de Wolfe's "Circus Ball" at the Villa Trianon, in Versailles. No expense was spared. The entertainment included trained Shetland ponies, satin-clad tightrope walkers, and acrobats building pyramids in the air. Six hundred bottles of Pommery et Greno 1926 and Veuve Clicquot 1928 were poured from an outdoor bar that was built like a merry-go-round encircling a giant chestnut tree. The British florist Constance Spry delivered three planeloads of red and white roses from London. Guests included the movie star Douglas Fairbanks Sr., the Hollywood producer Darryl F. Zanuck, and the socialite Elsa Maxwell. Coco Chanel was there in tiers of white lace, gardenias in her hair. Schiaparelli wore a gold-embroidered gown with a long shocking-pink scarf and white satin sandals with three-inch soles. Bromfield sat inside, eating lamb chops with mint jelly, bringing "screams of laughter," one attendee observed, from the guests at his table. The dance pavilion took its inspiration from Japan, with disappearing screen walls that opened onto formal gardens filled with marble statues and huge urns of cut flowers. "Even if you had been going to balls for 50 years, you could not have been insensitive to the beauty of the setting," wrote a correspondent from *Vogue.* Three orchestras played simultaneously at a distance—a black jazz orchestra from the Paris *boîte* Jimmie's Bar, a Cuban rhumba band, and an all-female Viennese orchestra—so you could walk from one musical world into another. De Wolfe had ordered a special dance floor from England undergirded with springs which gave dancers the impression of floating. To Bromfield, something about that night, and so many others like it, began to feel unreal. It was as if he had spent this whole expatriate period "living upon borrowed time in a dream" which was coming to an end.

The end came abruptly, on September 30, 1938. The agreement signed inside Adolf Hitler's marble-lined office in Munich, the Führerbau, horrified Bromfield. The British and French had capitulated in the face of Nazi aggression, essentially forcing Czechoslovakia to give Hitler the Sudetenland. The Munich diktat was not only a betrayal of a putative ally. It was also a major blow to the Republicans in Spain and their supporters, dashing any last hopes for an antifascist front that would include France and England. That fall, after the crushing Republican defeat at the Battle of the Ebro, the International Brigades disbanded. In December, Franco invaded Catalonia, forcing thousands to flee across the border. Hundreds of idealistic young Americans who had volunteered to fight for Spain in the Abraham Lincoln Brigade were trapped in internment camps or field hospitals. More than six hundred of approximately three thousand American volunteers had died in the war. Now the survivors—many wounded, shell-shocked, and penniless—had to get home.

Bromfield, as always at the epicenter of the American colony in France, stepped up. Earlier that spring, after the war began to turn in Franco's favor, Bromfield had asked the American hospital in Neuilly to set aside beds for the first wave of Americans. He then started negotiations with the French authorities for safe passage and visas. In June, he formally took charge of the Emergency Committee for American Wounded, formed at the Hôtel Lancaster. In open letters to the *New York Herald Tribune* and the *Washington Post*, he appealed to his fellow Americans on an emotional level, writing about the "pitiable" state of the young volunteers trapped in camps near the French border or lying wounded in a hospital at Figueres that had just been bombed by Italian warplanes. These boys, Bromfield wrote, urgently needed medical attention, as well as money, clothes, and cigarettes. He brought one of the wounded brigadiers, Harry Reubin, to meet with the American consul general in Paris to pressure the State Department to make allowances for the volunteers who had broken the law and violated the conditions of their passports by taking up arms in Spain.

Bromfield understood that this war was a divisive issue, that not all Americans were against Franco, so he modulated his tone with care. "The appeal is made to emotions and convictions which are above politics," he wrote. "These are American boys, who volunteered for service out of an idealism which is innately American. They are boys out of any 'home town' from every part of the United States. They might easily be our sons, brothers or cousins. Some of them are." A few expats gave Bromfield the cold shoulder. "Many a man who would put his hand in his pocket any time to help a stranded American home is deterred in this case by the belief that the beneficiaries are largely Communists, of which we have an abundant supply at home," wrote one. "Has Mr. Bromfield any information on this point?" Another letter to the *Tribune* described the Lincoln Brigadiers as "renegade Americans" who took up arms "for a foreign government guilty of atrocious crimes against the Christian religion."

Despite these detractors, the committee—described by newspapers as "the Bromfield Group"—was making progress. The first seventeen volunteers, whose injuries included bullet wounds and tuberculosis, sailed for America on the SS *President Harding* in June, after Bromfield hosted them at a farewell dinner in Paris. Hundreds more arrived in Paris over the next two months. "The task of the committee is not finished," Bromfield said in a letter to the *Tribune* on August 2, asking for more support: "Clothing, cigarettes, razors, toothbrushes are especially needed."

In all, the committee helped more than 1,000 Lincoln Brigadiers make their way home. For his work on their behalf, Bromfield would eventually receive the French Legion of Honor. But something broke in him after Munich. His contempt for the British prime minister was vast, bordering on irrational, and he blamed him for much of what would follow. "When Mr. Chamberlain debased the dignity of the British Empire, took his umbrella and overshoes and went to Munich to meet a second-rate adventurer, I, like any other moderately informed and intelligent person in Europe, knew that the dreadful thing was at hand, and that nothing now could stop it."

Bromfield's disgust with French and British appeasement was by no means a popular stance. Many in France were relieved that the country had, for the moment, avoided another war, whatever the costs. The French premier, Édouard Daladier, was greeted by thousands of weeping admirers when his plane from Munich landed at Le Bourget. But Bromfield knew that the peace was only temporary, its price far too high. He believed the European democracies had "murdered Czechoslovakia" and allowed "the murder from air of thousands of Spanish men, women and children." Furious, he wrote a thirty-two-page screed, a "literary brickbat" in the words of one critic, called *England, Dying Oligarchy*, in which he assailed Britain, a country he loved almost as much as France or America, for being led by "a clique of compromising undecided elderly politicians, decadent and full of cant, as easily terrified by the prospect of a general election as by the face-making of dictators." An English bookstore chain, Chester, withdrew all its Bromfield novels from circulation in response. "I have noticed lately," said a writer in the *Daily Mail*, "that gentlemen who yap loudest about the peace are those who are trying their hardest to cause other people to go to war."

He felt the Continent drifting away from him, normal life being overtaken by a ghastly geopolitical sideshow "in which all the drama was melodrama, all the acting shockingly exaggerated, and all the characters from Hitler to Chamberlain, from Mussolini to Laval, were caricatures. Even when you watched, at times with a kind of horror, you could not turn away."

———

Senlis had been in the path of German invaders during the Franco-Prussian War and World War I; there was no reason to expect it would be spared this time. Bromfield watched as the French government began to prepare for war. His automobile was requisitioned by the military. The city received a new garrison of soldiers. The mayor of Senlis issued a proclamation ordering residents to keep their windows dark at night. He said that the city's network of subterranean passageways and cellars could shelter people during a bombardment but that they could not protect against "toxic gas." Fearing for their safety, in September 1938, Bromfield sent Mary, Nanny White, and the children to the States. "I myself stayed on, partly out of a novelist's morbid interest in the spectacle, however depressing, and partly because, loving France, I wanted to be of help if there was anything I could do."

One night that fall, Bromfield went to visit Louis Gillet, a good friend whom he had met through Edith Wharton. Gillet was a literary critic and art historian, one of the "immortals" of the Académie Française. He seemed to embody for Bromfield something about French civilization itself, faced now with the prospect of destruction. Bromfield once wrote Wharton that he "never met a man with greater charm and wit, intelligence and humor." Gillet lived not far from Senlis in Ermenonville, where he worked as curator of the Abbaye de Chaalis, an eighteenth-century monastery that had been converted into an art museum.

Gillet, who wrote the introduction to several of Bromfield's novels

in French translation, described Bromfield in sweet if slightly condescending terms, saying that he gave off the impression of "a big irresistible child," possessing a "radiant vitality, like a young animal." Gillet
recalled a moment when Bromfield, stopping by the Pavillon Colombe
in a tuxedo on the way to some formal dinner, unleashed "a profusion of
anecdotes . . . in such a torrent that one could scarcely follow his words."
It was not the stories themselves that amused him but "the pleasure he
took in himself, the abandon, the devil-may-care attitude, and the naive
desire to share his good feelings."

On this day, however, Bromfield was much more serious. He had
come not so much to be convinced by Gillet of the need to leave France
but rather to have his guilt in doing so expiated. The two men took a walk
amid the ruins of the abbey, into the wild park that fronts the Château
d'Ermenonville, where Jean-Jacques Rousseau spent his final days. It was
the end of autumn; what few leaves remained on the trees were falling.
Gillet spoke of his family, his children whose lives were suspended awaiting news of war, and his own disbelief, shared by many Frenchmen of his
generation, that the madness hadn't been purged the last time.

> And as we walked about the great park among the lagoons and
> the seventeenth century gardens, surrounded by the evidence of
> all the glorious history of France, Louis Gillet talked brilliantly,
> humanely as he could talk when he was deeply moved. At last
> he said, "You must return home. There is nothing more you can
> do here that a Frenchman could not do. You can go home and
> tell your people what is happening here, what is bound to come.
> Tell them they will not be able to escape it—to be prepared
> and ready."

That night, after dinner and a glass of "good *vin rosé*," Bromfield
followed Gillet and his family into the forest to listen to the stags call,

an autumn ritual in this part of France since the Middle Ages. Smiling weakly, Bromfield sat on a blanket with the Gillets, his hand digging into the forest floor, and he experienced "a faint sickness" in the pit of his stomach. Louis Gillet would not survive the Occupation—he died in Paris in 1943. Two years later, Bromfield concluded his first memoir by saying how grateful he was to Gillet, "dead now of a heart broken by the humiliation of France, for the long talk of the evening in the moonlit forest of Ermenonville while we listened to the calling of the amorous stags, for he sent me back to the country where I was born, to Pleasant Valley and the richest life I have ever known."

—·—

By mid-November, Bromfield had left France. He was heartsick, but he was also home. He had decided at some point in 1938 that, rather than Maryland or Princeton or New York—places he had flirted with moving back to during his long sojourn in Europe—he was heading to Ohio, where he planned to raise his children on a "real honest-to-God farm." He joined his family in Oberlin, where they had rented a house while looking for land to buy. With the war coming, Bromfield had dreams of creating in this rich countryside a kind of bastion, a place where the vagaries of history could not so easily intrude on him. He was beginning, in his own confused way, to sketch out the contours of Malabar. It would be, he wrote, like "the medieval fortress-manor of France, where a whole community once found security and self-sufficiency . . . a place which, if necessary, could withstand a siege."

He had left France after a cocktail party at the Hôtel Lancaster in Paris attended by fifty of his closest friends. "Has the famous 'garden salon' of Louis Bromfield come to an end?" wondered the Paris *Tribune*. "With the lanky lord of the Senlis manor absent, Americans are asking themselves if the beautiful old house and garden where Mr. Bromfield's regular Sunday afternoon 'open house' united prima donnas and poets,

A page from the Bromfield family scrapbooks chronicling life in Senlis.

earls and advertising men, counts and couturiers, was to fall into decay."
Looking back on his fourteen-year expatriation, Bromfield admitted that
the hardest thing about leaving France was "not the loss of the intellectual life I had known there, nor the curious special freedom a foreigner

knows in a country he loves, nor the good food, nor even the friends I
would be leaving behind."

> The thing I should miss most, the thing to which I was most
> attached were the old house and the few acres of land spread along
> the banks of a little river called the Nonette. If I never saw it again
> a part of my heart would always be there in the earth, the old walls,
> the trees and vines I had planted, in the friendships that piece of
> earth had brought me.

Such sentimentality provided little comfort to the friends Bromfield
did leave behind, like Gertrude Stein, who pleaded with him to come
back, saying that he had made a terrible mistake. She considered his flight
a betrayal. "Et tu brute," Stein wrote to him toward the end of the year.
She also thought it was hypocritical of Bromfield to write articles criticizing Britain and France for pacifism from the safety of the American
Midwest. "Why don't you tell America to lay down its life for democracy? You are like a very large man standing and seeing two dogs biting
each other and saying with complete amiability, 'I think I am safe . . .
[it] will be best that they fight it out.'" Eventually, though, she let down
her guard, and said straight out what she was really feeling: "I might say
more about devotion and other things, but I love you and I mean that."

What upset Stein, ultimately, was not Bromfield's politics but his
absence; she missed him, she missed his Sunday lunches in Senlis, the
antics of his assistant, George Hawkins, and the shameless pleasure of
his garden, all of which seemed to be receding into the past with terrible
speed. That last winter of 1938 before everything changed, she visited
Senlis with Alice B. Toklas and the painter Francis Rose. Together, they
hosted a kind of impromptu wake.

> It is a bright white Sunday, the kind that was always so lovely only
> there are no Bromfields in Senlis . . . We went there and we went

in and we and the maid and the cook wept together it looked so deserted, don't tell me Oberlin and a farm is better cause it is not, and don't be so bitter about poor old europe, It has its little ways but it does give us and has given us awfully pleasant days, come back Bromfields come back to us all, so many [e]xiles must pray on as usual.

7

The Rains Came

After fourteen years in Europe, Bromfield returned to America a changed man. War and economic depression had made him yearn for the simple, self-sufficient farm life of his ancestors. Gardening in France had changed his relationship with the land. But there was one other ingredient necessary for the creation of Malabar Farm, and that was India. The country took him by surprise. His first trip there, in January of 1933, had been meant only as a diversion, a chance to sail somewhere warm while Europe froze and to lap up the luxurious lifestyle of a very rich new friend.

The Bromfields met Sayajirao Gaekwad III, the Maharaja of Baroda, the previous winter while vacationing in the Swiss ski resort of Gstaad. He was about seventy then, a small man with friendly, clear black eyes who suffered from gout and was often confined to a wheelchair. He seemed to lean heavily on his wife, Chimnabai II, the maharani, who was almost ten years younger. She walked, Mary said, "with a carriage so superb that you did not realize until you looked down at her that she was short." In Gstaad, the maharani wore Jaeger wool sweaters over her saris and jewels and spent most of her time playing cards inside the Palace Hotel.

Invited to join her one night, the Bromfields discovered that Chimnabai was "a rugged individualist at the bridge table." She cheated shamelessly, she cursed like a professional gambler in a mining camp, she made
up her own rules, and, when reproached, she merely chuckled. Bridge,
it turned out, was just a "polite and diplomatic" ruse, a way of ensnar-
ing them in a game she loved above everything else: poker. After losing
many hands, the Bromfields became friends with the maharani, which
led to introductions to other Indian royals who spent time in Europe.
That spring, they began visiting the garden in Senlis, landing, Bromfield
said, "like gaily colored birds in the grey old French town." The maharajas and their wives met Stein and Schiaparelli, ate strawberry shortcake,
drank rosé d'Anjou, and in typically extravagant fashion they repaid this
hospitality with invitations to their palaces in India. Toward the end of
the year, the Bromfields accepted. They sailed from Genoa on a course to
Bombay via the Suez Canal aboard the *Victoria*, a sleek new Italian liner,
then the fastest diesel-powered passenger ship in the world, and the first
to have an air-conditioned lounge (reserved for the Bromfields and other
first-class passengers).

Approaching from the Arabian Sea, they could smell Bombay before
they saw it. The hot winds of the mainland carried out to the ship a curious odor—a blend of drying fish, cow-dung smoke, copra, spices, and
jasmine. It seemed to Bromfield alien, intense. "The smell alarmed me."
Mary, who documented the trip in a frank and slightly xenophobic memoir, was more concerned by the sight of Bombay, the noisy crowds and
"Oriental dirt," which plunged her into an "agony of homesickness and
disappointment." As their luxury liner pulled into port, the Bromfields
saw thousands of Indians waiting below with wreaths of white flowers
on which they had sprinkled a sweet perfume that wafted up to the ship.
Disembarking, they were "buried from stomach to chin" in garlands.
Mary had just broken free from the thicket when a "most handsome
Englishman sprang up the gangplank calling for "Mr. Bromfield." He
held in his hand a large crested invitation to lunch with the governor of

Bombay. But Mary did not care about the governor of Bombay. "Nothing was mattering to me but heat, the craving for news of home, and the mistaken idea that we were going to a rare and comfortable and glamorous hotel, the Taj Mahal, where we would be waited on hand and foot by endless *ayahs* and bearers of the kind that I had read about in Kipling."

The Taj Mahal Palace, the most famous hotel in Bombay and a masterpiece of Indo-Saracenic revival architecture, struck them as a hideous mishmash of styles: Florentine and Moorish domes, Edwardian trellises, dull gray brick. It looked to Bromfield like the Indian equivalent of "a vast middle western county jail." They followed their luggage, which was conveyed by "far too many chattering untouchables," to a dirt-colored room with two twin beds covered in mosquito nets and electric punkah fans. Outside, porters slept on the floor, sometimes salaaming as they passed by. The Bromfields unpacked, read through the cables and letters that had arrived, and then went to the bar for a drink. They came down a grand hallway into an enormous room that looked like a "Klondike saloon," in which a jazz band played and bats flew about the ceiling. Several bartenders shook gimlets and gin slings and poured *chotapegs* (or small shots) of whiskey. All the white tourists looked dressed for "any eventuality"—safari, jungle romp, yellow-fever outbreak. The men wore pith helmets and the women were covered in flowing veils and suits of India silk, armed with parasols and guidebooks.

After drinks, the Bromfields toured Bombay by taxi: riding through the streets and alleyways and marketplaces. Mary observed that it was a feast day—"either of fertility or plenty, I forget which"—and many people had daubed their faces with red betel-nut juice. They saw women and children sleeping in gutters, crowded bazaars, "smells and color" everywhere. They were extremely hot, overdressed, and overwhelmed. Their taxi driver was their only guide. He took them to the southern part of the city, to a forked peninsula separating the harbor of Bombay from the Arabian Sea. On the western prong, the land rises gently, exposing rich homes and gardens. Then as now, Malabar Hill was the most exclusive residential district in Bombay. But the driver brought the Bromfields here not to gawk at the wealthy homes but to show them a special tourist attraction called the Towers of Silence.

These "Towers" were actually three circular temples where for three thousand years the Zoroastrian community of Bombay—known as the Parsis—have exposed their dead to be eaten by scavenger birds. Vultures pluck at the corpses until the bones are dry. The Parsis considered the gift of one's flesh to the birds a "final act of charity." This ritual, called excarnation, is both ecological and quick. Afterward, the bones dry in the sun and eventually drift into a central catchment, where they begin to decompose. Bromfield found the tradition fascinating, even though he could only see the outside of the temples, a fact about which the squeamish Mary was "relieved." Sometime afterward, they saw a Hindu funeral pyre and Bromfield was struck by the way the Hindus also seemed to deny the importance of the dead body. "It was as if they said, 'what is dead is dead' and hurriedly made off with the body to turn it back once more as quickly as possible before the sun set, into earth." This worldview seemed so different from the one he grew up with. "Here they *believed* the body was nothing and refused to honor it. In the West they only pretended to believe that the body was dust. In the West the clodlike body held people forever in subjection."

—·—

Bromfield was not the only Westerner who found himself drawn to India in the first few decades of the twentieth century, who sought in that country the possibility of some kind of spiritual rebirth. Many other writers came: E. M. Forster, Robert Byron, Hermann Hesse, and Paul Morand, to name just a few. Some were interested in India's ancient cultures, in the teachings of the Vedas or the mystical wisdom of swamis like Paramahansa Yogananda, whose lectures and books in the 1920s popularized yoga in the West. Others were moved by the country's modern problems: the yoke of the Raj, the plight of the untouchables,

Bromfield and Mary in Bombay in the winter of 1933.

the revolutionary fervor of Nehru and Gandhi. For these searchers, the subcontinent seemed to mark a kind of extreme of the European romantic imagination, which in those years was already oriented elsewhere. "I don't want to go north, don't want to *be* North," wrote D. H. Lawrence in 1929. "The North has all gone evil—I can't help feeling it morally and ethically. I mean anti-life."

While many writers came to "the Orient," as they called it, in search of answers to amorphous political and philosophical questions, there was another group of Westerners accompanying them—scientists, doctors, agronomists—who wanted to solve a much more basic, and pressing, problem: How best to feed the growing planet. At the turn of the twentieth century, the Earth could barely support its 1.5 billion inhabitants. Advances in sanitation and medicine meant that the population was expected to grow sharply, yet the total amount of food was capped by the supply of one important ingredient, which today is taken entirely for granted: fertilizer.

Whether it comes in the form of manure from an animal or the pebbly granules made in an industrial factory, fertilizer has always been essential to agriculture. Understanding why requires a brief science lesson. All plants must have certain basic elements to grow. Some of these elements, like sunlight, are readily available to them. But another element, nitrogen, is much more elusive. Yet all life depends on nitrogen—it provides the chemical foundation for the amino acids that nature needs to build essential proteins and genetic material, including our own DNA.

There is an abundance of nitrogen floating around in the Earth's atmosphere, yet plants can't access it unless it undergoes a chemical process that "fixes" it, or makes it usable by splitting the atmospheric nitrogen molecules and then pairing them with hydrogen atoms. This process occurs in nature in only a few ways: very quickly, when lightning strikes, which breaks apart the atmospheric nitrogen molecules and fixes a tiny amount in the soil; or very slowly, through the gradual decomposition of animals, plants, and their waste products, all of which feeds—indeed creates—fertile soil. Just how long this process takes might surprise you. For Mother Nature to build a single inch of topsoil, she typically requires at least a century.

Farmers, of course, could never wait that long. By growing crops in the same field for just a few seasons, they quickly depleted their soil of nitrogen and other essential elements. To restore fertility, they had only a few options. They could rotate in a crop of legumes (like clover or peas), whose roots play host to microorganisms that fix small amounts of nitrogen in the soil. Or they could use manure. Animal dung is rife with fixed nitrogen and, if applied correctly, can dramatically speed up the natural process of decay that leads to fertility.

The problem? There was never enough manure. In the nineteenth century, wars were fought in South America over natural, nonrenewable stashes of fertilizer, like guano and Chilean nitrate. In search of "chemical manures," industrialists spent massive amounts of money and energy creating machines to produce artificial lightning that would burn nitrogen out of the air. But they were running out of time. In 1898, the distinguished British chemist Sir William Crookes projected that, given the population trends, demand for fertilizer would outpace supply by about 1930, leading to widespread famine and plummeting population rates—a catastrophe famously prophesied in the late eighteenth century by the English philosopher Thomas Malthus.

Out of this impending global crisis emerged two divergent ways of thinking about food, two broad schools of agriculture that have endured in some form to the present day. For the sake of simplicity, let's call them the industrial school and the organic school. The industrial school has always been oriented toward the future. Its only religion was science. It treated the farm as a machine and the soil as a chemistry problem. Out of this school came the discovery that soil fertility relied chiefly on three essential chemical elements: nitrogen, phosphorous, and potassium, known by their periodic table initials, NPK. Out of this school also came, on the eve of World War I, the discovery of a method to artificially create a practically limitless supply of fertilizer. The Haber-Bosch process—named for the German scientists who developed it, Fritz Haber and Carl Bosch—used tremendous amounts of energy to force a chemical reaction between nitrogen from the air and hydrogen (usually from natural gas), creating fixed nitrogen on demand.

The industrial school essentially gave us the modern world. It solved the existential problem of fertilizer scarcity and provided enough food to triple the Earth's population over the course of the twentieth century, eventually replacing famines with obesity epidemics and making farming into one of the biggest global sources of pollution and greenhouse gas.

The organic school arose at roughly the same time as the industrial school and as a kind of violent reaction to it. It sought solutions not in the future but in the distant past. It tended to distrust new technology, to regard the role of science as limited, and to revere peasant traditions, especially those of Asian cultures. This school could be promiscuous in its religious and philosophical inspirations, sampling occultism and mysticism. It treated the farm not as a machine but as an analogue to nature, and the soil as a kind of cosmic mystery. Its progenitors included men like the Austrian philosopher Rudolf Steiner, the father of biodynamic agriculture, who in 1924 gave an influential series of lectures in which he claimed that the industrial school had cut off agriculture from its "deeper essences," that it did not look at the farm in its totality as a "living organism." Along with composting, Steiner suggested that certain "spiritual manures" could help maintain soil fertility. The most famous and widely mocked of his prescriptions was for a farmer to fill the horn of a cow with dung and then bury it at an appointed place and time, in order to collect "astral-ethereal forces," before digging it up and applying the manure on his fields.

Steiner was not the only hero of the organic school whose ideas were inspired by what he called "peasant wit." Another pioneer was the American agronomist F. H. King, author of the important book *Farmers of Forty Centuries*. A former bureaucrat at the USDA, King set out on a nine-month tour of the Far East in 1909 to get a crash course in peasant farming. He saw America's agriculture as wasteful and increasingly reliant on imported feeds and "mineral fertilizers," which he knew could not "be continued indefinitely." He wanted to understand how Japan, Korea, and China managed to feed a population of 500 million from fields that in some cases had been under constant cultivation for over four thousand years. America at the time had at least five times the amount of arable land per person yet was nowhere near as agriculturally self-sufficient. In King's travels, he found all the explanations he was looking for: The Asian peasants were brilliant intuitive farmers, they assiduously rotated their crops, they refused to waste *any* organic materials, even human excreta (known euphemistically as "night soil"), which they composted and used to enrich the earth.

King was interested in what the Orient could teach the West, so he overlooked deficiencies that plagued the East: like poverty, famines, deforestation, and environmental damage. The Asian peasants were, for him, noble savages, the custodians of a fixed, healthy, virile culture "which, with fortitude and rare wisdom, has kept alive the seeds of manhood and nourished them into such sturdy stock." King died in 1911, just before publishing his book, which was completed by his wife, Carrie Baker. While King's study succeeded in popularizing the ingenious methods of Asian farmers, it would take another member of the organic school to marry that ancient wisdom with modern science and create a scalable alternative to industrial agriculture. And he would create it in India.

Albert Howard, born in 1873, was the son of a farmer from Shropshire, England. He trained at Cambridge as a botanist and was posted throughout the British Empire, eventually landing at an imperial agricultural research center in Pusa, in northeastern India, in the early 1900s. He later opened his own soil institute in Indore, in Central India, in 1924. Howard, along with his wife and fellow scientist, Gabrielle, spent decades in India meticulously treating "the whole problem of health in soil, plant, animal and man as one great subject." The Howards discovered that the new chemical fertilizers did not necessarily produce a healthier plant and that their repeated use injured the soil. They wanted to put attention on the "quality as well as on the yield" of the crops they were growing. While animal manure was always in short supply, in India it was particularly scarce because most cow dung went to nonagricultural uses, like fuel. So the Howards needed to address two problems—the scarcity of natural fertilizer and the health of the soil—at the same time. They eventually developed an advanced method of composting, perfecting a technique that Asian peasant farmers had relied on for thousands of years.

This system, called the "Indore Process," allowed farmers, with a little bit of "starter dung," to create "an artificial product, closely resembling farmyard manure" that required no chemical additives whatsoever. Howard later credited the Indian peasants for inspiring his brilliant style of composting, calling them "my professors." But his approach to agriculture actually owed less to the methods of peasant farmers than to the way Nature farmed herself, which he described in a now-famous allegory.

> Mother earth never attempts to farm without live stock; she always raises mixed crops; great pains are taken to preserve the soil and to prevent erosion; the mixed vegetable and animal wastes are converted into humus; there is no waste; the processes of growth and the processes of decay balance one another; ample provision is made to maintain large reserves of fertility; the greatest care is taken to store the rainfall; both plants and animals are left to protect themselves against disease.

Bromfield visited Howard's soil institute in Indore in 1933. He later became one of the first people in the United States to promote Howard's work, calling his 1940 book *An Agricultural Testament*—which is the bible of today's organic food movement—"the best book I know on soil." Bromfield said that Howard's Indore method produced "perhaps the ideal fertilizer," one that reduced plant disease and raised yields per acre, creating "prodigious results in health, vigor and the productiveness of plant life." But he also knew that the painstaking process, which involved the hand-turning of compost piles and the collection of every ounce of animal waste, relied on cheap labor, the kind Howard had in abundance in India. If Howard's methods were to be useful in large-scale

Western agriculture, Bromfield realized, they would have to be adapted. Of course, such practical concerns were, for him, still a few years away.

——⁖——

Bombay was just a prelude for the Bromfields, a layover on the way to Baroda. The princely state was comprised of disjointed territories scattered across the scrub forests and semi-arid fields of Gujarat, a couple hundred miles south of India's present-day border with Pakistan. Over 2.2 million people lived in this state, most of them residing in the capital, Baroda City, which is now called Vadodara. The train ride there from Bombay took the Bromfields nine hours. Mary described the journey as "a nightmare of sheer horror." Despite the 90-degree heat, the train windows were sealed to keep dust from entering cars, yet the yellow-red dirt snuck in anyway, turning the melting blocks of ice meant to cool each cabin into cakes of mud. Every twenty minutes or so, the train stopped, and a team of sweepers climbed on with primitive brooms made of sticks. Their sweeping succeeded only at stirring up the dust, "choking the air of the compartment with it, and letting it fall again where it came from." The Bromfields passed the hours looking at the starving cows that dotted the parched landscape and feeding the mangy *pie* dogs—considered pariahs by the Indians—that gathered at every stop.

The maharaja's nephew, Bobby, was waiting for the Bromfields at the Baroda station. Seeing him on the platform, smiling in his jodhpurs and neatly wrapped red-and-gold turban, Mary immediately experienced a rush of relief. He somehow made India feel "cosy and friendly and less strange." He took them to their guest cottage, near the palace, part of a complex of white wooden houses built around a garden where they would take most of their meals. It was blessedly cool, and quiet except for the "sacred monkeys" (gray langurs), who had the full run of the courtyard—slinky things with black faces who flew from tree to tree, chattering, "imitating us," confident in the knowledge that no one dared to kill them because, legend had it, they had once defended the Hindu deity Rama in battle. The Bromfields were "fascinated" by the monkeys and could have spent a good portion of their stay sipping cocktails and watching them play—except that, as Bobby explained a little bashfully, they had a detailed itinerary to get through, planned down to the smallest detail by the maharani herself. Each day they would get a schedule and a private car and a royal escort would take them to various municipal sites: the museum, the music school, the redbrick libraries, the insane asylum, the prison, the agricultural institute, everything the reform-minded maharaja had built to yoke his people toward progress.

As the head of a "native state" with a degree of autonomy from his colonial overlords, the maharaja kowtowed neither to the officers of the Raj nor to homegrown religious zealots. He was a fierce critic of India's caste system, which he said had done "incalculable harm to our country." He hired low-caste servants in the palace; outlawed child marriage and bigamy; and joined his wife in urging girls to attend school. The Barodas were proud of the progressive state they built—and especially of its modern water system, which diverted the Vishwamitri River into a five-kilometer-long earthen reservoir that held the city's drinking water. A guide told the Bromfields how, during the monsoon of July 1927, that river overflowed and a "roaring torrent" nine feet high rushed through the city center. The damage was extensive—107 people died, 100,000 homes were destroyed, and half the season's crop ruined—but initial reports suggested the flood was apocalyptic, that the reservoir had burst open, and "thousands of people had been washed away."

That story lit a fire in Bromfield's imagination, which smoldered as he met more characters in Baroda: doctors, teachers, politicians, servants. He was introduced to an Oxford-educated museum curator and his beautiful wife who kept a pet crane in their living room and gave fabulous parties; to the head of the Baroda police, a Muslim who watched over a Hindu city; to a YMCA missionary who had just developed "a most successful method of irrigation." He thought about the world they were building, how refreshing their idealism seemed compared to the mood in Europe, where there was "no faith and very little good news."

The highlight of their week-long visit was a dinner given in their honor in the maharaja's 170-room palace, three times the size of Buckingham. Mary remembered birds flying around the ceiling, chandeliers covered with bees, the maharani's emeralds and rubies sparkling in a special gallery built into the glass-lined balustrades. Inside, there was no curtseying, little ceremony. Barefoot servants in turbans gave the Bromfields warm and vermouthy martinis ("a concession to European civilization"). The only other white guests were the resident British official, his pained-looking wife, and an American missionary family. Mary felt shabby and plain next to all the Indians, with their "dark smooth skin" and colorful clothes, the women in gold-tipped saris painted with flowers, the men in brocaded kaftans with jeweled buttons. They trooped up to a vast marble-lined dining room, with open windows covered in nets.

The meal was served on silver trays set with bowls of rice, curries with meat and fish, jellies, grated egg, and coconut. The Indians ate with their fingers. Mary thought the food "delicious" but "terribly hot" and the only way of enduring it was to resist "the fearful desire to drink between mouthfuls and just let the inside of your mouth go on burning." At a certain point in the meal, music began, coming from the court musicians who had assembled on the veranda. After dinner there was more music and dancing and then a magician, whose act was interrupted when the maharani abruptly rose from her chair and told everyone that the night was now over. "I have enjoyed seeing you all here so much. And I hope that you will all come back again some time."

The guests began to muster farewells. The Bromfields were the last to the door. As they approached the exit, one of the royal cousins drew Mary aside "with a good deal of mystery" and whispered: "Her highness wishes to see you immediately." They were led through a series of dark corridors, and finally up a flight of stairs to a sitting room with white-

and-gold walls. Inside was a small buffet—sandwiches, Champagne, coffee, cake—and, in the middle of the room, a table set for poker. Behind it sat the maharani "triumphant and alive again and ready for battle." They played until five thirty in the morning, when finally the Bromfields were led back through the twisting corridors, stepping over prostrate servants "like a bunch of conspirators," before emerging into the pink dawn. "So hypnotized were we that we didn't dare speak above a whisper until we were back in the guest house and safe in our own rooms."

———

Over the next two months, the Bromfields saw much of India: Benares, Calcutta, Agra. They were invited to visit the Barodas' daughter, Indira Devi, who was not only, Mary said, "the most attractive woman I've ever seen" but also the regent of Cooch Behar, another princely state in far eastern India, near Bhutan, in the foothills of the snowcapped Himalayas. They spent a week in her enormous Italianate palace, with "a heap of servants" at their beck and call. "Every time we wanted anything we clapped our hands," Bromfield said. "If we'd accidentally applauded anything we'd have been trampled." Each day after lunch twenty elephants appeared at the dining-room door and "everyone from old ladies to small children piled aboard to go off into the jungle."

In 1936, Bromfield came back to India for a second time with George Hawkins, a bachelors' trip, in the company of two American women, Maggie and Peggy, about whom little is known. They explored teakwood jungles and hunted bull bison. They saw a king cobra dance. They toured agricultural schools and irrigation ducts. In a street market in Madras, they found a gray mongoose with a "delicate pink nose" and "brown shoe-button eyes" being viciously dragged along on a string by a Pashtun with a foot-high turban. "There seemed to be only one way of rescuing her and that was to buy her," Bromfield said. "After some double talk haggling," he bought the animal for 13 rupees, and put her in the pocket of his coat. For a name, Bromfield chose Rikki-Tikki-Tavi, after

Indira Devi, the Maharani of Cooch Behar, speaking to
Gertrude Stein in the garden of the Presbytère.

the mongoose in Kipling's *Jungle Book.* He eventually brought her back
to live in the garden at Senlis, where she became quite the conversation
piece. "She had tiny brown paws which gave her the effect, when she sat
erect, of a very chic lady wearing brown gloves."

Bromfield loved the landscapes of India, the music, the temples, the
food. He was happier there, he told Gertrude Stein, "than I had ever
been in my life." And he could not stop thinking about that first week in
Baroda, the people he met: the wise old maharaja, the wily maharani, the
Muslim police chief, the idealistic American missionaries. They all put
their faith in modernity, in the university, and the waterworks. Bromfield was struck by how fervently they believed in this future knowing
full well that a host of calamities—famine, disease, earthquake, religious violence—was waiting for them around the corner. What if the
river flooded again, as it did in in 1927, and this time it wasn't only the

maharaja's exotic zoo animals who drowned in their cages but the entire
modern city that they had worked so hard to create?

Somewhere in all this was a novel. He had begun it in Cooch Behar
in 1933 but it took him almost four years and half a dozen drafts before
he had finished. The final work, *The Rains Came*, clocked in at 240,000
words—longer than *Moby-Dick*. At the novel's center was a man much
like Bromfield, Tom Ransome, a hard-drinking Anglo-American, who
paints and gardens, who idealizes his farmer grandparents, who had
given up on a money-grubbing America and a decadent Europe, who
felt like "a useless liberal in a sick world which demanded violence and
ruthlessness and revolution to set it right." He ran as far away as he
could and landed in the fictional native state of Ranchipur, a spitting
image of Baroda, with its modern infrastructure, gouty maharaja and
poker-playing queen.

Ransome and the royals are just a few of the forty named characters
in the novel—Indians and Westerners, idealists and cynics, religious
fanatics and nonbelievers. The book unfurls, a bit like Thornton Wild-
er's *The Bridge of San Luis Rey*, as a series of interlocking portraits of
people on the edge of some great catastrophe. First we are introduced in
long interior monologues to Ransome, then a Brahmin doctor, then an
American missionary family, then a British tycoon who's taken time off
from plundering the Orient to buy the maharaja's prize horse, then his
nymphomaniac wife, Lady Esketh, and so on. They are all parched, sun-
stroked, awaiting the monsoon, which arrives late but with a vengeance.
After the rains come, Ransome watches the vines in his garden "writhe
and thrust" in a kind of "vegetable ecstasy." But the rains do not stop.
By the time Bromfield connects the lines between his waterlogged characters, there is an earthquake. The reservoir—having been dammed by
a European conman posing as an engineer—bursts, unleashing a great
flood. As if the symbolism wasn't head-smackingly obvious, Bromfield
makes it explicit: "The dam had been in a way a kind of symbol—the
symbol of Oriental faith in Occidental practical achievement and hon-

esty, organization and superiority, a faith which like the dam itself had long since cracked."

Out of the violent paroxysm comes first destruction, then disease, then death, and finally, for the few characters who survive the ordeal, something akin to rebirth. The book was his dirtiest novel yet, featuring words like "slut" and "bitch," dashed-out curses and a loveless liaison in the palace that Bromfield compares to "the *accouplement* of two *pie* dogs." The plot contained elements of a trashy soap opera, stretches of very repetitive prose. But it had the sweep and atmosphere of a genuine epic, one leavened with comedy and sharp social observations. Yes, it was overdone. Yes, it was overly romantic. It was, after all, a Louis Bromfield novel.

And so it was also a massive success when it came out in the fall of 1937, perhaps the strongest-selling American novel since Margaret Mitchell's *Gone with the Wind* appeared the previous summer. In its first year, *The Rains Came* went through thirty-two printings in America and spent a total of sixty-eight weeks on the bestseller list. "It seems to me a magnificent and noble piece of work, by far the best he has done," said Edna Ferber. "I shouldn't wonder if it is the best anyone has done in the past 20 years." Pearl Buck agreed, saying that the novel "accomplished something of a miracle—the Indians themselves liked it." Krishnalal Shridharani, a poet and freedom fighter, wrote Bromfield to say how much he appreciated the nuanced portrait after the stereotypical treatment of the "India problem" in books like Katharine Mayo's *Mother India*: "You know how sensitive we Indians are to all forms of 'imperialism,' literary or otherwise," he said, calling the book "the first 'real' novel on India by a non-Indian."

Twentieth Century Fox bought the movie rights, and the film's budget quickly ballooned to $2.5 million—an almost unprecedented sum. A studio executive described the film as the biggest picture Fox had ever attempted. Major Hollywood stars were cast for the leads: Tyrone Power (in brownface) as the Brahmin doctor, George Brent as Ransome, Maria Ouspenskaya as the Maharani. For the part of Lady Esketh, Tallulah

Bankhead, Kay Francis, and Marlene Dietrich all competed. Bromfield shamelessly sent Francis, Dietrich, and Constance Bennett identical telegrams saying each would be "perfect" for the role, which eventually went to Myrna Loy. Five thousand people worked on the production. The director, Clarence Brown, said because they were shooting "in almost continuous rain" all cast members would need "a daily physical examination," otherwise the insurance company would not cover losses.

The resulting picture left most highbrow critics cold. "The film version is the merest skeleton of the Bromfield work," wrote the *New York Times*, "completely a romance now; not the composite biography-romance-social treatise that became a best-seller." But the Oscar-winning flood and earthquake sequences—which required more than 4,000 extras and 400,000 gallons of water—were unlike anything moviegoers had ever seen, eclipsing in technical proficiency earlier disaster pictures like *Hurricane* and *San Francisco*. The film debuted in September of 1939, the year cinema historians regard as Hollywood's *annus mirabilis*, when 365 movies were released and moviegoers bought tickets at the rate of 80 million a week. That year produced *Stagecoach, Mr. Smith Goes to Washington, Of Mice and Men, The Wizard of Oz, Ninotchka*, and *Gone with the Wind*. Despite such stiff competition, *The Rains Came* still managed

Crowds in September 1939 at New York's Roxy Theatre lined up to see *The Rains Came*, a lavish Hollywood adaptation of Bromfield's best-selling novel based on his travels to India.

to become the fifth highest-grossing film of 1939, raking in $9.4 million, roughly the same box-office haul as *The Wizard of Oz*.

The movie, and the lucrative Hollywood career that it sparked, made Bromfield a rich man (at least momentarily) and gave him the means to build one of the most influential farms in American history. He would never forget where the money came from. He chose to name his place "Malabar" after one of the first sights he had of India—that of the hills above Bombay Harbor, where the Parsis fed their dead to the birds and their bones to the soil, a kind of human compost heap that fully embraced the cycle of life. He said later that "nothing could be more appropriate than giving the farm an Indian name because India made it possible."

PART TWO

FARM

(1938–1956)

Everybody, that is, everybody who writes is interested in living inside themselves to tell what is inside themselves. That is why writers have to have two countries, the one where they belong and the one in which they live really. The second one is romantic, it is separate from themselves, it is not real but it is really there . . . The middle nineteenth century American generation were like that about England, my generation the end of the nineteenth century American generation was like that about France.

Of course sometimes people discover their own country as if it were the other, a recent instance of that is Louis Bromfield discovering America . . .

—GERTRUDE STEIN

8

Seeding

Bromfield was hardly the first writer to embrace agriculture. About 2,600 years before him came the Greek hillbilly poet Hesiod, badgering his lazy brother to bring in the hay: "Don't put off till tomorrow or till later/No barn is filled by a procrastinator." Xenophon, in the fourth century BCE, delved into practical matters like how to fertilize a field with a leguminous cover crop such as lupins or clover, which "enrich the soil as much as dung." The Romans lionized the farmer: "Of all the occupations," wrote Cicero, "none is better than agriculture, none more profitable, none more delightful, none more becoming to a freeman." Varro ranked manures, while Virgil wrote verse about dairy cows (the best are thick-necked and "fierce of feature").

Renaissance men also picked up the plow, sometimes clumsily, like the wine-grower Michel de Montaigne, who could barely find the way through his Bordeaux vineyards but who nevertheless hoped his final act in life would be an agricultural one: "I want death to find me planting my cabbages, but careless of death, and still more of my unfinished garden." Voltaire must have enjoyed that line. He famously urged his readers to cultivate their gardens—and took his own advice. In Ferney, by the Swiss border, he built not just a garden but a whole progressive agrarian estate, complete with five hundred beehives, poultry yards, vineyards, orchards, and his own personal pasture—called "Monsieur de Voltaire's field"—which he worked by hand into his seventies. "To have cultivated a field and made twenty trees grow," he said, "is a good which will never be lost."

American literature was practically inaugurated by an agricultural tract—*Letters from an American Farmer* (1782)—which became the first international bestseller to come out of the newly independent colonies. It was written by a "simple cultivator of the earth," the French-born New Yorker J. Hector St. John de Crèvecour, who worshipped the "precious soil."

> What should we American farmers be without the distinct possession of that soil? It feeds, it clothes us, from it we draw even a great exuberancy, our best meat, our richest drink, the very honey of our bees comes from this privileged spot. No wonder we should thus cherish its possession, no wonder that so many Europeans who have never been able to say that such portion of land was theirs, cross the Atlantic to realize that happiness.

Thoreau, who planted a field of beans (as well as potatoes and peas) by Walden Pond, also knew the farmer's happiness, as well as his hardships: the backbreaking labor, the woodchucks that ravaged his fields, and "those Trojans who had sun and rain and dews on their side"—otherwise known as weeds. Yet he considered growing crops an extension of his education as a naturalist: "What shall I learn of beans and beans of me?" And his bean field provided him not only sustenance but also—after he sold the surplus at a neighboring market—a tidy profit.

For Bromfield's generation, the agrarian ideal seemed especially appealing—a respite from the unpleasantness of war, industry, and the modern unhealthy city that seemed to characterize their age. Before he fell in love with literary Paris, Ford Madox Ford fell in love with pig farming. He spent several years as a farmer in West Sussex, raising not only swine but also rabbits and potatoes. His farm, Red Ford, drove him to the brink of financial ruin. The last straw came one day in the early 1920s, when an old literary acquaintance passed Ford's pigsty while he was feeding a sow called Anna and covered with mud up to the eyes. Despite the surprising context, the man recognized Ford: "Didn't I once meet you at Henry James's?"

Ford was only one of Bromfield's literary peers who experimented with the pastoral life. Edna Ferber, John Dos Passos, Dorothy Parker, E. B. White, Archibald MacLeish: they all had farms at one time or another. But they were amateurs, dabblers, at best gentleman or lady farmers who treated their rural seat more as backdrop than subject. Bromfield was different. He would make agriculture into literature in a way that none of his forebears or contemporaries had. He was the first major writer to give himself over completely to the problems and possibilities of agriculture, to get down into the dirt of it, to become a modern farmer. Farming became for him a calling, a platform, almost a religion. He wanted not just to farm for himself but to change the idea of what the farmer was or could be. His celebrity, his creativity, his money—all of it would eventually go into the compost pile.

Of course Bromfield realized none of this upon his return to America at the end of 1938. All he knew then was that he wanted to raise his children on the kind of farm that had sustained his grandparents, the kind he glorified in his autobiographical novel: a self-sufficient world, cut off from war and politics and economic privation. But he had not the faintest idea that, in pursuit of this romantic ideal, he would turn himself into an authority not just on agriculture but on ecology and the conservation of natural resources. He could not know that he would play a major role in launching the organic food movement and postwar environmentalism. Within a few short years of his return to America, Bromfield would become one of the country's leading ecological voices, and he would eventually convert thousands to the cause. But like any evangelist, first he needed to be born again.

He remembered the landscape from his childhood, from those horse-and-buggy drives into the countryside with his father, when they would hunt for underpriced cattle or visit eccentric relatives like Phoebe Wise. Sometimes, when they used to drive past farmers at work in the fields, they would offer to help ring hogs or husk corn in exchange for a midday dinner. This country was in his bones. He knew its marshes and mill-races, its fishing holes and Indian caves, but that knowledge had been scrambled by time and nostalgia. Now, he wrote, finding his way back through these hills was like retracing one's steps through "the maze of a vaguely remembered dream." Everything he saw was out of proportion to his recollection of it: that small hill should have been as big as the Matterhorn, that stream as wide and deep as the Mississippi. "Be careful!" his father used to warn as he approached the water. "You could drown while I have my back turned." *Drown?* Now, after twenty-five years, he could probably wade across it without getting his knees wet. That is, if the creek hadn't been frozen over, like the rest of the eastern Ohio landscape.

It was December 1938, just weeks after Bromfield's return, and he was driving in a new Ford station wagon vainly in search of a farm that he thought he remembered from his youth. In the car with him was Mary, buoyant and supportive, and George, impatient and wisecracking. They had already seen dozens of places but none was right. Now he was losing the daylight. He remembered later feeling nervous, wondering whether returning to Ohio was the right move. He looked almost unrecognizable to the old school friends who met him for lunch at the Leland Hotel in Mansfield. They remembered him only as the "gangly long-legged boy who left here more than 20 years ago." Now he was "a big, husky chap," weighing 180 pounds, dressed in a three-piece Savile Row suit, wearing a Cartier wristwatch and lighting his cigarettes with a sapphire-studded gold lighter. He was nearly forty-two. He had thickened out, ripened into middle age. Crow's feet spread from the corners of his eyes—the result of days spent digging in the sun and nights spent at the bottom of the bottle.

They had driven down from Oberlin, passing through the flat lake country of Ohio into the hillier zones of Holmes and Ashland Counties, where the first foothills of the Blue Ridge Mountains ripple across the landscape. He turned onto a winding country lane called Pinhook Road. "Beautiful," Mary said. "What a lovely, friendly valley!" Pleasant Valley, it was called, with a kind of flat, unpoetic, Midwestern accuracy. He made a sharp right onto a road that ran between two high sandstone ridges, wooded on each side, all the trees encased in snow. Bromfield felt he was finally on the right track. The farmhouses looked familiar to him, and he recognized the old Dutch and English family names hanging on the barns and the mailboxes: Shrack, Mengert, Berry. They drove a few minutes longer before stopping at a small house with a large cupolaed barn.

The buildings sat "on a kind of shelf" halfway up a long hill. He noticed approvingly the way the hill "turned its back on the north winds." The treetops on each ridge were "tinted with the last pink light of the winter sunset." The valley had a kind of snow-globe perfection, the air cold and "luminous like the unreal blue of skies on the cyclorama of a theater." Later he wrote that he felt like Brigham Young, who, upon seeing Salt Lake Valley, declared "This is the Place." Mary did not foresee the family's destiny quite as clearly, but she thought the farm had about it a sense of "snugness," and that the view from the house would be lovely, "not of wild and overpowering beauty—but a view across the fields and the hills, with a creek wandering through the pastures." Bromfield was excited. He got out of the station wagon and told Mary and George to wait in the car. He walked through the snow to the house. He wrote later that he felt like he was "knocking at the door of my long-gone boyhood."

Mrs. Herring, a woman he recognized, opened the door. When he told her his name, she remembered him vaguely "as a small boy who used to camp" at the place next door and fish in Switzer's Creek, the stream that ran through her property. She looked much older. She had a bad case of arthritis and kept her hands wrapped in her apron. She brought him hot coffee and spiced cookies. Bromfield surveyed the kitchen and felt welling up inside him a sudden, stupid, childish delight, which he attributed to the familiar smell of woodsmoke, apple butter, and pork sausage. The kitchen was bathed in gaslight. He looked at the walls of hand-cut stone, quarried from the cliffs behind the house; he saw the parlor, the room the Herrings reserved for weddings and funerals. And then he asked Mrs. Herring if her farm was for sale. She said she didn't know but that her husband was on the place, and they could go ask him. She put on a shawl and led Bromfield to the barn, where Clem Herring sat on a stool milking a Guernsey cow. Bromfield was hit by more familiar smells, these a bit more particular—hay, grain, and steaming manure, which he would later describe with a straight face as his version of "the perfumes of Araby."

The Herrings could not decide if they wanted to sell until they spoke to their children, so they offered him another cup of coffee, which he accepted. This gave him more time to survey the property. He liked their house very much—the simplicity, the country workmanship. It was "warm like the nest of a rabbit," the kind of house that could grow over generations with a family. After Bromfield finally said his goodbyes to the Herrings, he walked back to the car knowing that he would have their farm just as he knew he would have the Presbytère. By January 1939, he had prevailed upon them to sell the place for $20,000. He also bought all the neighboring pastures with their simple farmhouses and rundown barns, as well as an adjacent 70-acre marsh that he eventually called "the jungle." In total, the property was about 600 acres. He did not have enough cash to buy it all outright—royalties from *The Rains Came* and other Hollywood projects would not come rushing in until that fall—so he took out a bank loan for $34,000.

———

Bromfield had no intention of moving into the small Herring farmhouse as he found it. He wanted rather to make the 34-foot-wide gabled structure the "nucleus" of a vast manor house, which looked "as if it belonged there on that hillside shelf." He had learned of an architect in Mansfield, a man of distant French extraction named Louis André Lamoreux, who smoked a pipe, wore bow ties and berets, drank heartily, and fancied himself an authority on the pioneer farmhouses of Ohio. "I might not have been the *most* informed individual regarding the Western Reserve period," Lamoreux wrote in a touchy memoir about building Malabar, but: "I was one of them."

The two men met for the first time in the architect's office early in the afternoon of Friday, January 13, 1939. Bromfield asked Lamoreux if he would be interested in "remodeling an old farmhouse" and then drove him 11 miles southeast of Mansfield to show him the site. The landscape that had swept Bromfield to such emotional heights looked to Lamoreux "pretty dismal." The best he could say about the Herring place was that it had "a nice old native sandstone foundation" and an appealing background of rock and evergreens, but he thought it was a bit too close to the barns for most clients' comfort.

Bromfield, of course, was not most clients. Lamoreux listened to the famous author's vision with a mixture of wonder and alarm. "He was not easy to follow," Lamoreux said. "He'd go off on tangents" and had an "utter disregard for material things." Bromfield began by saying that he wanted a "good unostentatious farmhouse which will be beautiful, authentic and simple." Yet it wasn't so simple. He wanted the house built in the Greek Revival style of his hero, Thomas Jefferson. Such architecture was prevalent in the grand farmhouses of rural Ohio, he said, and its stately, classic lines would blend with the family's antique French furniture, which Hawkins had recently brought back from Senlis.

Bromfield also told Lamoreux that the house had to suit its occupants—"*big* people, big physically and rather big and loose and careless in our living. None of us, including George and Nanny, down to Ellen the youngest could be said to have a dovelike submissive personality." He told him that George needed a kind of "hideaway, neatly kept," where he could "entertain his friends." He said that Mary needed a "feminine nest," with considerable "*froufrou* and disorder." He wanted the children put in their own separate wing, apart, like in a French or English middle-class household. Bromfield believed that "children and adults living in too close proximity can cripple each other's personalities." For himself, he needed "a big rambling room with a lot of light and lot of big comfortable chairs and sofas on which a tall man could lie on the base of his spine and where you could talk for hours undisturbed with friends about farming or politics." The room would be a place to sleep, take breakfast in bed, work, read. It would have a door onto the garden, and be connected to a smaller room with a sink where Bromfield could make flower arrangements. It would also have to have a trapdoor where his dogs could come and go as they pleased. Bromfield had procured two boxer dogs—Rex and Regina—the progenitors of a multigenerational clan that in time would become the drooling mascots of Malabar Farm.

Lamoreux was overwhelmed. He brought some early sketches to the Bromfields' rented house in Oberlin. The design meetings were always conducted with the whole family—the three daughters, George, Nanny, and Mary all offering their own suggestions. "The conversation was almost a bedlam," Lamoreux said. The early sketches mostly showed Lamoreux what not to build. There was a major problem of scale—as Bromfield added rooms, the frontage grew to well over 200 feet, dwarfing the small Herring house and making the design appear ungainly. Bromfield insisted that, whatever shape the final house took, the original Herring place must be preserved at all costs. Lamoreux disagreed. "It would have been more economical to destroy that building," he said. "In fact, a good fire would have been a blessing."

Every night, Lamoreux took his work home with him. Many times solutions or ideas would come to him in the middle of the night. Once, when he awoke and couldn't find his usual drafting pad, he "resorted to many sheets of toilet paper." (Bathroom stationery, he later called it.) Bromfield learned of this story, and whenever he saw Lamoreux's wife in town would say: "If and when your husband has more toilet paper, ask him to redesign" the back porch or the children's suite or the main entrance. Months passed, hundreds of sketches came and went, Lamoreux did more research. He found a scholar at the Cleveland Museum of Art, I. T. Frary, who had written books about early Ohio homes and Jeffersonian architecture. They studied photographs and illustrations; they referenced century-old carpentry handbooks; they combed through the back roads of Ohio in search of suitable models. Late one afternoon, in Kinsman, by the Pennsylvania line, they found the Peter Allen House, built for a country doctor in the early nineteenth century with Greek Revival columns that were roughly the same scale as the Herring house. This was a start. Then they found other examples of local architecture to ornament and amplify the design. From homes along the Ohio River they copied porticoes with cast-iron pillars in a filigreed pattern of grapes and leaves. From the original Mormon settlement at Kirtland, Ohio, they took a simple but beautiful fanlight for the main entrance. For the dormer windows, they took inspiration from the German utopians who created the historic village of Zoar, just south of Canton. The final design, Mary said, "was a kind of museum of Ohio architectural detail."

Bromfield liked what he saw, until Lamoreux shared with him the projected costs, which approached six figures. He felt "some thousands" could be cut out of that estimate. He had "no desire to build a cheap house," he told the architect, but he wanted the maximum on investment, to use only simple materials and to "OK" all the fixtures. "I am not a gadgeter and do not go in for glass-walled bathrooms." He asked Lamoreux if they could use local red sandstone because of what he called "my complex against brick": "If we can construct the whole house without a brick showing, I will be happy. Brick, in these days, seems to me synonymous with suburbia." He was starting to nitpick. If there was any "grumbling" among contractors or stonemasons, "tell them all to go to hell, and we'll go elsewhere."

On April 14, 1939, Bromfield sent Lamoreux a long, irate letter with eight bullet points. He was annoyed by the whispers of his neighbors in Mansfield. There had been a report in the local newspaper that Bromfield's "desire to purchase a farm near here is merely a whim." Another story quoted the wives of farmers expressing skepticism. "I don't know whether I'd like a man like Bromfield to move into our community, or not. Seems to me he might do more harm than good," one said. "He'll make his place into a beauty spot. He'll have it landscaped and fenced in with a high hedge and maybe he'll raise blooded horses." Another woman said, "As farmers I bet they'll be laughing stock—and if Richland county gets a tinge of French and Indian and Oriental into its agriculture, it'll be strong seasoning." Bromfield told Lamoreux he was "fed up with the rumors and the stories," that "there is too much curiosity and too much of a smell of goose-plucking about the whole 'thing.' "

> All the pressure in Mansfield is toward making me make this a show suburban place. In the first place, I hate that kind of place, and in the second, it psychologically sets me apart from my neighbors who are really the people I want to be closest to. Also, I should myself feel uncomfortable in such a house. In spite of opinions to the contrary, I am a farmer and can and do run the tractor and the manure spreader and milk on the hired man's night out. . . .
> As the house is to be the basis of my existence for the rest of my life, as well as the sum total of my experience up to date (which, if I do say it myself has been a pretty wide one), I see no reason to run ahead and build something I am going to tear apart almost at once because it doesn't suit me. . . .

Lamoreux thought he had to go back to the drawing board, to simplify and refine the designs yet again. But Bromfield was really just stalling for time. He had run out of money. "I won't know until July anyway exactly how finances stand," he conceded. When a big check from Hollywood finally came in later that spring, Bromfield sent word to Lamoreux: "Go ahead with the contracts. Let's build."

———

As the farmhouse took shape, Bromfield spent many weeks in the winter and spring of 1939 shuttling between New York and Washington. War was coming to Europe, he was convinced, and though he felt calmer that his family was no longer trapped between Paris and the Maginot Line, his humanitarian work took on a new sense of urgency. Shortly after he arrived from France he hosted a benefit for Jewish refugees at the Algonquin Hotel. A few days later he was at the Hotel Astor, close to tears as he spoke to an audience of five hundred about the despair of the people of Britain and France. His call for Neville Chamberlain's resignation received rapturous applause. "You cannot appreciate the menace of Hitler and Mussolini. You cannot believe the atrocity stories you hear and read. But they are all true." On December 15, he and the heavyweight boxing champion Jack Dempsey were part of the welcoming party when 149 of the last Lincoln Brigadiers arrived from the war in Spain on the liner *Paris*. He joined them in a procession to the flagstaff of the Eternal Light in Madison Square Park, where they laid a wreath in memory of their fallen comrades.

Then he traveled down to Washington, vainly hoping to lift the arms embargo that prevented the sale of American weapons to the Spanish Republicans. He believed that a repeal at that moment "would be worth 10 battleships to us in five years." Journalists interviewed him beside the Spanish ambassador, Fernando de los Ríos. Bromfield listened as the diplomat calmly explained why American Catholics, who were inclined to be pro-Franco like their pope, should instead throw their support behind the beleaguered Republicans. "The ambassador has made his argument too mild," Bromfield said. "I have just returned from there, after fifteen years in Europe. No person who calls himself an American has any business defending a Fascist cause." Bromfield accepted the chair of Spanish Intellectual Aid, a committee formed to rescue six hundred artists and writers jailed by Franco who faced "certain death" because of their anti-Fascist positions.

He was invited on national radio to discuss foreign policy. He consulted with officials at the State Department and lunched with the powerful politico Jim Farley, Roosevelt's campaign manager, who was now the head of the Democratic National Committee. Then he dropped into the Washington salon of the columnist Evie Robert. "Much to my pleasure," she said. "He has one of the greatest stores of wit and humor I've ever seen." In interviews, he was bracingly impolitic. He described isolationist senators like Gerald Nye and Hamilton Fish III, as well as members of Charles Lindbergh's "America First" party, as "gutless" and "Jew-baiting." He said that members of the German-American Bund, a pro-Nazi organization representing citizens of German descent, "should be treated as spies." Eleanor Roosevelt, who saw him speak at a PEN conference, thought he had a future in politics. "Here is a man who has lived for fifteen years in different parts of Europe and watched the political scene. . . . His family came from Ohio, which has a way of producing politicians . . . now he is back on a farm in Ohio where, instead of writing books, I gather he is deep in political questions and much interested in the American scene." A journalist described Mrs. Roosevelt's "fondness" for Bromfield as being both "personal and literary." Their friendship would fall apart within a few years, but for the moment, she told readers of her syndicated column *My Day*, she found him "delightful."

Given Bromfield's political engagements and social schedule, it was sometimes difficult for Lamoreux, the architect building Malabar, to get answers to pressing questions. "He was traveling constantly," he said. And constantly making changes to the design. While Bromfield would not relinquish control over building decisions, he would also sometimes ignore Lamoreux's requests for answers about details that did not interest him—like plumbing or hardware or lighting. At one point, Lamoreux got so frustrated with delays that he lined up appointments at fixture shops in New York and hopped a plane, tracking down Bromfield at his usual perch, the Algonquin. He waited for Bromfield to finish a double old-fashioned and then they picked out fixtures together before the men settled in for dinner at "21." Lamoreux recalled how a pair of "vivacious and attractive women" appeared "out of seemingly nowhere." One was the actress Eleanor Harris, the other the eccentric oil heiress Millicent Rogers, who just a few years earlier had enjoyed canoeing in the Nonette. Lamoreux left out of his memoir the fact that he got extremely drunk that night trying to keep pace with Bromfield, and quite possibly hazarded into an illicit liaison—for the next day he needed to enlist Bromfield's help to cover his tracks. "Here's the story I told the family," he said in a letter, before relating some complicated alibi. "I never should leave town."

———

In the spring of 1939, the Bromfields moved into one of the outlying farmhouses at Malabar, a simple, cheaply constructed clapboard building that couldn't have been more than a few decades old. Bromfield hated the place, which he dubbed the "mail-order house," since it looked like it had been bought in some cut-rate catalogue, but it served as a good base of operations from which to direct construction of what he was starting to call "the Big House." In all, the construction took twenty-one months, from April 1939 until December 1940. "Louis's inability or unwillingness to study the drawings," Lamoreux said, "resulted in fantastic revisions." Walls had to be torn down, partitions removed, doors enlarged, the pitch of steps altered. Whole rooms were moved from one end of the house to the other. Bromfield at times knew he was being difficult but could not help himself. "I possess, unfortunately, a hopelessly unmechanical mind," he said, "and an utter inability to understand blueprints or to visualize final results." He only knew what he wanted, or didn't want, once he saw it. He would constantly walk through the site, looking at plans for outlets and wiring and fixtures that he thought they could do without: "Hell, we won't need that." Hawkins, walking behind him, would make a face to Lamoreux that meant: *Ignore him.* "Louis thought he had saved a lot of money," Lamoreux remembered. "And everybody was happy." The architect kept a tally on the paperwork—the sixty-odd floor plans, the twenty-one separate work contracts, each of which was "changed from one to 19 times."

As the months wore on, it became clear to Lamoreux that Bromfield, in his elliptical way, was building not just a house but a story, a kind of architectural novel, with a discernible chronology, that began in the early nineteenth century, with the Herring place, a simple, no-frills farmhouse of the kind built by country carpenters as Ohio emerged from the log-cabin era. That house had grown and changed along with the family's size and circumstances. Wings were meant to look architecturally distinct, their floors built at different levels and with cornices and details done in different styles to give the impression of having been added slowly over a period of a hundred years or more. "We felt that as crops might have failed, though a family increased, the unnamed original owner had of necessity simplified the work," Lamoreux said. Bromfield claimed that, before long, the fiction became a kind of fact around the construction site. "All of us, family, architect, carpenters and stonemasons came in a way to believe the story."

The only thing clashing with the narrative was a stone statue of the Hindu deity Ganesha, the remover of obstacles, which Bromfield had bought in Jaipur and wanted installed in a niche above the main entrance to the farmhouse. Lamoreux thought this was an unnecessary expense and that the sculpture would clash with his Jeffersonian façade. But Bromfield was typically inflexible; he said he wanted that sculpture "more than anything in the house." As spring turned to summer, Lamoreux and Bromfield began to realize they were creating something significant, far more

In a niche above the entryway to the Big House, Bromfield
installed a statue of the Hindu deity Ganesha, the remover
of obstacles, which he had bought in Jaipur.

significant than the "simple unostentatious farmhouse" he had asked for
in the beginning. "I'm afraid," Bromfield said, "it's going to be the kind
of house people will come from all over the world to see, damn it!"

The final nineteen-room, six-bath farmhouse stretched 137 feet along
the hillside terrace. The facade was painted ash white, the roof and shutters pine green. The two-story house looked east, so the sunrise coming
through the valley hit it straight-faced. The hall and the living and dining
rooms ran clear through the house, just as Bromfield wanted, and the tall
French windows opened onto a series of breezy verandas and porches. An
artificial pond, fed with water from a nearby spring, had been dug beside
the rockery, where Bromfield would lay out a magnificent terraced garden. In no time wisteria climbed over the cast-iron pillars and sparrows

built nests around the elephant-headed Ganesha. "The effect was such, when all was completed, that it was difficult to remember, even for those who lived here, which had come first: the old orchard behind, the great white barn below, the broad-leafed catalpa and giant black walnut trees on the lawn, or the house itself, so comfortably shaded, so at ease in its setting that it might have been there for centuries," wrote Ellen.

Yet the apparent simplicity of the Big House disappeared as you walked into a grand entry hall—white walls decorated with a pattern of gold wreaths—and looked up at two huge walnut staircases lined with plush red runners. Ellen remembered how her father, with his "fanatic hatred of the protective fussiness of middle-class housewives," proceeded to walk up those stairs daily with boots muddied from working in the fields. Niched into the wall of each staircase were replica Houdon busts of Jefferson and Lafayette.

The whole thing was a mixed bag, a combination of stately grandeur and random whimsy: in the entry room there was a tiger rug from India and candy-striped Davenport settees from Mary's childhood home. In an adjacent powder room there was a gilt mirror, red velvet curtains, and a framed photograph of a fat and bonneted woman that was captioned: "*Restroom—hell, I ain't tired: Where's the can?*" The living room was dominated by a pink marble fireplace that Bromfield had found in an antique shop in New Orleans. Above it was a mirrored wall with a giant bas-relief of an American eagle spreading its wings over thirty-eight embossed gold stars. "Those stars represent the Democratic states," Bromfield told a visitor. "I didn't count the ones that went Republican." The adjoining dining room brought the outdoors in with large bays, plants in wrought-iron stands, a birdcage, and walls painted soft green.

"Any woman would gush over Mrs. Bromfield's room," wrote a local society columnist. It looked like the lair of an aging Easter bunny in pastel shades of blue and yellow, with powder-blue carpet, turquoise chintz draperies, and a yellow marble fireplace. Much attention was paid to Mary's bed, which had been designed by her sister-in-law, the noted

Bromfield shared his bed with his favorite boxer, Prince.

New York decorator Ruby Ross Wood. Painted in frilly letters on the headboard were all the titles of Bromfield's best-selling novels, with the 1927 novel *A Good Woman* occupying the centerpiece. (The fact that the "good woman" in that book was actually an overbearing, self-denying harpy modeled on Bromfield's mother was not commented on.)

The southern end of the house belonged to Bromfield. "My room is a combination bedroom, study, library, living room and farm office," he told a visitor in 1940, "but it looks like a depraved night club." Here Lamoreux had designed an enormous, ten-foot-wide walnut desk, shaped like a horseshoe, covered in leather. It quickly became a repository for a mountain of paper, books, and ashtrays, and Bromfield used a small card table to do all his writing. He chose for the walls the bright acid green "of the painter Veronese." The carpet was black, there were more Indian tiger skins on the floors, black-green and flame-red lamps, and a corduroy armchair. There was, as requested, his own personal "flower room," with vases, baskets, containers, and shears. And there was a secret door, leading to a stairway that went up to Hawkins's office and bedroom. Lamoreux conceded this was an "unorthodox" setup but added that "the nature of their work necessitated such an arrangement."* George's studio, clad in waxed cypress and with red pile carpet, was designed to resemble the suites he stayed in at fancy hotels like the St. Regis in New York. An urbanite banished to the countryside, he could close his wood shutters and pretend he was still in the city.

There were many other rooms in the Big House: a sitting room, a parlor, a children's wing with its own living room, servants' quarters, and guestrooms that were always occupied. Just a few years after it was finished, Bromfield wrote that the house had been "mellowed" by use and even looked shabby in places. This he liked.

> There is no parlor and no spare room kept empty with the shades drawn. Every inch of it has been in hard use since it was built and will, I hope, go on being used in the same fashion as long as it stands. Perhaps one day it will belong to the State, together with the hills, valleys and woods of Malabar Farm.

---

* Predictable rumors circulated in Mansfield about the unusually close relationship that Bromfield had with Hawkins, but there are no letters or memoirs suggesting that Bromfield was gay or bisexual.

9

Germination

MALABAR FARM, 1939

When Bromfield bought the Herring place, he got ten cows, two old draft horses, an ancient plow, a few chickens, some geriatric ewes, and a collection of run-down barns. He intended from the beginning that his would be not only a working farm but a profitable one. His self-conception, something in his upbringing, demanded that Malabar not be a showplace. "Look at that soil!" he told a visiting journalist shortly after he settled in. "That's paying dirt." He said it, he might have even believed it, but it was not remotely true. When the snow melted that first spring of 1939, he saw that his land was practically worthless. Most of the sandy, loose alluvial topsoil had been washed off the hills, down Switzer's Creek, to empty out eventually into the Ohio and the Mississippi Rivers. Wind and rain cut up the bald fields, digging deep gullies in the landscape. Only cocklebur, Scotch thistle, and meager "poverty" grasses grew on the brown pastures. Seeking more nutritious fare, whatever animals lived on the farm had been let loose to browse the woods. All the big trees had already been cut down by previous owners to raise cash, and the livestock ate whatever seedlings were left. It was a disaster. No rural banker, no country real-estate agent, no self-respecting farmer would

After the snow melted in the spring of 1939, Bromfield
saw that the land on which he'd hoped to build his dream
farm was badly eroded and starved of nutrients.

have ever invested in this property. Bromfield had bought a dream, and
now he saw that it was empty.

The change of season brought him a few consolations. The overeaten
woods sprouted dogtooth violets and other wildflowers and the farm
filled with the slightly sweet smell of thawing earth and manure. The

family got to work, doing whatever they could themselves. They planted corn and potatoes. They rooted willows by Switzer's Creek to stem the runoff. Nanny White set to work in the garden, potting petunias and planting roses and lilacs. A few old ewes died after dropping orphans, which the seven-year-old Ellen fed from Coca-Cola bottles filled with cow's milk. Bromfield had bought goats, which immediately proved a nuisance, eating manuscripts that he left on the porch of the mail-order house, climbing on the Ford station wagon and burrowing holes in its roof.

As the Big House rose, Bromfield must have realized he was building his manor on a mud pile. Nothing in his "experience"—gardening in Senlis, writing *The Farm*, watching his grandfather fondle peaches, watching his father lose money flipping old pastures—had prepared him to reclaim these 600 barren acres. "It wasn't a job I could do alone," he confessed. So he put out feelers for a farm manager, and interviewed several candidates. Some were scientific farmers, the products of agricultural schools who could quote chapter and verse from Morrison's *Feeds and Feeding*. Others were eggheads and "rabid theorists," with no feel for the land, "innocent of the hard work involved in farming." And others were old-fashioned dirt farmers who seemed stuck in the past, too "sot" in their ways.

Bromfield had almost no respect for the average American farmer, including his neighbors in Pleasant Valley. He thought of them as pig-headed, incurious people who had brought poverty upon themselves "by ignorance, by greed and by a strange belief inherent in early generations of American farmers that their land owed them a living." He thought many farmers only stayed on the land because "they have not the energy to quit and go to the cities and factories where they properly belong." Later in life, Bromfield would give his definition of a "good farmer," and it was both lofty and long. A farmer, he said, should be "a horticulturalist, a mechanic, a botanist, an ecologist, a veterinarian, a biologist and many other things." He should have an open mind that was "ready to absorb new knowledge and new ideas." But knowledge was "not enough." He needed, most importantly, two traits which "could not be acquired," which were "almost mystical qualities." These were "a passion for the soil" and an "understanding and sympathy with animals." In other words, Bromfield thought, a good farmer needed to be a little *teched*.

> To the good farmer, his animals are not simply commodities without out personality destined only to be made into pork chops or beef steaks or to produce milk all their lives. To a good farmer, each animal has its own personality. A good farmer cannot himself sleep if his animals are not well fed and watered and bedded down on a cold winter night. Watch any good farmer showing his sheep or cattle or hogs at a county fair and you will understand how much he respects the animals that are linked into the chain of life which explains and justifies the whole of his activity.

It was a very tall order. The man who came closest in Bromfield's estimation was named Max Drake. He was thirty-two and came from a family of Ohio dairy farmers. Ellen Bromfield Geld described Drake as "a darkly handsome young man" with "strong square hands, good humor and soft, unruffled speech that one finds among those who have been raised in the country." He had tried to read *The Farm*, which was required reading in his high school. "I got through a couple chapters but found it so dull I couldn't finish it." Drake had an agriculture degree from Ohio State and worked for a time as a county extension agent. Bromfield interviewed him twice, first in Oberlin and then on the farm over a boozy lunch. "He tried to get me drunk that day," Drake recalled. "He was on his third martini and he got me into two of them. I think he enjoyed seeing how folks would react when they got more under their belt than they should have. That's the way he knew what they were really like."

In the winter of 1939, Drake and his wife, Marion, moved into an old cottage downhill from the Big House. Over the next few months, Bromfield and Drake had a series of conversations in that cottage late into the night. Marion brought them beer, pickles, and sandwiches. Years later Ellen remembered those talks, how the farm plan was hashed out in clouds of cigarette smoke as she sat in a shabby armchair. She understood little of what was being said but was "fascinated" by the energy in the room, by her father's lionlike passion and the look on Drake's face, which changed from enthusiastic to dubious to terrified depending on the subject.

Out of these conversations emerged "The Plan," always written with a capital *P*. Bromfield began, typically, with fiction. Malabar was not, he said, just 600 worthless acres but "a small kingdom" of farmland and streams and woods that they, the two of them, would bring back to life. They were not just devising a crop plan but the "recreation of a world." He began to lecture. He said that he was haunted by "the terrible economic insecurity which a mechanized and industrial civilization imposes upon the individual." He had lived through hyperinflation and strikes, through violence and food shortages. He had seen a newspaper in Germany cost 9 million Reichsmarks. He had seen the banks close in France. And he knew America was no more immune to disaster than Europe. He had watched his own family be pushed off the farm before he went away to the Great War and then he saw that process repeat itself a million times over during the Depression.

What he wanted to build was a "thrifty island of security" that could be not only a refuge for his own family and friends but also an example for other American farmers. He told Drake that farmers didn't need to be poor, or live poorly. He told him about wealthy winegrowers in Alsace and Burgundy who made enough money to send their sons to university and about his peasant heroes Picquet and Bosquet, who lived richly off the land despite the fact that they were, by American standards, dead broke. Malabar, he said, would achieve a similar kind of self-sufficiency. This meant they would have to produce as close to "everything as possible." Not just chickens but guinea fowl and ducks and geese and turkeys which, he said, "could live off the abundance of the farm" in a "half-wild state" a bit like "the birds that live in the *basse-cour* of a prosperous French farm."

But Drake had never been to Alsace and Burgundy, and he did not know what a *basse-cour* was. What he knew, far better than Bromfield, was how to farm in the Midwestern United States in the twentieth century. His own father had been a farmer, a "general farmer" of the kind Bromfield apparently admired, but when Drake was young his father had to give up his hogs and focus his energies on the dairy. The cost of farm equipment and labor had outpaced his earnings. He could not afford to hire anyone and he could not do all the work himself. Drake had long ago internalized a rule of modern agriculture: To survive, you had to specialize.

"Damn it!" Bromfield sputtered. That was *exactly* what he wanted Malabar to disprove. He hated specialization, hated reading about those desperately poor sharecroppers in the South who were forced by greedy landowners to grow cotton up to their front porches only to spend money they didn't have in midsummer buying canned vegetables. His farm would be a direct challenge to them and to the "great mechanized farms which were more like industries." He did not believe that "the impulse of our times" toward economies of scale—doing everything bigger, faster, cheaper—"necessarily represented progress." Why, he wondered, must they live in a world where the rising cost of feed and fertilizer and farm machinery meant it was practically impossible for a single family to live off the land?

No, Malabar, he said, would be a *general farm*. It would produce *everything*. Not merely eggs and butter and milk and vegetables—the "things which many foolish farmers buy today"—but also asparagus, grapes, watermelon, peaches, currants, gooseberries, cantaloupes, strawberries, and so many other things "which could be had for the mere planting." Ellen remembered how Drake nearly fell off his chair with excitement as Bromfield spoke about how the spring ponds at Malabar would produce a constant supply of fish, and the long-dormant maple bush would make sweet syrup, and they would get thousands of bees to produce honey and pollinate the crops. The Plan called for 75 to 100 beef cattle; for 10 Guernsey cows to provide milk; for 100 hogs, 5,000 laying hens, and 250 ewes. They would have a program where meat was quick-frozen for storage and sale. They would have a cellar (a "cave of abundance," Bromfield called it) filled with home-canned goods and preserves: peaches, tomato juice, sauerkraut, sausage put down in lard, bins of apples, potatoes, carrots, turnips, and squash, baskets of black walnuts, hickory nuts, butternuts. If they produced too much, Bromfield said, they would sell the surplus or leave it to the birds and the raccoons.

As for the economics, Bromfield thought the solution lay in a Soviet-style collective scheme. "We accepted its principles only in a large and rather loose way," he said. Naturally, this socialist utopia placed Bromfield at the top of the food chain. "I, myself, as the capitalist, was substituted for the state." Under the plan, Drake's family and others that would soon join them would have their house rent-free, with all utilities included and all food provided except things that did not come off the farm (coffee, spices, sugar). Working families would also receive a salary—in Drake's case, $2,400 a year, which Bromfield rated "above average" and Drake thought "low." Bromfield would finance "the adventure" until, he said, "we came to the point where we turned a profit." (That they would reach this point was beyond doubt.) Once the profits came rushing in, Bromfield would skim 5 percent off the top and then the remainder would be divided "*pro rata* according to the salaries paid each worker, which varied according to their education, skill and value to the common enterprise."

Drake was sufficiently dazzled to agree to everything. Privately, he may have wondered how, exactly, they were going to achieve any of this. But Bromfield did not stick around long enough to answer that question. By May of 1939, he had set off with Hawkins for Hollywood.

—+—

Bromfield spent much of Malabar's first year in Los Angeles, barking directions via letter and telegram to Drake and Lamoreux. The fortune Fox had invested in *The Rains Came* made the Bromfield name hot, and Hawkins stoked the fires. Within months, Bromfield had four more film projects in production at three different studios and was being described as "America's best-selling author in Hollywood." For Darryl F. Zanuck at Fox, he was writing a biopic of Brigham Young and a drama about the origins of the Salvation Army, *Marching as to War*. He had also sold Jack Warner the rights to his 1936 short story "It All Came True." And MGM had given him a check for $50,000 to option his next novel, *Night in Bombay*, a tawdry rehash of *The Rains Came* set in the Taj Mahal Palace Hotel. When that book came out, in the spring of 1940, Harper reported that advance sales exceeded that of any other title published by the house in the previous decade. Bromfield's career had by now progressed to the point that he could sell his novels to Hollywood based only on a conversation and a handshake. He pitched an executive at Columbia Pictures his idea for a Civil War novel about New Orleans—*Wild Is the River* it was eventually called—and was given another $50,000. The easy money produced in him a kind of smug cynicism. "Every line I write is sold to Hollywood before I write it," he bragged to a journalist. "They want my name on the story. Even if I should make a hash of it and a couple of Hollywood writers rewrote it, my name would still appear on the screenplay. That's all they want." He looked at the movie business as little more than a bank; he was only in Hollywood to raise money for Malabar, and maybe to have a little fun on the side.

Bromfield and Hawkins usually based themselves in a rented villa at the Garden of Allah, a complex of Spanish bungalows on Sunset Boulevard that was the address of choice for literati like Robert Benchley and John O'Hara. An English actress remembered spending the afternoon with Bromfield poolside. "He stayed under so long we were becoming

alarmed about him. Just as we were about to do something, he came to
the surface, spouting like a porpoise. 'My bathing trunks came off!' he
stuttered, 'and I didn't dare come up.'" Hawkins and Bromfield attended
parties in Palm Springs and the Hollywood Hills, met Bette Davis, went
sailing between Catalina and the coast on Humphrey Bogart's thirty-
six-foot boat, *Sluggy*. Bromfield was often seen with beautiful actresses:
relaxing on-set with Myrna Loy, waltzing with Patricia Morrison. He
seemed especially keen on Kay Francis, with whom he spent so much
time that gossipmongers like Hedda Hopper and Ed Sullivan began to
hint that they were romantically involved. "I get a kick out of that magnificent laugh," he told the columnist Sheilah Graham. He and Francis
went everywhere together: to the Trocadero, to Ciro's, to Hedy Lamarr's
birthday party at the Beverly Wilshire Hotel, to the gala premiere of *Of
Mice and Men*. Bromfield was kicking up so much news that the local
paper back in Mansfield could barely keep track: "Bromfield Bulletin No.
9,963" it wrote, before relating the latest item. In letters to Lamoreux,
who was becoming something of a confidant, he would talk about all the
pretty celebrities on his dance card: "Kay Francis, the 'oomph girl' [Ann
Sheridan] or Dorothy Lamour." "I spend my days working hard," he told
the architect, "and my evenings among the stars."

As much as he enjoyed cutting loose, he said Hollywood was "dull
as hell, compared to the farm." Every columnist and movie star he met
had to listen to him whine about missing the lambing season or the
spring planting. "No, I'm not playing at farming. I'm a dirt-farmer . . .
and we're going to make the farm more than pay its way. Oats, corn,
soybeans, wheat, alfalfa, chickens, cattle, some horses, hogs and goats."
Some of his witty colleagues saw right through the rustic persona. "It's
very strange," said James Thurber, "I've met Louis in London, Paris, New
York, Hollywood—and every time I see him he says: Have you heard?
I'm living on a farm in Ohio." Others fell for the act. The columnist
Louis Sobol, after seeing Bromfield for cocktails in New York, thought
that Malabar had transformed him. "You almost imagined when he

Bromfield and his youngest daughter, Ellen,
inspecting the corn at Malabar, circa 1939.

entered the Stork Club or Twenty One you saw a wisp of straw trailing
from the lapels of his dinner coat."

Mary planned to join him in Hollywood that first summer of 1939,
but he kept on delaying her visit. "*Of course* I don't want to go out till
you're ready for me there," she wrote to him. "I understand perfectly."
If Mary was worried about Bromfield spending his evenings with star-
lets, she did not mention it in her letters. "Have you seen Bette Davis?
How do you like Myrna Loy? I liked the picture of you with her." Her
only mention of Francis seemed perfectly innocent: "Give lots of love to

Kay." Most of her letters were filled with reports about Malabar. "The new cattle heifers are lovely and the lambs are beginning to romp about in a foolish fashion in the field opposite." She said the family was happy picking raspberries ("hard and black but good for jam"), shopping for horses, watching Drake get the barns in order, and helping where they could. "Great excitement," she said in another letter. "The bees have just arrived!" By July, she said the hay had already been cut and the wheat was being cut now. "Everything is shooting up like arrows," she told him. "I wish I could describe to you some of the small events and the constant excitement of this place. Everything assumes such vast importance and we're all involved in it with Nanny at the center."

She sent updates about the children, how her fair and blond middle daughter, Hope, age ten, seemed to be growing up so quickly. "She is going to be one of the most attractive women that ever lived—everything about her fascinates me, her looks, her quiet, her grin, her understanding and her sense of humor." Mary was delighted by the bravery of her youngest daughter, Ellen, age seven, who took to the farm work like her father. "Ellen unsaddles and unbridles [the draft horse] Red all alone, scrubs him down and feeds him." She was a "born horse-woman—I never saw such a seat." The workers at Malabar took to calling Hope "the Lady" and Ellen "the tomboy." Of Mary's eldest daughter, Anne, the one who most resembled her in looks with dark hair and a full face, she kept quiet. Now fourteen, Anne preferred to be alone, avoided eye contact, had trouble picking up on social cues and expressing herself in conversation—today she possibly would be diagnosed with an autism spectrum disorder. She spent most of her time reading, writing poetry, or drawing pictures that sometimes upset young children visiting the farm.

Perhaps Anne inherited some of her brooding, solitary nature from her mother, who often slipped into depressions, which were aggravated by Bromfield's inattention and the huge gap she perceived between his success and her own. Mary never developed her gifts as a writer, and as the girls aged she left most of the mothering to Nanny. "Wednesday was my birthday," she wrote her husband in an undated letter, "and I was most depressed A. Because I don't like to get old. B. Because it reminded me of myself and that I was born with all the talent in the world and all there is left is a fair amount of adaptability and tolerance and nothing else." During Malabar's first summer, Mary went into Mansfield to get her picture taken—not for "you personally" but for a magazine article about Malabar—and she found the photos "so repellent that I don't see how I can ever appear in public again without a veil." Later, when she found bedbugs at the mail-order house, she called a fumigator and wrote to Bromfield: "I wish I'd gotten into the house by mistake when the poison gasses were doing their deadly work." In the very next line, without transition, she wrote of arranging a picnic to celebrate Hope's birthday. The depressive notes may have been calibrated to get Bromfield's attention and sympathy. None of Bromfield's replies survive in his papers, so one can only speculate about how he reacted to such dramatic cries for help from his wife.

When he left for Hollywood, Mary wrote to him: "I felt very dismal after you left yesterday. I had made up my mind that I wasn't going to miss you, that I was *glad* you were going. Then my poor foolish mind changed on me and I was crying away all alone, felt horrible all day and all night. Fools we are, especially women." She signed her letters "the old lady" or "your old woman" or "your old shoe (if not always too comfortable)."

When Mary wanted to please her husband, she knew the way to do it was to wax romantic about the farm. "Louis, I love this place more and more and I can't tell you what feeling of peace it gives me. Even though I'm not a farmer, all the things done on a farm are so fascinating . . . I tried to love Senlis to please you but I don't think I even got away with pretending. I always felt as if I was in prison in a suburb—waiting to be free and breathe. Time passes almost too quickly here." As Bromfield's Hollywood sojourn drew to a close, she became giddy at the prospect of his return. "You will find the place entirely changed. I didn't realize till

I looked at it from the Herrings last night—that bit by the creek that we cleared up is absolutely overgrown and the whole field is long grass."

———

Max Drake did not wait for Bromfield to start turning Malabar into a modern agricultural operation. With the blessing of "Mr. B"—as he was increasingly called around the farm—Drake bought a tractor and a secondhand silo (Mary said it looked like "a medieval turret") where he fermented Malabar's first batch of grass silage, or cow fodder. He planted corn, oats, and soybeans. He seeded pastures with clover and sprinkled lime and welcomed the first batch of leghorn chickens—484 of them, at 5 cents a bird. He remodeled all the old barns and outbuildings, painting them in the white-and-green color scheme of the Big House. He kept Bromfield apprised about the weather and the first vegetables: the cucumbers, peas, celery, and potatoes. His sense of humor was bone-dry. "Things are growing well," he said in June of 1939. "Even the weeds."

Yet at some point during Malabar's first year, Drake made a unilateral decision. He knew that Bromfield could never have the agrarian paradise he had sketched out in the cottage without first restoring fertility to the land. Perhaps Drake underestimated Bromfield's interest in the minutiae of the farm, thinking not unreasonably that he was a famous author busy with Hollywood contracts, geopolitical maneuvers, and building his dream house. Drake contacted a friend from Ohio State, Herschel Hecker, who worked at the Soil Conservation Service outpost at nearby Mt. Gilead. The SCS was a New Deal agency established by Congress in 1935 in the wake of the Dust Bowl crisis to halt "the wastage of soil and moisture resources on farm, grazing and forest lands" that had become a "menace to the national welfare." Many of the methods employed by the SCS were on the cutting edge of agricultural science. They offered farmers interested in restoring their eroded land a chance to become demonstration farms, where free government labor and technology would be deployed in the hopes of setting an example for other farmers about how poor land could be made rich again.

Hecker completed a survey of Malabar, which showed the condition of every field and pasture. The results were bleak. Most fields had lost between 50 and 75 percent of the topsoil. "The gullies were big enough that you could lose a horse inside, bury it, and nobody would ever know it was there," Drake said. There were rotted old fences dividing fields so small that modern farm equipment could not work on them. Hecker and Drake began to sketch out a plan, with a lowercase *p*, that was far more scientific and pragmatic than Bromfield's version. They got in touch with the local leaders of the Civilian Conservation Corps. This was yet another New Deal organization meant to put the unemployed back to work on conservation projects that would improve the land and restart the rural economy. Hecker convinced them that there was valuable work to be done at Malabar and proposed this free labor source to Drake. "Well, I'm supposed to be in charge," Drake said, "so bring 'em in!" Beginning in the summer of 1940, fifteen CCC enrollees were transported daily to the farm from a nearby work camp. They pulled the old fence posts and bulldozed gullies and seeded pastures and refitted the fields. Within a few months, Drake said "everything was changed around and you wouldn't know the farm."

When Bromfield came back from Hollywood and saw the heavy equipment and government workers, he exploded at Drake in an expletive-laced tirade and then stormed off toward the Big House. Drake was about to pack up; he assumed he had been fired. But then Bromfield returned. His fury had now been replaced by curiosity. "What the hell has been going on here?" So Drake told him the outlines of the plan, and now it was Bromfield's turn to be schooled. They had three related problems, problems that hundreds of thousands of farmers around the country were also facing: (1) They had to check the erosion of the topsoil caused by harsh winds. (2) They needed to make sure that rainwater penetrated into the soil instead of carrying it off the hills. (3) They needed to restore nutrients and fertility to the long-neglected fields.

First, the water. Drake explained that almost 70 percent of the rain that fell on Malabar ran down its hills into the streams. The acute lack of water burnt the fields out and dried up some underground springs. So they had dug a 15-foot diversion ditch around the contour lines of the hillsides to catch the floodwater so it stayed on top of the hills and slowly seeped down into the soil instead of rushing across and cutting deep gullies. Next, they had to deal with the soil itself. The pastures where livestock had grazed were full of cow droppings, so there was probably plenty of nitrogen; but they lacked other essential minerals, which could be added by applying ground limestone and phosphorous. Hecker devised a whole program of crop rotations, alternating between plants that robbed the soil of nitrogen (like corn) and those that gave it right back (like alfalfa). On the top fields, usually kept bare in winter, their plan called for leguminous cover crops—like vetch and red clover—which not only minimized erosion but also, when plowed or disced into the earth, served as "green manures" that would enrich the soil. Now when they planted, they would do it not in straight lines as was customary but along the natural contours of the landscape, creating beautiful waves of sea green and gold that were interspersed with bright green strips of sod to catch more water. On the steepest slopes, they would grow only green hay and grasses that helped bind the earth. And to rebuild the overeaten woods, they would plant new trees and shut out the cattle so the forest could become green once again.

Once all these conservation measures were put in place, Bromfield saw remarkable changes within the first couple of years. "It is marvelous the quickness with which nature responds," he said. "Where there was once little, we have abundance." The swampy hog lot below the Big House had been transformed into a garden with a clear spring stream running through it that no longer dried up in the summertime. Concord, Niagara, and Golden Muscat grapevines clambered over the garden fences. In the shade, Bromfield let healthy brambles of raspberries and blackberries run wild—never cultivating them but just mulching

Max Drake, Bromfield's first farm manager, helped turn
Malabar into a modern farm and gave Bromfield his first
lesson in the principles of soil conservation.

once a year. Where once there was a gullied hillside, he now saw flowering shrubs and rich fields. When it rained, the water no longer rushed
down the hills in brown torrents that cut the earth. The contoured rows
of crops hugged the landscape. In the apple orchard, a thick layer of
sod grass had grown up around the old trees. And new trees had been
planted: peaches, plums, and pears. Bumblebees, working "in platoons,"
pollinated the fruit trees as well as the pastures of clover and alsike. He
planted a row of locust trees to feed the bees—and to pour more nitrogen
into the soil (since locusts are also a legume). He loved the smell of their
blossoms that drifted into the Big House. He loved seeing muskrats swim
across the pond in the moonlight. He loved standing in a field of corn in
midsummer and listening for the "faint crackling sound" as "the stalk
increases its circumference cell by cell."

For him, this kind of work was the greatest pleasure, better than the Pulitzer, than Paris, than the garden in Senlis. "My travel, my experience—nothing I have ever done has given me nearly as much satisfaction as this bit of land and what we have been able to do with it. I take deep pleasure in going out every morning and seeing the miraculous changes which have happened, and which are happening, and which will go on happening until the end of our lives."

10

Victory Garden

ST. LOUIS, MISSOURI, 1941

He is the greatest patriot who stops the most gullies.
—PATRICK HENRY, BEFORE THE VIRGINIA ASSEMBLY

On December 5, two days before the Japanese sneak attack at Pearl Harbor, Bromfield told the audience at an anti-Nazi rally at the Chase Hotel in downtown St. Louis that America was already in the war. "The choice of war is not ours," he said. "It was decided by Germany and Japan." Yet he felt the country was then facing a "greater menace" than the Axis powers. Perhaps he was blinded by his newfound passion for conservation, or maybe he could just see farther into the future than everyone else. Whatever the case, Bromfield would take every chance he had during the war years to tell Americans—whose sons were dying on foreign soil—that protecting the environment was as vital to national defense as a strong army or navy. "We are in more danger of destroying ourselves," he said in 1942, than of "being destroyed."

The history of environmental activism in the United States during World War II is little known outside of academic books and articles, but it is a vital chapter if one hopes to understand how this country transitioned from the depredations of the 1930s to the recognizably modern environmental movement of the 1960s, from the Dust Bowl and *The*

A visit to Malabar often culminated with a speech from Mount
Jeez, named sarcastically by George Hawkins because it is here
where Bromfield preached the gospel of soil conservation.

Grapes of Wrath to Earth Day and *Silent Spring.* Bromfield described the
movement that was born in those intervening years as nothing less than
"a revolution," one that he would foment and help direct.

The revolution had actually begun earlier, in the 1930s, sparked by
the same national crisis that had led Bromfield to write *The Farm*. When
Franklin Roosevelt took office in 1933, a major priority of his administration was fixing the broken farm economy. Because of the Depression,

there was a glut of food on the market; crop prices had collapsed; and American farmers were being dispossessed of their land by the millions. In the first hundred days of the New Deal, Congress established the Agricultural Adjustment Administration (AAA), under the leadership of the secretary of agriculture, a brilliant, dreamy-eyed Iowa farmer and agrarian theorist named Henry A. Wallace. The AAA's job was to raise crop prices by artificially creating a scarcity in the market. Wallace tried to achieve this, in the summer of 1933, by slaughtering 6 million piglets and plowing under 10 million acres of cotton. "It was a truly terrifying strike," said Russell Lord, a Maryland-born conservationist who was then working at the AAA. "All the more terrifying because the government was not only permitting sabotage but paying for it." Lord remembered watching cotton farmers weep as they drove their crops into the earth. The harsh measures—and government checks—kept many farmers on the land, but Lord said the spectacle of waste horrified Americans from all walks of life, arousing "a sense of shame and an instinct of repair" that spread from rural towns to cities. As Wallace put it, "To have to destroy a growing crop is a shocking commentary on our civilization."

Wallace, Lord, and other early advocates of what is today called sustainable agriculture did not use only the Depression to make the case that the country needed to radically change its approach to the land. If economics was their Exhibit A, the weather was Exhibit B. On the morning of April 2, 1935, a giant dust storm that had originated in northeastern New Mexico began to drift east, across the Great Plains and into the Ohio River valley. Hugh Hammond Bennett, a soil scientist and New Deal bureaucrat, was watching the storm closely. He was about to make his case to the Senate Public Lands committee to permanently establish a Soil Conservation Service. The storm arrived in Washington like "a dreadful miracle" just as the hearing was getting under way. For the senators, seeing the topsoil of the western United States suddenly airborne and blotting out the sun above the Capitol Building forcefully illustrated the abstract problem of soil erosion. "When it arrived, while the hearing was still on, we took a little time, off the record, and moved from the great mahogany table of the Senate Building for a look," Bennett said. "Everything went nicely thereafter." On April 27, 1935, Congress voted to permanently establish a Soil Conservation Service, the first federal agency devoted to preserving a natural resource since Theodore Roosevelt created the Forest Service, in 1905.

—·—

So began a propitious period for early environmentalism. From the common farmer to business leaders and government officials, Americans seemed finally to realize how badly they had mistreated their land. Paul B. Sears, an Ohio-born ecologist then at the University of Oklahoma, published *Deserts on the March*, which made a scientific argument in plain English that America was farming itself to death—just like long-extinct civilizations in the Near East. In 1934, the ecologist Aldo Leopold, with the help of various New Deal agencies, began the country's first major soil and watershed restoration project in Wisconsin's Coon Valley. Albert Howard had returned to Britain from India and was piecing together his experience, devising the tenets of what would soon be called "organic" agriculture. In 1936, the Roosevelt administration bankrolled a short film, *The Plow That Broke the Plains*, which made the same case as Sears with melodramatic language, shocking images, and powerful music by Virgil Thomson. Though Hollywood refused to distribute the film, calling it "New Deal propaganda," its director, Pare Lorentz, found three thousand independent cinemas to show the picture to an estimated 8 million people—making it something like the *Inconvenient Truth* of its era.

Books, movies, and heart-stopping photographs (by Walker Evans, Dorothea Lange, and others supported by the Farm Security Administration) brought much-needed attention to the soil crusade, but the conservationists wanted their message to travel not only from the top down but from the soil up, for it to be carried into the 4-H Clubs and masonic houses and garden clubs and suburban living rooms and city soda fountains. They felt a sense of urgency. The problem of soil erosion was by no means confined to the Dust Bowl but was present in nearly every state. Bennett estimated in January 1936 that 100 million acres of once-fertile land—roughly equivalent to the size of California—had been effectively destroyed and that two-thirds of the country's remaining acres were suffering from "serious erosion." But the conservationists also felt a sense of possibility, with the New Deal afoot, the country in flux, and disaster on the brain. By the late 1930s, Americans were not only reading books about environmental calamities—from *The Grapes of Wrath* to Bromfield's *The Rains Came*—but also experiencing those crises firsthand, from the last dust storms in the Plains to a devastating fifty-year flood that hit Los Angeles in February of 1938 to a Category 5 hurricane in New England that September that killed more than six hundred people and destroyed over fifty thousand homes.

Among those most concerned with the state of the land was Morris L. Cooke, a Pennsylvania Quaker and social reformer who had devoted his life to rural development and preserving freshwater resources. His work often required taking long flights over the Midwestern United States, giving him a bird's-eye view of the soil crisis. He began discussing with men like Bennett and Lord the idea of a nonpartisan, nongovernmental organization, allied with the Soil Conservation Service, that would bring the mission of conservation to thinking farmers and "city people" throughout the country. It would not have a specific pet cause, like the Audubon Society (birds), the Boone and Crockett Club (big game), or the Sierra Club (forests and wilderness). Instead, it would look at the whole picture, the interdependency of all aspects of nature, from soil to air to water to food to animal and human health. On January 23, 1940, Cooke, Lord, Bennett, and a few others met in the Department of the Interior's Office of Land Use to sketch the outlines of the new society, which they called the Friends of the Land. Out of those first meetings came a remarkable manifesto, which today sounds like Greenpeace by way of the Book of Daniel.

> Any land is all of one body. If one part is skinned, bared to the beat of the weather, wounded, not only the winds spread the trouble, dramatically, but the surface veins and arteries of the nation, its streams and rivers, bear ill. Soiled water depletes soil, exhausts underground and surface water supplies, raises flood levels, dispossesses shore and upland birds and animals from their accustomed haunts, chokes game-fish, diminishes shoreline seafood, clogs harbors and stops with grit and boulders the purr of dynamos.
>
> Eroded soil is in some part dead, devitalized. Soil debility, soon repeated in nutritive deficiencies, spreads undernourishment. Evidence on this point is far from complete; but the trend of accumulating findings is unmistakable. If the soil does not have it in it, plants that grow there do not; nor do the animals that eat those plants; nor the people throughout a country who eat those plants and animals. Soil debility soon removes stiffening lime from the national backbone, lowers the beat and vigor of the national bloodstream, and leads to a devitalized society.
>
> We, too, are all of one body. We all live on, or from, the soil.

—·—

In March of 1940, the Friends of the Land held their first public meeting over two days at the Wardman Park Hotel in Washington, DC. Just sixty people attended: farmers, scientists, doctors, government officials, writers, concerned citizens. They chatted on the hotel's sun porch and listened to a string of inspiring speeches, led by the social theorist Stuart Chase. "We are creatures of this earth, and so are a part of all our prairies, mountains, rivers, and clouds. Unless we feel this dependence, we may know all the calculus and all the Talmud, but have not learned the first lesson." What the friends had in passion, however, they lacked in funds. When the hat was passed, Lord was dismayed to discover the organization had collected only $500. How would they pay for future meetings, publish a journal, and fan out across the country? "Do we first start a magazine that hatches a membership," Lord asked, "or start a membership that supports a magazine?" The public dismissed the event as "a meeting of extremely long-range visionaries," and the mission of the Friends was subsumed by war preparations. "One hundred days after its founding," Lord wrote, "our high-hearted little society fell flat on its face."

Right around this time Lord received a letter from Louis Bromfield. He apologized for not attending the inaugural meeting—he would have been there, he said, but he detested Washington, DC, especially now that it was bloated with "small-fry" New Deal bureaucrats who reminded him of nitpicking French *fonctionnaires*. Nevertheless, he said, he was devoted to the mission of the Friends of the Land. He told Lord about what was happening at Malabar, his conservation revelation, the work with Max Drake. And then he invited the Friends to Ohio for the first of many "field trips." For Lord and his colleagues, it was as though a switch had been flipped. With a world-famous author, they could perhaps draw enough attention and membership to get off the ground, even with a war coming. "I think that had we had him with us from the first we might have bypassed some wishful thinking and wasted motion," Lord said of Bromfield. "He is a great romantic, but when it comes to practical measures, a realist—a peasant in a large way."

The friends arrived in Columbus, Ohio, in July of 1941. The meeting was to begin with a day of speeches at the Deshler Hotel, to be followed the next day by visits to Malabar and other conservation sites. Lord hoped the event could draw a hundred people, but five hundred showed up on the first day. When Bromfield arrived at the Deshler, he saw every session overflow into corridors and galleries. The Friends seemed to receive "the spontaneous co-operation" of local press and women's clubs, of the Farm Bureau, of sportsmen's and business organizations. Bromfield, Sears, and Chase all spoke. Their styles were different, but their messages overlapped and merged into a general sense of alarm that grabbed the attention of everyone in the audience. "Every one of us lives by virtue of the hospitality of the continent of North America," said Chase. "For three centuries we have outraged that hospitality, until the soil itself revolted." The men spoke about rich pastures becoming desert, about forests being cut down without replacement, about acute water shortages in cities and rural towns while farms were being washed away by floods. The time had come, they said, to do something about it. "We can never think again the way we thought before the banks closed in 1933, and before France fell in 1940," said Chase. "There is a chance, and a fair one, that our new thoughts will be not only different but better. There is a chance that our thoughts will turn toward giving to our country rather than taking from it."

They did not just give these environmental problems lip service. The next day, Bromfield led a motorcade of about a hundred cars through the state. They toured southern Ohio, to see where strip-mining coal operations had turned once-rich farmland into wastes and where great forests had been reduced to scrub. It was a countryside "pillaged," Bromfield said. As the caravan moved through the state, to model farms and government soil research stations, its numbers seemed to grow. Bromfield spotted license plates from Kentucky and West Virginia and Pennsylvania, and realized at some point that they had all joined the motorcade heading toward Malabar. News of a picnic that Bromfield was giving had been printed in local papers. The meal he had planned for 150 guests, Bromfield realized, would now need to feed at least 500. He called the caterer in Mansfield, asked to quadruple the amount of shrimp and potato salads, cold ham, sandwiches, beer, cake, coffee—and to set everything up on big tables on the lawn under the black walnut tree.

Malabar was only three years old then, but Bromfield could already point to signs of progress. He showed them the lower pastures, where the addition of lime and phosphate had created an "extravagant lawn." He pointed to the thick contours of clover and alfalfa alternating with strips of corn. He pointed to the woods, where a new crop of tiny oaks and beech and ash was restoring the forest. He walked them through the meadows, drawing attention to the tingling scent given off by the crushed wild mint underfoot, and then he stopped his audience beside the large spring pond. This was one of his favorite parts of the farm, a place that always brought out the sentimental storyteller in him. The once-muddy pond, now ringed with forsythia and green, semi-weeping *Babylonica* willow to stem erosion, had been transformed into a great stage set for nature. It was the scene of tragedies (like when an ancient snapping turtle preyed upon the baby ducks) or comedies (like when a gray Toulouse goose gripped an old sow by the ear and dragged her away from the cornfield).

The methods used to create all this life, to reanimate this landscape, were cheap and available to most farmers, Bromfield told his audience, exaggerating shamelessly. The philosophy was simple: "We have sought merely to build as nature builds, to plant and sow and reap as nature has meant us to do."

For some, the experience of visiting Malabar was life-changing. Bromfield watched them turn into "evangelists, some very nearly fanatics." Soon the Friends of the Land would be flooded with requests for Bromfield to speak. He became the organization's vice president and during the first half of 1942 gave at least sixty speeches across the country. No venue was too small: the Moose lodge, the Kiwanis Club, PTA assemblies, corn roasts. He traipsed around America on his own dime, a happy alarmist. "I hope to scare the daylights out of you," he told the Garden Club of Harrisburg, Pennsylvania. He insulted farmers: "Not ten per cent of America's farmers are as good as the average European peasant." He lost his patience: "When I see abuse of the land it makes me almost physically sick." On tours through the South, he alienated ranchers in Kentucky by calling their cherished bluegrass a "noxious weed."* And he infuriated peanut farmers in the Black Belt of Alabama and cotton farmers near Atlanta by blaming their poverty on a heritage of cash-crop monoculture, which had taken almost everything from the soil: "It wasn't General Sherman who wrecked your country. You did it yourself before Sherman ever came."

Bromfield sometimes brought his farm manager Max Drake with him to Friends meetings. One night, in Des Moines, Iowa, Drake listened as Bromfield painted a dire picture of the effect local farmers were having on the environment. He said the thick, black silt that turned the nearby Raccoon River "into a stream of oily muck" during a downpour was not just the earth flowing downstream but the prosperity of that city, representing wasted health and economic opportunity. Then he began to extol all the conservation techniques at Malabar, how he and Drake had not only stopped runoff and revived their land but also doubled, tripled, even quadrupled, their crop yields. Drake felt himself blush. He was in a room with six hundred of the best farmers in Iowa, and Bromfield was scolding them like little children. Worse, much of what he said was exaggerated for effect. "Every time he pulled a fact out of the air like that, I scooched down in my chair a bit further." After the speech, Ding Darling, a famous editorial cartoonist and one of the founding members of the Friends, could see the shame written on Drake's face. "Max," he said, "don't worry about it. Somebody's *got* to scare the bejesus out of them."

Bromfield was the Friends' star speaker, but its greatest platform was

---

* Kentuckians were so outraged by this slur that, in 1951, they chartered two planes and sent a delegation of fifty farmers, led by the state's governor, to Malabar to debate Bromfield on his home turf. The group came armed with a case of bourbon and a Kentucky ham from a bluegrass-fed pig. In an effort at conciliation, Bromfield told the governor that Kentucky bluegrass was far better than the Canadian variety. Then he served the group a round of mint juleps.

The Land, a quarterly magazine, edited by Lord with beautiful scratch-board drawings by his artist wife, Kate. It soon became a cult hit among progressives, selling out its first issues. "*The Land*," said Eleanor Roosevelt, "should be on everybody's table." Articles and letters came in from Albert Howard, Henry Wallace (who became the US vice president in 1941), John Dos Passos, E. B. White, Aldo Leopold. Through its magazine, the Friends also helped promote the "world-shaking theory" of an Ohio farmer named Edward Faulkner. He believed that the venerable moldboard plow—used in agriculture for centuries—harmed the soil and had been a major cause of the Dust Bowl. The Friends helped Faulkner publish his 1943 book, *Plowman's Folly*, which instructed farmers to leave the vegetal residue of previous crops to decay on the surface of the soil rather than plowing, which exposed the soil to wind and rain and buried organic material deep underground.

Plowman's Folly was nobody's idea of a hit book—one editor quipped it would be "folly" to publish it—yet it became a surprise bestseller, selling 340,000 copies in its first two years and sparking an international debate that moved from the pages of *The Land* into general-interest magazines like *Time* (which described the controversy as "the hottest farming argument since the tractor first challenged the horse"). Today Faulkner's book is regarded as one of the foundational texts in the canon of sustainable agriculture and his technique of "trash farming," now labeled "no-till agriculture," is employed by farmers around the world to reduce soil erosion.

One reason the book succeeded so dramatically was Bromfield's promotion of it in *Reader's Digest*, which at the time was among the most widely read American magazines. Bromfield not only submitted his own articles about the soil crusade to the *Digest* but also convinced the magazine to republish articles from *The Land*. "It is a tremendous joy," its editor wrote to him, "to be able to give a circulation to Friends of the Land, for the objectives of your work are incomparably basic." The Garden

Clubs of America also participated in the crusade, distributing 100,000 copies of Bromfield's *A Primer of Conservation* to its members.

By the middle of 1942, Bromfield felt like they were making progress. Conservation districts, soil experimental stations, and reclamation projects had sprouted in almost every state. America's top documentarian, Robert J. Flaherty of *Nanook of the North* fame, came out with a film about the soil crisis, *The Land*, financed by the USDA, that received a full-dress opening at New York's Museum of Modern Art. Lord had worked on the script and Bromfield promoted the picture with his usual lack of reserve: "*The Land* seems to me the most important documentary film ever made in the United States." The director and his wife, Frances Hubbard, traveled more than 100,000 miles across the country, capturing haunting images: Southern plantation houses with porticoes rotting away, desiccated farms, the Arkansas River filled with so much eroded topsoil that it looked like you could walk across it, a little boy who worked in the fields for slave wages and whose fingers kept moving even as he slept. (His mother told Flaherty that he still thought he was picking peas.) The message was simple: "When soil fails, life fails."

But the film ended on a hopeful note, with Flaherty's voice rising and the violins racing as he pans over rich fields ribboned with contoured crops and sod strips.

> A change has come over the land in the last few years. Farmers are turning to a new way of working it—a new pattern . . . new furrow lines, new terrace lines . . . to hold the rain where it falls, to prevent it from forming into torrents. It is a pattern that will always hold the soil, no matter what—the slash of wind or the wash of rain. Fields enriched with clover turned under, enriched with lime, with phosphate, enriched for the hearts and minds and bones of our children and our children's children. It is a *new* design. The farmers talk it over. It looks practical. It *is* practical!

—┼—

In the fall of 1942, the Friends held their first big national conference, in Louisville, Kentucky. Several thousand people attended. Bromfield was invited to give the keynote address, right before a speech by Henry Wallace. Bromfield, looking sharp in his pinstriped three-piece suit and silk tie, had had a few drinks, per usual, and he began by ribbing Wallace for being sober. "I beg the indulgence of the Vice President, who drinks only lemonade; I am not of that category." There was laughter, a tight smile from Wallace. Then Bromfield continued to loosen up the crowd. Perhaps, he thought, a little ethnic humor? He said the only people—other than Americans—who knew anything about having fun were their new allies, the Russians. "The French can't; too cautious. The English can't. In all friendliness, I know of nothing sadder than an Englishman trying to have a good time. They call it a 'binge!' As for the Germans, they drink beer. And nobody ever got anywhere on beer!"

Those who saw Bromfield speak could never quite understand why he was so good at it. "In his platform demeanor, he breaks all the rules," said Lord. He would lean sideways on the podium, slouch, jangle loose change in his pockets, drop his head from time to time as if talking to himself. Yet the performance was often riveting, mostly because Bromfield seemed to have no idea of what he was going to say until it was too late. As the laughter dissipated, the Louisville speech abruptly turned. Now Bromfield was going to talk about the war. It is doubtful that anyone in America at this time could have made World War II seem like a *bigger* deal than it already was, yet Bromfield tried his best, wrapping the massive geopolitical struggle and his conservation crusade into one giant, age-defining conflict.

> This war is a revolution. It is about many things that don't appear on the surface. It is about an accumulation of inequalities, of disorganization, of destructive waste. It is about the impact of man's

criminal neglect and exploitation of the earth. It holds out to us the prospect of a new world, ours for the making, good or bad. We have got to think about it. . . . When Pearl Harbor broke upon us, we were simply 135 million selfish individuals, not a nation. We were engaged with all our might in wrecking ourselves . . . We fell on a rich country like a plague of locusts. We were living a happy-go-lucky, pilfering life, the days of which are gone and gone forever. Today, the people are waking up. And if they are successful in asserting themselves, we shall have a decent world. Otherwise, there will be no end of aggression, war, spoliation and inhuman discord.

One newspaper editorialist called Bromfield a "miracle man" for having so thoroughly transformed himself from best-selling novelist into a pioneering agricultural reformer. But he still thought that Bromfield and all his Friends of the Land had their "heads in the clouds." It was 1942, the Nazis were in Paris, surely there were more important things to talk about than the environment. "It is hard, for most people, to win a war and build a Utopia at the same time."

11

Food Fight

MALABAR FARM, 1942

Bromfield tried to wage his war on two fronts. Through the Friends of the Land, he fought for a healthier agriculture, which he believed was a matter of national security. But he also did everything he could to support the home front in traditional ways, through relief work, fundraising, and political advocacy. As the war dragged on, however, these two separate campaigns began to clash, forcing him to make tough choices. Starting in 1942, Bromfield, a lifelong Democrat, began a political metamorphosis that would alienate his two most powerful friends in Washington—Eleanor Roosevelt and Henry Wallace—and lead him to support a Republican candidate, Thomas E. Dewey, in the 1944 election. The cause of this political transformation was not ideological. It was basic. Bromfield began to believe that, barring major changes on the home front, wartime America might starve to death.

He had begun the war as a bleeding-heart liberal. "If Jesus of Nazareth came back today, He'd be a Democrat," he said upon his return from France. "If Thomas Jefferson were reincarnated, he'd be a New Dealer." He was far to the left of Roosevelt, a fixture at Socialist mixers or "a parlor pink"—as H. L. Mencken once described him. He submitted the odd article to the *Sunday Worker* and sometimes called Stalin "Uncle Joe." Immediately upon his return from France, Bromfield allied himself with a string of aggressively liberal organizations. He served as the president of The Friends of Democracy, a political advocacy group that attacked isolationists—one of its more persuasive pamphlets was titled "Is Lindbergh a Nazi?"—and protested the exclusion of immigrants from the war effort based on their national origin. As a result of such involvements, Bromfield became a target of right-wing newspapers, like the *Chicago Tribune*, which attacked him for his "prominent" roles in "several communist front organizations." J. Edgar Hoover's FBI pegged him as a "radical writer"—"definitely tied up with left wing organizations"—and began surveilling Malabar. In a confidential memo, a special agent assigned to the case expressed alarm at "the unusual number of visitors" who came to the farm from "other parts of the world," including those "who have been under suspicion" by the bureau.

After France fell in the spring of 1940, Bromfield lobbied hard for America to break off relations with the collaborationist Vichy regime and to recognize Charles de Gaulle's Free French Forces. He was elected the first president of the French-American Club and secured a list of powerful speakers, including Eleanor Roosevelt. He also wrote a propagandistic novel about the Nazi occupation of Paris, *Until the Day Break*, and helped publish a charity cookbook, *Les Spécialités de la Maison*, with recipes from his famous friends like Lucius Beebe (Steak Diane), Tallulah Bankhead (Southern Fried Chicken), Charlie Chaplin (Sour Cream Hotcakes), and the First Lady herself (Mrs. George Washington's Crab Soup). The proceeds of the book's sale, Bromfield wrote in the introduction, "will go to those who are fighting for civilization. And in civilization the art of cooking holds a high place." In August 1942, De Gaulle sent a telegram thanking Bromfield for his efforts on behalf of Free France.

More quietly, Bromfield also made sure that whatever money he had hidden under the floorboards of the Presbytère in Senlis—as well as about $60,000 worth of his French royalties—would be diverted to the

Resistance. An anonymous letter, smuggled out of Occupied France in the summer of 1942 and eventually published on the front page of the *Boston Globe,* said that the money had been received and put to good use. "I would appreciate if you saw Louis Bromfield or sent him a note to tell him I was able to get his royalties out of German control and have used part of them according to his instructions to help some of the most urgent cases . . . He will find lots of people tremendously grateful to him when he comes back over here."

The work for France was just a small part of his wartime contribution. He also made arrangements to house a number of English refugees on his farm. The first of them arrived in August 1940: Mrs. De Winton Wills and her two daughters, Venetia, twelve, and Edwina, seven, who were "happy in the peaceful surroundings." Working with other well-known writers like Clifton Fadiman and Dorothy Parker, he sold millions of dollars in war bonds.

By the fall of 1942, he had become so busy with different aspects of national affairs that the editors of the *New Yorker* thought it would make an entertaining "Talk of the Town" piece to record his movements in detail over the course of a single week. The article begins after he takes a sleeper train from Malabar to New York, arriving at ten a.m. on the morning of October 27, 1942. "He went right to the hotel, where he was visited, in rapid succession, by a delegation of Fighting French, two Negro second lieutenants, three Austrian refugees, a child who wanted to interview him for a school paper, an English lady who wanted help in getting permission to return to England with her two children." The reporter tracked Bromfield as he met with two Hollywood executives for a contract negotiation, lunched at "21" with naval officers, wrote a script for an upcoming radio broadcast, and took a nap. After Bromfield awoke and dressed, he traveled to the Astor Hotel where he made the seating arrangements for a charity dinner and then chewed the fat with a motley collection of union bosses over cocktails. After dinner, more drinks—at the Plaza, at El Morocco, and finally at the Stork Club,

Direct contact with agriculture gave Bromfield credibility
in the 1940s when he took it upon himself to become a
national spokesman for the average dirt farmer.

where the gossip columnists Leonard Lyons and Walter Winchell took
down "every word Bromfield said, as if they were working on the New
Testament."

Immediately after Pearl Harbor, Bromfield had taken it upon himself to
become a national spokesman for the average dirt farmer, who, he said,
was "unorganized and inarticulate" and therefore easily exploited. In the
fall of 1941, even before America entered the war, Roosevelt's new agriculture secretary, Claude Wickard, had called for the "largest production
in the history of American agriculture to meet the expanding food needs

of this country and nations resisting the Axis." But after Pearl Harbor and mobilization, Bromfield saw a problem emerge. The farm labor force that was required to produce this abundance was suddenly disappearing into America's military machine. If farmhands weren't drafted, then they were leaving in droves to work in munitions factories, where they earned double or sometimes triple the wages.

Alarmed, Bromfield wrote an open letter to Secretary Wickard, which appeared in the *Farm Journal* and then was picked up by the Associated Press and the *New York Times*. He said it was "impossible" for the farmer to compete with the "roaring factories," that the serious "drain" on farm labor would soon become "devastating." Farmers were being asked to give up their tractors and other rubber-tired equipment, and to go without spare parts. "Everything possible is being done to hinder farm production" at the very moment it was most needed. Bromfield wanted dairymen, poultry men, and market gardeners to be given an outright exemption from the draft as "skilled labor necessary to war production." He called the farmer a vital—"perhaps the most vital"— element in the war. This article, calm and measured compared to what would follow, was applauded across the farm belt. A farmer's wife from Arkansas said: "We need more of your kind of plain talking and facts." A cattleman from Wisconsin wrote: "MORE POWER TO YOU!" A county extension agent from Ohio: "We appreciate very much the help you are giving us."

He spent the rest of 1942 holding his fire, criticizing Wickard only occasionally as a "small man behind a very big desk." He was busy enough with Free France, the Friends of the Land, and Malabar, and he was also encouraging Americans to fight food scarcity in their own backyards by planting "Victory Gardens" (22 million of which were planted during that year alone). Yet as he traveled the country, listening to what cattle ranchers and grain farmers were telling him, his alarm about the food situation only grew. In September 1942, Wickard further rationed farm machinery. That fall, Bromfield drove down to Mansfield from Chicago and saw field after field of corn and soybeans that "had not been harvested" and were now "lost." Short-staffed farmers were wasting precious time navigating between a half dozen agencies that managed the wartime food system. One Southern farmer told *Harper's* that, to help the war effort, he had tried to triple his production despite the fact that both of his farmhands—who were also his children—had left for the war (his son was drafted; his daughter enlisted as a nurse). He plowed 100 acres for beans, yet could not find the seed he needed because it had been "frozen by some bureau in Washington." When his tractor broke, he had to go "drivin' all over the country like a crazy man" to search in vain for a replacement part. "I swear if they don't quit hogtyin' us with priorities an' restrictions an' regulations the only thing us truck-farmers'll be able to do is close up."

In October, a few weeks after seeing Wallace during the Friends' conference in Louisville, Bromfield sent the vice president an intense four-page, typewritten letter that confessed to a "growing loss of confidence" among farmers in the FDR administration—even among those who, like himself, had previously "fought for the New Deal."

> I have always been a Democrat. I believe passionately in most of the New Deal program. But I confess that I am bewildered. I have lived half my life in Europe and know that end of the stick as well as I know America. I have had great advantages over the man in the street, but . . . I understand no better than he does where we are being led.

Bromfield felt that the food crisis was symptomatic of mismanagement across government. The White House, he said, had been taken over by "smoothies" like Roosevelt's powerful adviser Harry Hopkins and his attorney general, Francis Biddle, who were seen by the average rural American as dictatorial bureaucrats—"flippant Jesuitical New Dealers" in Bromfield's parlance—who were burying the home front in red tape.

He said that farmers hated the treasury secretary Henry Morgenthau Jr. for his "scolding, school teacherish attitude and know-it-all stubbornness" and had been driven around in circles by Wickard's USDA. "The farmer feels, and rightly that Wickard has done *not one thing* to help the farmer, but has only kept repeating that the farmer and their families must work harder." Wallace replied, calling the letter "very thought-provoking," and adding, "I am halfway minded to send it on to Mrs. Roosevelt but I certainly will not do so until I hear from you." Bromfield said go ahead, although he thought there was no use in pressing his case with Eleanor. He had already tried that, months ago. "She was inclined to laugh it off and to refuse to take seriously the things I was saying."*

By January of 1943, Bromfield could see a crisis developing. The normal production of farm machinery had been cut by 80 percent. About 1.5 million farmhands had been drafted or lost to factories. And now Wickard was demanding that farmers somehow exceed the previous year's food output, which—owing to almost perfect weather—proved to be the most productive year in America's agricultural history.

Bromfield could no longer contain himself. In February 1943, he launched a one-man, all-out assault on American public opinion. It began with a letter to the *New York Times* that called Wickard an "incompetent" figurehead proposing only "absurdities" to cover his utter failure to come up with a workable plan. He signed the letter: "From a Democrat

---

* Bromfield's meeting with Eleanor could have been the one she described in a newspaper column that March: "My Children and I who were lunching together yesterday, quite unexpectedly met Louis Bromfield. We invited him to join us, and that led to much exciting and vehement talk among Franklin, Jr., Ethel, Mr. Bromfield and myself. It is a delightful combination to be a farmer and a writer. The kind of farm Mr. Bromfield runs must be an exciting adventure. Farming on a scale large enough to have the workers on the place [be] your partners and really make it a business. It is one of the things which, if I were young, would appeal to me. On one thing, at least, Mr. Bromfield and I did agree, in spite of many arguments. We decided that to work on something you enjoyed was an essential part of life. . . ."

who once believed that the New Deal was a program instead of merely a gigantic improvisation carried on from day to day and week to week at the expense of American citizens." (How quickly he had forgotten that the Soil Conservation Service and Civilian Conservation Corps—which had given him free labor and expertise to revive Malabar—were also New Deal agencies.) Members of the Roosevelt administration were disturbed to see one of their most ardent supporters break rank. Eugene Casey, the president's special executive assistant, sent Eleanor Roosevelt a note: "Louie, whom I believe you know quite well . . . is off the reservation today."

The next salvo was a four-part series trashing Wickard and his food program (or lack thereof) in the anti-Roosevelt Scripps-Howard newspapers. Bromfield used Malabar as an example of problems faced by farmers across the country. He said he could not find fertilizer "at any price," that he lost two of his best farmhands to the draft and a third left to work in a war factory where he received triple the wages, that when he appealed to the US Employment Service he was told there were no replacements. "Not even a tramp or an alcoholic." Bromfield warned of impending shortages of eggs, meat, and butter. He lamented the half measures of the administration, how the government's price ceiling on milk was putting dairymen out of business, how there was a price ceiling on chickens but not on the expensive feed that the farmer must buy to produce them.

One reporter described Bromfield as "the Paul Revere of the harassed farmers," striving through "press, radio and personal interviews to awaken the country to the fact that vital food shortages are coming on the food front, faster than any one realizes." An Oklahoma dirt farmer said she was "wholeheartedly in accord" with Bromfield and had spoken to "dozens and dozens" of farmers who felt the same way. The president of a Pennsylvania milk conglomerate wrote in to say that "Mr. Bromfield's articles, instead of being an overstatement of the seriousness of the plight of the farmer, are an understatement."

The Scripps series produced such an outrage that Wickard was forced to respond with his own two-part series, in which he dismissed Brom-field's attacks as "intemperate and inaccurate" and blamed any tempo-rary shortages on the war. Many onlookers thought Bromfield was only criticizing Wickard to raise his political profile with the White House. Leonard Lyons claimed there was nothing between Bromfield and FDR that couldn't be resolved with "a two-minute meeting" in which "the president would say, 'I hereby appoint you Secretary of Agriculture.'"

Yet as the winter wore on, conditions on the home front showed that Bromfield's alarm was at least partially justified. "The American people have been caught short on food," Wickard finally admitted. A multimillion-dollar underground economy for meat and other rationed foods developed, with housewives joking that they bought their Sun-day roast from "Mr. Black" or "the meat-legger." "Everywhere," declared *Time*, "the people could see that a year's indecision and vacillation had finally caught up with Claude Wickard and the Administration." Spring came with bad weather: floods in the Midwest, late frosts in the South. Wickard finally confessed that his earlier crop forecast was, as the histo-rian Maury Klein wrote, "a scrap of useless paper." The "food front" was now in peril: "There was still food aplenty. But it was at the wrong places, it was going to waste, it was being badly mismanaged." For the moment, Bromfield looked prophetic. The chairman of the House Agricultural Committee now called the food situation "desperate." Wickard finally fessed up to the seriousness of the "food shortage," saying that Americans needed to "tighten [their] belts." In March, Roosevelt appointed Chester Davis, a friend of Bromfield's (and one of the Friends of the Land) to head a new War Food Administration.

Yet Bromfield continued to sound the alarm. "We are witnessing an extraordinary spectacle—that of the richest nation in the world facing a catastrophic food shortage." He began warning about an impending "famine" and "food riots." Millions listened to his prognostications on national radio programs like *Cavalcade of America* and *Town Meeting of the Air*. Suddenly, Bromfield found himself being egged on by former enemies: Hamilton Fish III, the isolationist right-wing senator, quoted one of Bromfield's articles to burnish his case about the folly of the New Deal. Herbert Hoover appeared with him on news programs like *The March of Time* to discuss the food crisis. At times Bromfield's vitriol bordered on the unpatriotic: "If the New Deal had hired Nazi propaganda minister Goebbels to think up a U.S. farm policy, he could not have done half the damage that has already been done by the administration."

By June of 1943, a bipartisan congressional delegation demanded that Roosevelt eliminate the price controls. Bromfield wrote a cover story in *Collier's*: "It's a Farmer's War, Too," in which he speculated that America might end up on "starvation rations" like Germany and foresaw a meat shortage that will "make the present situation seem like an abundance." If there is a drought, "which seems likely," he wrote, "not only will western corn burn out, but cattle and hogs will die even before they reach the corn-feeding stage, from want of pasture and water." He spoke of grave shortages of machinery, skilled and unskilled labor, animal feeds, fertilizers, and farm equipment. "By December this year we shall really feel the gravity of the food famine," he wrote. "Some of those in the know are predicting food riots. I have no opinion, save that the situation will be bad."

In August, Bromfield published a similar, even more dire, article in *Reader's Digest* entitled "We Aren't Going to Have Enough to Eat." "We are already rationed. In every city in America there has been a lack of such staples as potatoes and beef and milk and poultry . . . I would rather not think about next February. By then most of our people will be living on a diet well below the nutrition level."

Yet Roosevelt had already begun to respond. Farm machinery production had been increased. The War Manpower Commission announced that no more essential farm labor would be drafted. And other factors were helping. The weather was improving. Fresh vegetables from Victory Gardens were starting to make up for some food shortages. Hundreds of thousands of civilians from the Woman's Land Army of America—

dismissed earlier by Bromfield as a "fantasy army"—had begun to replace male farmhands in the fields. Even as Bromfield was making his most dire predictions, dairy farmers were setting new highs for milk production and hogs were going to market in record numbers.

There would be no famine, and Bromfield received much blowback for his scare tactics. Newspapermen dismissed him as a "first-rate alarmist" and a "man of letters posing as an authority on agricultural affairs." A *New Republic* correspondent taunted him: "How you eating, Brommy?" The gossip columnists had a field day. "Some time in April, the month designated by Louis Bromfield as the time when our food shortage will begin to be felt, Bromfield's friends will present him a $14 fund they had raised and earmarked: To keep the Prophet of Starvation from Starving." Another said: "Mr. Bromfield earns the ration ticket for the prize boner of the season." In January 1944, Senator Joseph Guffey of Pennsylvania told reporters: "I have before me the latest figures of the Department of Agriculture on the food production of 1943. They show that total food production exceeded that of the miracle year, 1942. Livestock products, including milk and eggs, were eight per cent above 1942 and thirty-one per cent above any earlier year . . . All the false prophets from Dewey to Louis Bromfield should have this magnificent American farm record thrust down their throats."

Yet Bromfield took it all in stride. "Nobody is happier than I that there is food and that my prediction of a food shortage this month did not come true. I hope the supply continues," he said, adding that the "strong-arm methods" used in his "campaign" had achieved their goals: securing an exemption for bona fide farm labor and increasing the production of farm machinery. "So everybody's happy." Even Secretary Wickard, the target of so much of Bromfield's ire, conceded in 1944 that his tactics had, in a way, helped matters. "You'll recall that Louis Bromfield, the author, made a widely publicized prediction last year that there would be a food famine by February . . . I think the prediction did some good, however, because it scared people to the extent that they

planted and preserved more food than they might have done otherwise."
As Bromfield told Leonard Lyons: "We'd have had a famine, if I hadn't
written the article."

—•—

Throughout the war, throughout the soil crusade and the food scare,
Bromfield maintained a strong connection to Hollywood. This was where
his money came from, this was where his best friends lived, and he could
use their stardom to publicize Malabar and its mission, to burnish his
reputation as a person of influence, or to cover up his mistakes—be they
literary or political—with a veneer of celebrity glitter. One columnist
described Malabar as an "auxiliary health resort and junior pump room
for hosts of celebrities traveling between the coasts." Over the years, Joan
Fontaine, Ina Claire, Clifton Webb, and James Cagney all visited. Kay
Francis came at least four times. On one of her visits, she sat down to
dinner with the Bromfield family, a visiting Lutheran minister, and two
European refugees. The meal was interrupted when one of Bromfield's
Guernsey cows gave birth and "all the dinner guests went to the barn to
welcome the newcomer."

Yet no movie star came to Malabar as regularly as Humphrey Bogart.
In March 1942, a visiting newspaper reporter described him, wearing
a heavy cardigan and fedora, "warily" offering to feed the cattle while
listening "with an attempt at serious interest as Bromfield pointed out
his crops." The New York City–bred Bogart may have had no rural han-
kerings himself, but he was amused by how much pleasure the squire
of Malabar could wring out of his fields. Once asked about his taste in
friends, Bogart said that he hated Hollywood "phonies" and preferred
spending his time with real "characters"—"wonderful guys," he said,
"like Louis Bromfield."

Bogart, then forty-two, usually came to Malabar with his third wife,
the actress Mayo Methot. They had a famously combative relationship,
complicated by the fact that both of them were drunks. When angry,

Methot liked to throw various domestic objects at her husband, especially phonograph records, which, she once told a reporter, made "such a satisfactory crash." At Malabar, Methot had to make do with whatever happened to be lying around. Ellen recalled a typical incident during one of the couple's visits: "One of my mother's favorite Venetian lamps went whizzing past Bogie's ear, and in an instant the entire room exploded into a cyclone of books, ashtrays, whiskey bottles and all imaginable items that could be lifted, swung and hurled."

Methot's relationship with Bogie effectively ended in 1944, when he was cast as the lead in the Hemingway adaptation *To Have and Have Not*. The reason for the breakup was Bogie's costar: twenty-year-old Lauren Bacall, a tall, cat-eyed actress described in the press like a man-eating serpent. She was "slithery," "sulfurous," "languorous." She was also deeply in love. "There was no way Bogie and I could be in the same room without reaching for one another, and it wasn't just physical," she wrote in her memoir. "It was everything—heads, hearts, bodies, everything going at the same time." As Bogart's affair with Bacall heated up, Methot desperately tried to hold on to her marriage. Bogart felt trapped, so he started drinking more, sometimes calling Bacall late at night when he was deep in his cups to say that he missed her. Methot was not the only thing keeping them apart. "Baby," as Bogart called Bacall, was twenty-five years his junior. "I could be your father," he told her. In a confessional letter to Bromfield (whom he jokingly addressed as "Dear Father Bromberg"), Bogart wondered if the reverse wasn't actually true: "She's too old for me—and I'm too young to be married."

In January 1945, after finishing work on his next picture with Bacall, *The Big Sleep*, Bogart headed for a two-week visit to Malabar to decompress and plot his next steps. Bacall met him on the farm later that month. Around this time, gossip columnists began reporting on the affair and Bogie finally owned up to it. Asked if he intended to marry the young actress, Bogart said, "You're God damn right. But I'm not divorced yet so we've got to put it off." The press seemed confused by Bogart's where-abouts. "The mystery of the week in Hollywood," read one wire report, "was why Humphrey Bogart journeyed 2,000 miles to an Ohio farm to announce his romance." (The reason, Bogart told Walter Winchell, was "to try and convert" Bromfield back into a Democrat.)

George Hawkins was waiting in the Ford station wagon to pick up Bacall and her mother (who came as her chaperone) when they arrived at the Mansfield train station. Bacall later wrote about this visit in her memoir, describing the farm covered in snow and the Big House filled with "beautiful antique French country furniture and seven boxer dogs." Bromfield struck her as "a very tall man of enormous charm and good humor. We got on well immediately." As for the farm itself, she said, "I was agog."

> Malabar was more beautiful than Bogie had described it in his letters . . . The food was wonderful, the atmosphere really back to the earth. There was rationing because of the war, but one couldn't tell with the fresh eggs and great slabs of butter that the day started with. . . . There were roaring fires and screaming games of hearts, Bogie and Louis' affectionate ribbing of each other about Hoover and Roosevelt. There were dog fights under the table and boxers breaking wind at all times. Louis took me all around the farm, and in a barn, for the first and only time in my life, I saw a calf being born. It was a happy, healthy, peaceful way of life. I envied them all.

The visit ended with Hawkins and Bromfield "insisting" that, when the time came, the couple should have their wedding in the Big House. Bacall thought this was a "lovely idea."

By the middle of March, Bogart's lawyers had worked out a settlement with Methot that included real estate, two-thirds of Bogart's cash assets, his life-insurance policy, and several investments. Guilt-ridden to be leaving his wife in such a state, he was, according to his biographers, "buying himself out of the marriage." As part of the deal, Methot would spend about a month in Reno, Nevada, to fulfill the residency requirement for a divorce, which was granted in early May. The wedding at Malabar was set for May 21. *Life* magazine asked if their photographer could join the couple on the train from Los Angeles to photograph the run-up to the nuptials. "Great," Bogart sniffed, "maybe he'd like to photograph us fucking?"

They boarded the *Santa Fe* on May 18. Because of a transfer in Chicago and the couple's shooting schedule, they would have only a two-day window in Ohio for preparations and the ceremony. All the arrangements fell to Hawkins: the blood tests, the marriage license, keeping the press at bay. He found a local judge, Herbert S. Schettler of the Mansfield Municipal Court, to waive the customary five-day waiting period for a license. Requests for invitations poured in "by the hundreds," Hawkins said. "We have been forced to give the same answer even to the closest friends of Mr. and Mrs. Bromfield." Many people asked if they could "help out" with the preparations: a wedding singer from Akron volunteered to come at his own expense; sorority sisters offered to help Miss Bacall with her makeup. Hawkins got the local sheriff to post guards at entrances and outlaw parking on the road leading to Malabar. Nevertheless, he said, "It seems certain Miss Bacall and Mr. Bogart will not have the quiet ceremony they so urgently desire."

Hawkins told an AP man that the preparations were driving "me out of my mind . . . This is the first wedding I've arranged and if I get through this one, it's going to be my last." The day before the wedding, Bromfield took Hawkins fishing to calm him down.

May 21 fell on a Monday, not traditionally the most festive day of the week but the weather was bright and clear and Bacall remembered that the Big House was "shining," with every table waxed, and the brass polished: "It was truly beautiful." Newspapers across the country were following the event closely. "Today's the Day!" wrote one. "The plot— matrimony. The cast of characters—languorous Lauren Bacall and merchant of menace Humphrey Bogart. The setting—Malabar, novelist Louis Bromfield's 1,100 acre estate."*

The couple rose early for their blood test and the visit to the Richland County Courthouse to get the license. "Bogie and I were ridiculous, holding hands like teenagers (I almost was one)." After they returned, Bacall started to feel nervous. She ran a bath. Following an old tradition, she laid out something blue (a slip with her name embroidered on it), something old (a bracelet), something borrowed (a handkerchief from her mother), and something new (everything else). She put on a two-piece belted doeskin suit and wrapped a dark scarf around her neck. Hawkins knocked on the door, calling her by the same name Bogart used. "Are you ready, Baby?" In her simple outfit (a concession to wartime fashion standards), she looked even younger and skinnier than on-screen. Bacall and Hawkins hugged each other, and then she gave him the ring and felt herself begin to shake with a mix of fear and excitement.

"Hope's at the piano, ready to start," Hawkins said. Nanny White, Bacall's mother Natalie, the farm workers, and their families had all assembled in the grand entry hall, which was decorated by Bromfield with white snapdragons and tall ferns. Hawkins said that Bogart was getting "itchy" waiting for her. "Shall I give the signal?"

"Okay," she said, but then she told him to wait a minute: She had to run to the bathroom.

---

* Throughout its history, Malabar was described in the press as ranging in size from 500 to 1,500 acres. The original farm encompassed only 600 acres; the larger numbers were usually a result of journalistic sloppiness, Bromfield's tendency to exaggerate his holdings, and the fact that he often leased neighboring pastures, which temporarily expanded Malabar's total acreage.

"Where is she?" snapped Bogart from downstairs.

"Hold it," replied Hawkins, adding with romantic discretion: "She's in the can."

Bacall emerged. Hawkins led her to the top of the stairs. Hope began to play the wedding march from *Lohengrin* as they descended. "My knees shook so, I was sure I'd fall down." She caught sight of Bogart, in his plain gray flannel suit and dark tie. He had had a few martinis to calm down before the ceremony and now looked to her "so vulnerable and handsome." Bromfield, the best man, towered over him in a blue three-piece suit with a flower in his lapel. His favorite boxer, Prince, the only dog invited into the wedding party, had sat himself down at the center of the altar, on Judge Schettler's feet. Bacall took her place beside Bogart as the judge began the ceremony. She remembered feeling so nervous that the "enormous, beautiful white orchids I was holding were shaking themselves to pieces." She saw tears coming down Bogart's face. When it was over, he leaned in to kiss her lips, but she shyly turned her cheek. Bogart said, "Hello, baby," and then she hugged him. At the end of the ceremony, Bacall turned her back to the audience and tossed her bouquet, which Hope caught. Then, Bacall wrote, "all hell broke loose with the press."

> Cameras were whipped out, the outsiders were let in, the cake was brought out—three beautiful tiers, with a bride and groom standing under an arbor on top—and we were photographed from all angles—cutting the cake with Louis watching, me feeding Bogie a piece. . . . Champagne was flowing—we all went outside for more photos—Louis finally could stand the blue suit no longer and changed into his dirty old man-of-the-soil corduroys—and newsreel cameras followed us around the farm.

"Every photographer in the world was there," said Ed Clark from *Life* magazine. "God there was just a swarm of us." For a gift, Bromfield gave the couple a boxer puppy, and 1 acre of land at Malabar for them

The media circus surrounding the May 1945 wedding of
Humphrey Bogart and Lauren Bacall in the Big House established
Malabar Farm's national reputation. Hawkins is at right
and Bromfield's middle daughter, Hope, is at far left.

to build a cottage—which turned out to be only a symbolic gift, since
they never did. But Bacall fantasized about it. ("The picture was always
complete with me in an apron carrying [a] milk bucket.") This celebrity
wedding accomplished something that Bromfield—despite his stature
as a novelist and a pundit—could not have achieved on his own: Now,
practically every American knew the name of Malabar Farm.

12

Erosion

He decided to write up the whole story of Malabar: the escape from France, finding the farm, building the Big House, the Plan, the soil crusade—putting it all in a drippy memoir called *Pleasant Valley*. Parts of the book were charming, especially the stories of the farm animals: Gilbert, the implacable turkey who tried to move into the Big House; Haile Selassie, the Karakul ram who developed a taste for chewing tobacco; and Hector, the Nubian he-goat, who spent his afternoons swaying on the porch swing. "The trouble with the animals on this farm," George Hawkins said, "is that they all think they are people."

The book also told the story of a *teched* farmer named Walter Oakes—a fictional character that Bromfield dishonestly presented as one of his real-life neighbors—who turned his shaggy 90 acres into a living memorial to his dead wife and farmed the earth "as if it were the only woman he ever loved." In other chapters, Bromfield introduced many ordinary Americans to Albert Howard and Edward Faulkner, whose ideas were coalescing into a movement that was now being called "organic" farming. Most important, he offered a new view of agriculture as a higher calling, a profession as demanding and urgent as any other, its satisfactions perhaps even greater. A good farmer, Bromfield said, is "the happiest of men for he inhabits a world that is filled with wonder and excitement over which he rules as a small god."

Pleasant Valley became a national bestseller, a random agrarian tract in a nonfiction list dominated by titles about the war by the likes of Ernie Pyle and Gen. George C. Marshall. To some, it seemed that, by writing about Malabar, Bromfield had finally found his great subject, his natural voice. "For a good many years Louis Bromfield has been working up to this book," wrote a critic for the *New York Herald Tribune*. "But not until he found the land he dreamed about, his own native land in Ohio, and began doing what he really always wanted to do, could he write his Testament of Beauty." Bromfield was flooded with letters from would-be farmers, many of them newly discharged GIs who now dreamed of making their own Malabars: What kind of land should I buy? What types of cover crops should I raise? To plow—or not to plow? He wrote another, more practical, book to answer their questions. *Malabar Farm* (1948) also sold strongly and inspired, among other things, a delightful 123-line poem in *The New Yorker* by E. B. White.

> *A farm is always in some kind of tizzy,*
> *But Bromfield's place is really busy:*
> *Strangers arriving by every train,*
> *Bromfield terracing against the rain,*
> *Catamounts crying, mowers mowing,*
> *Guest rooms full to overflowing,*
> *Boxers in every room of the house,*
> *Cows being milked to Brahms and Strauss,*
> *Kids arriving by van and pung,*
> *Bromfield up to his eyes in dung,*
> *Sailors, trumpeters, mystics, actors,*
> *All of them wanting to drive the tractors,*
> *All of them eager to husk the corn,*
> *Some of them sipping their drinks till morn [. . .]*

The farm books powerfully conveyed the comedy, adventure, and mission of Malabar, but they also overflowed with Bromfield's failings as a writer: exaggeration, sentimentality, sloppiness, repetitiousness, and pretentiousness—especially pretentiousness. He bragged about how he made "lots of money" and his books were "translated into every language in Europe and even into Chinese and Bengali." He bragged about how, at Senlis, "every Sunday Rolls-Royces and automobiles labelled *Corps Diplomatique* stood before my door." He bragged about his enormous crop yields, his "humble stock of wisdom and experience and humility," his wide knowledge "not only of agriculture but also of world and market conditions." Sinclair Lewis, a Nobel Prize–winning novelist, found *Pleasant Valley* insufferable and penned a vicious satirical review, "The Boxers of M. Voltaire," for *Esquire.* Lewis thought Bromfield had boldly set out to create a twentieth-century *Walden* only to half-ass it, becoming in the process both the perpetrator and victim of a "literary tragedy."

> And just there is the tragedy: that, with the enthusiasm and perhaps with the power to make an enduring book, a true *Walden*, he should have cluttered and botched it with all the pert vanities of the money-grabbing, socially-climbing Paris-Broadway-Hollywood literary gent. He did not listen to the quiet of his own fields and of his own heart. Into the valley he had to drag columnists and business managers and five damn big noisy boxer dogs . . . Once, in novels like *The Green Bay Tree* and *The Strange Case of Miss Annie Spragg,* he promised to rank with Hemingway and Cather and Dos Passos, but he grew tired of being the priggish sort of writer who thinks that it is of some importance to write.

Whatever remained of Bromfield's reputation as a serious novelist did not survive the war years. Left-wing journals like the *New Republic* and the *Nation* had already given up on him in the 1930s, after the string of uninspired novels between *The Farm* and *The Rains Came*. H. L. Mencken categorically refused to review his books, calling them "trashy stuff." His sales were still in the hundreds of thousands, his stories were still getting optioned by Hollywood, but the New York daily critics who had supported Bromfield for so long now began to turn on him. Orville Prescott, a leading reviewer for the *New York Times*, thought he had "abandoned literature for a mess of popular-magazine potage and the fleshpots of Hollywood." A critic from the *Herald Tribune* was even harsher: "There is no more uneven writer practicing fiction than Louis Bromfield. When he is good he is good enough, but when he is bad he is horrendous."* In 1944, in *The New Yorker*, Edmund Wilson performed a lengthy vivisection on his latest novel, *What Became of Anna Bolton*, which was so brutal that the magazine's editor, Harold Ross, wrote to Bromfield in advance to apologize.

He pretended not to care. "Don't worry about Eddie," Bromfield replied. "He just has an in-growing case of liberalism and can't get out of the Twenties. I think a dose of about one per cent of my public and royalties would probably cure the congestion. It's been going on ever since the Left Bank." But his daughter Ellen said that such harsh criticism cut Bromfield to the quick, and partially explained why, in later years, he began to denigrate the whole enterprise of novel-writing, calling it "simply a way of making a living" and "not a very satisfactory or even self-

---

* This review, of Bromfield's 1947 novel *Colorado*, was typical of his postwar critics. The book was intended to be a joke about western genre fiction but no critic found it funny. The setting was "canvas and plaster," the characters were "hand-me-down costumes." Bromfield's plot included not one but two broken-down musicians—who both wore toupees. Despite the critical barbs, MGM bought the rights for a reported $125,000 and paid Bromfield $3,500 per week to adapt his own story. The book eventually sold more than 1 million copies—a record for Bromfield, and perhaps the most stark example of the gap between his critical reputation and popular acclaim.

"Oh, dear! I see Louis Bromfield is still three ahead of me."

Bromfield often wrote novels faster than his fans could read them,
as this 1943 *New Yorker* cartoon by Helen E. Hokinson suggests.

respecting one." Why bother inventing stories, Bromfield asked, when
"your daily newspaper is more exciting than most novels?"

———

Most critics did not connect Bromfield's preoccupation with agriculture
to his descent as a writer into what Wilson called the "fourth rank."
But George Hawkins certainly did. Hawkins had patiently typed up
every Bromfield work since 1930. In addition to decoding his illegible
longhand and adapting his stories into lucrative movie treatments, Hawkins also edited Bromfield's prose and was his most honest, harshest,
and ultimately most valuable critic. He loathed reading Bromfield's writ-
ings on farming. "Here's your humus, mucus, retch and vetch, all 140
pages of it," he would say after typing up the latest chapters of *Pleasant*

Valley. "And that, thank Christ, is that." His attachment to Malabar was "perfunctory," Ellen said, and he often fled to New York or Hollywood or closed his shutters to block out the pastoral scene. He hated seeing how, in the presence of farmers and agricultural bureaucrats, Bromfield turned from a sophisticated writer into a "dreadful, hogwash-preaching old bore." And he lamented all the time Bromfield wasted lecturing to garden clubs. "You, Mr. B.," he once said, "are getting to be nothing but the Sinatra of the Soil for middle-aged women!"

As Bromfield's reputation as a farmer grew, Hawkins sought to puncture it at every available opportunity. He liked to make a fool of himself while Bromfield led Sunday tours around Malabar. One summer day, he waddled out of the Big House, wearing only a Scotch plaid bathing suit, and addressed a collection of garden-club ladies who were waiting for an audience with Bromfield: "God will be with you in a moment." Then Hawkins plopped himself on a lawn chair and promptly dozed off.

"George had no innate desire to improve the world," Ellen wrote. "He felt it was good enough as it stood, as long as one picked and chose one's pleasures in the right places and didn't look for trouble." While he could be lovable, even cuddly, few got to know the person underneath the jovial surface. Only shreds of his biography were known: He had grown up in Patchogue, on Long Island, the son of a postmaster; he had spent his twenties as a seaman, traveling the world; he had turned up in Hollywood, where he became a joke writer and studio fixer. But that was about it. "To pry into the privacy of that strange soul," Ellen wrote, "would have been unthinkable."

On April 9, 1948, Hawkins, who had been in New York for business, was found in bed in his hotel room at the St. Regis, dead of a heart attack. He was just forty-five. The Mansfield newspaper announced the news with a banner headline on the front page. Telegrams and letters poured in from all quarters: Hollywood, New York, the farm belt. One of the owners of the "21" Club wrote, so did Hugh Bennett, chief of the US Soil Conser-

Hawkins played the role of jester in the
Bromfield family; in this photo he is dressed
in drag as a Paris call girl, an American
tourist, or some combination of the two.

vation Service. "Your telegram late last night about George Hawkins was
terrifically shocking," Bennett said, adding that he and his wife "both
loved George. I think most everybody did . . . We can only extend our
condolences to you and Mary. We had associated George with you as practically part of yourselves." Mary was devastated but letters like Bennett's

consoled her. "They keep him alive," she wrote to Bromfield. "And the nicest thing and the thing that makes me proud and happy is that so many people write to us *both*—it means that we stood as a *trio* of friendships and affection . . . The house isn't sad because George left *years* of gaiety and wit and fun behind him and deep affection, too. It's all around us."

Everyone grieved for George—everyone, seemingly, except Bromfield. In Ellen's memoir, written in the 1960s, she called her father's reaction to the death of his best friend "incomprehensible" and "so disturbing that even now it is difficult to write of." It was as though Bromfield had been "relieved at last of a great burden." The chaos and lighthearted amusement that Hawkins represented suddenly seemed of no importance to him. He was just happy to have control of his own affairs, to have to answer to no one. "You have no idea," he told Ellen, "what a relief it is to me to have my papers in order for the first time . . . George was really hopeless." Hawkins was no longer around to defend himself. Why Bromfield turned on him is unclear, but his secretary's death seemed to mark a shift: From this point on, Bromfield would never again write a runaway bestseller (to say nothing of a critically successful novel), and he would devote his energies almost entirely to agriculture.

It took the better part of a year to find a suitable replacement for Hawkins. First, Bromfield hired Lauren Bacall's mother, Natalie, as a temporary secretary, and then Woodrow Wyant, a former professor of animal husbandry at Ohio University in Athens. Finally, he settled on a plump Englishwoman named Annie Rimmer. She had followed her eighteen-year-old son, David, whom Bromfield had taken on in 1948 to care for the gardens at Malabar. David was a dashing young man with fine brown hair—Mary described his face as almost "seraphic"—who had just graduated from an agricultural institute in Wales. Bromfield often took him on the road, and enjoyed showing him off to journalists. "There's no such thing as a good American gardener," Bromfield said when introducing David. "So I had to go outside of America to find one."

Under Bromfield's direction and David's care, Malabar became more beautiful in the late 1940s—the fields thicker, shaggier, greener; the edges hemmed with flowers and vines. Bromfield started to plant hedges of multiflora rose, which he used as a "living fence" to separate the pastures. They bloomed in white blossoms and sheltered pheasant and quail. "All the shrubbery and willows have reached the point where they make the picture I wanted in the beginning," Bromfield wrote around this time. "All around the house the flowers and shrubs show through a sort of hazy curtain of trailing pale green weeping willow." It reminded him of a painting by John Constable or Claude Lorrain, the landscape at its romantic height.

13

Four Seasons at Malabar

BASED ON FARM JOURNALS, 1944–1953

Winter

The flies have disappeared from the barns. The red leaves on the maple and sumac trees have fallen. The Sunday visitors have stopped coming. But it is not quiet at Malabar. Everyone, and everything, is hard at work: the new Graham plow and the pike-tooth harrows and the manure spreaders. By the first week of December, the winter wheat is a few inches high. Once the other fields are plowed and the rest of the winter grains sown, the barns must be cleaned out, the deep-freeze replenished. The lambs are slaughtered first, which is done in a cement-floored room adjacent to the dairy. All the implements are here: knives, cutting table, hanging hooks, hose, hot and cold running water. A man named Kenneth does the butchering. The children watch him and learn. Ellen is most interested. Death on the farm has become prosaic to her: the issues are timing and technique, controlling what you can, preparing for what you cannot.

Rabbits move closer to the house, picking up corn spilled from cribs and the beans and oats left out for the turkeys and guinea hens. Most of the birds have flown south, but the house sparrows stay on through the winter. In his farm journal, Bromfield notes that they prefer "people and bustle and sociability." One sleeps every night on a ledge inside the portico covering the front door. Even when he turns on the light, she does not go away but watches him "very quietly with bright little eyes." On the coldest nights, he goes out to check on the cattle, clumping his way through the snow to the barn, where the cows lie bedded down in straw, dry and warm in their shaggy winter coats. They are mostly blue roans, crossbred from Angus and Shorthorns. Plenty of cattlemen, favoring purebreds, look askance at these mutts. "We're not interested in pedigrees or show cattle," Bromfield writes, "but in producing quality, top-market beef with a minimum of sickness." He turns on the lights in the barn. The sleek calves stand up, stretch themselves, come toward him. He throws them an extra bale of alfalfa but "they only nuzzle the hay and push it about because they are already filled up. It gives you a remarkable feeling of security and well-being, so rare in the world today."

On wet days, the winter air creeps inside the house, freezing everyone's toes despite the moccasins and heavy rugs. A Brahms concerto plays on a gramophone. Two dozen people move through nineteen rooms, slamming shut doors that five drooling boxer dogs proceed to scratch open. A friend, Inez Robb, calls Malabar "one of the most luxurious dog houses in America." She always visits during the holidays and files her national newspaper column from the farm. The guests are "stacked like cord wood," she writes. "Since my arrival the dining room tables have never been set for less than twenty-two." The cook, a tiny lady named Reba, wipes off a cast-iron pot, which Bromfield snatches to make supper. "Pans don't even have a chance to get cold in this house!" Reba says. At five o'clock, a bell summons everyone for cocktails. Dinner is country-fried chicken, or leg of lamb with mint jelly, or turkey with chestnut dressing. Bromfield often prepares the meal himself. "He is a marvelous cook," Ellen says of her father, "but has a mania for dirtying as many pans as possible and then only washing the first two."

Unlike her father, the teenage Ellen doesn't like drinking liquor ("expensive gasoline with ice in it") but she likes a warming winter grog with spiced rum, which makes "everything in sight gay, cheerful and spirally." After a few, she washes the dishes and they "just float out of the sink and into the cupboard." Christmas arrives with evergreen needles on the floor, garlands of pine, holly, and mistletoe hanging over the doors. The tree is too big; it looks like it is growing through the ceiling. In January, they butcher hogs. A visiting French farmer teaches them how to make boudin noir, or blood sausage, so they can make use of every last bit.

It feels like forever before the lower pastures turn from brown to green, the winter wheat heads out, the silver pussy willows appear in the garden. By March, everyone is hoping for deep freezes at night followed by sunny days, which will make the sap in the maple trees run. Metal buckets are attached to their trunks. When they are full, Ellen carries them to the sugarhouse, an old unpainted shack—three walls and an open front. A porch swing is the only furniture, covered with a dirty sheepskin rug. There is a stove lined with brick and iron tubs on top. She pours the sap into a tank just outside the shed and then siphons it into the tubs through a large funnel. She can't fall asleep for long, so she drinks coffee and stokes the log fire, watching the syrup drain and boil until it has "the strong, sweet and smokey taste of the woods."

Spring

The guinea hens announce the change of season, annoyingly, waking everyone up at six thirty with their metallic squealing. Slowly the air warms and the earth softens. Ellen notes the coughing of a two-cylinder tractor, which she finds reassuring, the sound "of life picking up again." Switzer's Creek has melted and runs clear. The dogwoods are blooming in small green flowers and marsh marigolds have come out in "the jungle." The field tools are removed from their black tarp covers. Manure is being hauled out of barns. The oats will go in first, then the corn, which they will plant in a field that had been enriched with nitrogen from a cover crop of ladino clover. They use a chisel plow to dig grooves in the earth and a big Seaman tiller to chop the soil and roots into the right consistency. Fertilizer is mixed in, then the corn seeds are planted nine inches apart. Crows follow as they plant, gobbling up the earthworms that had recently been multiplying—"a good sign." Bromfield often works the soil himself, driving his Ferguson tractor at high speed, throwing up weed seedlings and bits of earth into the air.

When he shuts off the engine, he can hear tree frogs crying out for rain. This is a dangerous time of year. Drought is obviously bad, but an excess of water can also be a problem—it makes the earth too wet to plow. A hot March brings out everything too early—the alfalfa, the fruit blossoms, the perennial flowers—exposing them to frost if the weather turns cold. When this happens, Concord grapes are scalded, magnolia flowers burned, crab blossoms pinched. By April, when the grass turns green and the forsythia and plum trees are in bloom, the weather is a consuming anxiety. "The question of whether there will be a killing frost becomes the most important thing in the world, far more important than what Stalin is doing in the Kremlin or Mr. Truman's quarrels in Washington." Bromfield gets up in the middle of the night to go outside and watch to see if his breath will freeze in the air. He goes back to sleep with his fingers crossed, awakening to sunshine and only a slight hoarfrost in the trees, too light to do any harm. "So today I feel fine." Easter, the idea of resurrection, makes sense on the farm.

By May it is busy in the garden by the Big House. Ellen dips a bucket into the pond and brings up tadpoles. They plant peonies and climbing hybrid perpetual roses and carefully try to transplant a few ragged robins and lady's slipper collected from the woods. Down the hill from the garden is the dairy, home to forty Guernsey cows and Mummy, a female tiger cat who keeps the place clear of mice and rats. She walks on a concrete ledge along the feeding trough and is sometimes licked by the tongues of the cows as she passes. "When this happens," Bromfield notes, "she will stand quite still, arching her back and purring." Once she got

Intercropping, which encourages soil biodiversity, was one of many
ecological farming techniques that Bromfield practiced at Malabar.

too comfortable and was taken in the mouth of a fat cow named Eileen,
who shook her until her tail ballooned and she emitted "furious squalls."
Such hysterics are a consolation for Al, the dairyman, who rises at four
a.m. He has an intern, a young Frenchman named Gérard. They work
in shifts, caring for the small calves and the nursing cows and inspecting
the herd. They know every cow by name, treat each "according to its
own mood and personality." This is important; the amount of milk the
cows give depends on how comfortable they are. The radio plays while

the cows are being milked—they seem to like country music and base-
ball games. The milking parlor can accommodate eight cows at a time,
with two Surge milkers and a Westinghouse cooling system. The milk is
poured through a cooling strainer so it enters the cans cold, limiting the
time it is exposed to the air.

Bromfield likes to visit the dairy but he prefers watching his beef
cattle in the open pastures. On late spring evenings, he studies their
movements: the way they congregate at the bottom of a shady ravine
where the damp sandstone ledges make the air too cool for flies, how
they feed their calves at prescribed hours before gathering them into a
"kind of kindergarten," hidden in a copse, while the herd goes roam-
ing. The king of the herd is Blondy, a coal-black Angus bull who can be
affectionate—sometimes he comes up to Bromfield in the field to have
his ears scratched. But he is also unpredictable, and very attached to his
cows. Once, when Bromfield tried to separate him, he smashed through
the wall of a barn and broke through a floodgate and several fences to
rejoin the harem.

Summer

Bromfield sees a goldfinch on a thistle, plucking out the thistledown to
make his summer nest. The leaves of the thistle are green, the blossoms
purple, the thistledown white, and the goldfinch, "as delicate as a Cellini bird," bright yellow and black. The woods are thick now and so are
the fences, hidden by a growth of blackberries and sassafras, themselves
hiding pheasants, thrushes, and quail. The dragonflies over the ponds
look to him like "gaudily painted miniature planes." He fishes until
sunset, sitting beneath the willows and watching a crescent moon in
a sky that changes from scarlet to gold to pale mauve and then finally
to dark blue. Mary and the girls are shelling peas. Some visiting children yell whenever they hook a silver spotted trout. They put whatever

they catch in milk cans and transfer most of the fish to the smaller spring ponds.

Before it is completely dark, he likes to go up to the highest pasture, the Ferguson Place, where there is a very old peach orchard, with small yellow clingstone peaches, a bit misshapen but delicious—the hot, dry weather seems to concentrate their flavor. Some of the peaches have sharp teeth marks from the possums and foxes. Also here are the wild apple trees, which he thinks might be the descendants of those planted in Pleasant Valley more than a century earlier by Johnny Appleseed. Their fruits are small and sour, appreciated more by raccoons than people.

The garden is full of weeds. Ellen pulls them out by hand or hoe. It is getting too hot to work through the days. The boys hired for the season spend their mornings filling bushel baskets with vegetables and take a break around noon to jump in the pond. For supper, there is cold Guernsey milk, broiled chicken, mashed potatoes, sweet corn dripping in butter churned that week, and Nanny's pickles. For dessert: tart apple pie with whipped cream.

They are making hay now, which is hard work, and Bromfield mows until late at night. He is joined by the barn swallows, which sweep over him catching the insects driven out of the grass by the mower. "Sometimes they brushed my head and I could feel the rush of air from their wings." As night falls, a new moon appears and the wind turns north and the air becomes a bit cold, which, he writes, "augurs well for the hay"—a thick, protein-rich mix of emerald-green alfalfa and lettuce-green brome grass. "I almost envy the cows feeding on that next winter."

When he comes back from the field, the kitchen is still at work: making jams and juices, chopping, scraping knives, marking jars. The plums have to be cooked down and then pushed through a colander and recooked with sugar to make plum butter. "It is the longest, sloppiest, stickiest process I have ever been through," Ellen writes. The peak of the tomato harvest comes in August. Bromfield sits in front of a big tub, washing tomatoes with a hose and supervising an assembly line. "Them that works, eats," he says before dumping a fresh load on somebody's lap. They are peeling, chopping, and blending the garden's surplus (tomatoes, onions, celery, spinach, parsley, garlic, bay) into a concoction that will last all year. Nanny calls it "Doctor Bromfield's Special Vegetable Compound and Celery Tonic." To Ellen, it's just "glorified tomato juice."

Twenty thousand people visit Malabar each year, and summer is the busiest season. On Sundays, schoolchildren and celebrities come, delegations of cattlemen, garden-club ladies, families from Cleveland, Columbus, Pittsburgh. He most enjoys meeting the farmers. Some are underexperienced and overeducated, back-to-the-landers who have read all of Bromfield's books. Others are local dirt farmers, skeptical, wanting to see what the fuss is about. They arrive around lunchtime, picnic, take a drink from the springhouse, inspect the beehives, the cattle barns, the hay lofts. Then Bromfield appears in his work clothes and offers them a "quick look around," which takes up the whole afternoon. He leads his "faithful tribe" up a long, winding lane to the highest hill at Malabar, Mount Jeez, named sarcastically by Hawkins because it is here that Bromfield proselytizes, here that he gives his weekly sermons on the mount. And from here, Malabar does look like a land of milk and honey, with its contoured fields, its tall native trees and its Lombardy poplars— planted nostalgically one year when he was missing France.

Mount Jeez is not only for sermonizing. At the end of the summer, they gather everyone on the farm for a big party, forty people climbing onto a hay wagon covered with straw bales, which is drawn up the hill by a big John Deere tractor. There is a local troop of Boy Scouts, the hired hands who bale hay all season, and the executive committee of the Friends of the Land. They build a big fire from wood cut from an abandoned apple orchard ("there is no better firewood") and eat Reba's potato salad and meatloaf. There are two giant, very crisp watermelons, beer, a couple of bottles of bourbon. They sit on straw bales and somebody starts singing the "Battle Hymn of the Republic," and then everyone joins in. "It may sound sentimental but it seemed like a spontaneous hymn of thanksgiving for the peace and the beauty all of us experienced there on the top of Mount Jeez."

Giving thanks does not insure against trouble, like drought. The contour plowing and strip-cropping mean that the soil at Malabar is not as parched as in the neighboring farms, and water does not need to be hauled around, but a few weeks without rain is still a major problem. The early corn is nearly ruined and the pastures are short. In late August, Bromfield says, *To hell with it.* He turns all the hungry beef cattle and the hogs into a 50-acre field of alfalfa in which rows of corn and soybeans are also growing. For the first few days, the neighbors come by to tell him the livestock are in the corn—to them "a violation and a sacrilege." But Bromfield likes seeing the animals "in paradise," unable to decide whether they prefer the corn, the soybeans, or the alfalfa. The hogs are almost overwhelmed by the choice, chewing big mouthfuls of grass and then dashing "with grunts and pig excitement" into the corn to snatch up the ears knocked off by the beef cattle, then getting into the soybeans—a "three-course menu." As for the cattle, they pick carefully at the corn and alfalfa, before wandering off to find dock and mint and coarse weeds. "They are seeking something," Bromfield writes, "probably minerals or even flavors, which the shallow-rooted bluegrass and white clovers do not contain." The animals seem to know how to balance their own diet better than "any professor or feed merchant." So Bromfield sees his job as only giving them a "diverse selection."

When the rain finally comes one night, it is soft, "scarcely loud enough to disturb a cricket," yet it wakes him up and he lies in his bed, afraid to go back to sleep in case it will stop. He gets up, walks out onto the terrace to feel the rain. Two of the boxers, Prince and Baby, come with him, "enjoying it as much as myself." Baby, "the natural clown," lifts his head, opens his mouth, and lets the water dripping from the eaves fall onto his tongue.

Fall

The raccoon comes in September when the corn is high, sometimes with his cubs, who look like small bears trailing behind him. Instead of claws he has delicate little hands that are "deft at catching cray fish and opening the latches of chicken houses and washing the apples he eats." Racoons are "great thieves" of sweet corn. Bromfield admires their discrimina-

tion. "They like the corn exactly as you like it, neither too green nor too tough and they will go along a row of sweet corn delicately tearing open the husks until they find an ear exactly to their taste." Bromfield's solution to this problem is to plant "enough corn for both the raccoon and ourselves."

The air is cooling and the ground is filling with hickory nuts that crunch as he walks the fields. When it rains, Bromfield gathers the season's first mushrooms, filling his hat with them. They are "fresh, young and damp, some of them no more than buttons, others opened up with the gills showing tender and flesh-pink." The grapes have all ripened—yellow leaves cling to their vines, and the jelly they make tastes a bit like wine. Visitors are still frequent. One night, dancers from the American Ballet Theatre drop by after a show in Cleveland. Bromfield has decked out the Big House in autumn finery: pumpkins, squash, bouquets of brome grass hay. After dinner, the dancers fall into easy chairs, drinking martinis or Scotch around a fire. One of the principals, Dimitri Romanoff, gives a brief performance, mostly as a joke, and Bromfield joins him with "a great deal of heel stamping and clicking of imaginary castanets," writes Ellen. In the morning, after a hearty breakfast and a quick trip up the maple leaf–strewn path to Mount Jeez, the ballerinas leave and the family gets back to work.

Winter is coming, and the farm must be made ready, so they work every day now, even on Sundays, when the neighbors rest. "I am sure the Lord understands," Bromfield writes. By the first frost in November, everything is more or less in its right place: the buttermilk, apples and potatoes in the cellar, the quick freeze and silos full. On Thanksgiving, they take a hard-earned break. There is turkey, peas, mashed potatoes, roast pumpkin, and mince pie. Afterward, they sink into the sofas in the living room, hands over full bellies. Bromfield slouches in an armchair, sipping his drink, asking for another. He sits cross-legged, stroking the head of the boxer that is usually in his lap.

It is always nice, after long trips to Hollywood or New York, to see the dogs again, and his homecomings have settled into a kind of routine. All the boxers—Prince, Folly, Smoky, Baby, and the matriarch, Regina—appear at the front door. They bark, which signals to Mary that he is home, and she appears at the door to greet him. He loves all the dogs, but Prince is the only one who sleeps in his bed and follows him around the farm. "People came to say that I did not own Prince: he owned me." One evening, upon returning from a fishing trip up in Michigan, he sees the usual rush of dogs, except Prince is not there and Mary does not come to the door. Instead it is Tom, a farmhand, walking to him from the kitchen. Tom doesn't even say hi, just begins taking his bags out of the car, before turning and blurting out what Bromfield already fears is true. Prince had been coughing badly. He was sent to the vet and died overnight. Mary did not come out of the house because she couldn't bear telling him.

They have friends over that afternoon, cocktails as usual. Everyone says they're sorry. "They couldn't know how I felt." When the company leaves, he turns to Mary. "I think I'll go have a look at the farm before dark." He takes the Willys jeep, army-issue, a new addition to Malabar, which the dogs like because it is open and they can easily catch all the smells on the breeze. Baby, Prince's brother, comes along. He's a "self-contained dog," less affectionate than Prince, which is why Bromfield is surprised, halfway up the lane, when Baby jumps on his lap and begins to lick his ear—"exactly as Prince had done so many times." He pushes the dog away. *Let me alone. I have to drive.* But the gesture strikes him as curious, and he wonders whether Baby's personality will change now that Prince is gone. It reminds him of what Emerson had written about compensation—all the mysterious ways nature finds to make up for a loss.

14

On the Hill

Some of the first serious congressional hearings about the danger that synthetic pesticides might pose to public health took place in a small sub-committee room on the third floor of the Cannon House Office Building, just south of the US Capitol. Rep. James J. Delaney, Democrat of New York, invited a series of witnesses—agronomists, chemists, doctors, PhDs whose statements were filled with complicated graphs and foot-notes. A director from the American Cancer Society came. So did lobby-ists for the chemical companies. Among the issues debated was whether the chemicals that had invaded American gardens and croplands since the end of World War II—especially dichloro-diphenyl-trichloro-ethane or DDT—were sickening citizens, polluting stream beds, and killing off wildlife. There had been a few isolated reports: birds falling from the sky; poisoned fish washing up on beaches; a rosarian with intestinal hemor-rhaging. The proceedings moved slowly, the debate clouded by the kind of pointy-headed crosstalk that is still common in Washington. Congress-men vented frustration about the available research, which seemed con-tradictory. Some scientists claimed that DDT was harmless to humans; others said it caused chronic illnesses. One study revealed that young turkeys died after ingesting alfalfa laced with DDT; another experiment reported that rats thrived after eating the same substance in meat. "I am not interested in rats," snapped a congressman from Nebraska. "I want to know what happens to babies who drink milk loaded with DDT."

In six short years since the American military made DDT available to consumers, its use had more than tripled across the globe—from 33 to 106 million pounds per year. Its developer had won a Nobel Prize in 1948. Many smart people thought that DDT was a miracle, as important to the cause of progress as antibiotics or atomic energy. It eradicated insect-borne diseases like malaria and destroyed pests like the Colorado potato beetle and cabbage worm that had long harassed farmers. Its value seemed obvious—and many experts lacked the data, or the courage, to question its cost. Bromfield had no such problems. On May 11 at 10:15 a.m., the committee's chief counsel called him to the stand. "Mr. Bromfield, will you come forward."

This was not his first time as a congressional witness. As the country's most famous farmer, he was frequently invited to Washington to weigh in on contentious matters of food policy. His presence never failed to make these matters more contentious. In 1949, he came to Congress representing dairy farmers, whose interests were being threatened by margarine companies that wanted to eliminate a ban on coloring their product yellow so it could better compete with butter. Margarine was made from the oils of row crops like corn, soybeans, and cottonseeds, which were grown in huge, soil-depleting monocultures—the very kind that Bromfield and his Friends of the Land had spent the past decade fighting against. Bromfield's case against margarine started strong—its packaging was "deceptive," its health claims "dubious"—but his testimony quickly devolved into a shouting match with senators after he suggested that American housewives were lazy, alleged that chemical companies were forming a "communist"-style cabal, and repeated his line that King Cotton had done more damage to the South than Sherman's March to the Sea. When a Chamber of Commerce group asked Bromfield to speak at another congressional hearing, they gave him a few pages of prepared remarks so he would stay on point. He began his testimony by flinging them on the table. "I'm not going to give you this statement because I disagree with it."

For the pesticides hearing, however, Bromfield stuck to the script, which he wrote himself. This was an issue to which he had devoted much time and study. Just weeks after DDT was released for civilian use in the fall of 1945—and seventeen years before Rachel Carson would publish her legendary indictment of it in *Silent Spring*—Bromfield came out strongly against the chemical. In a nationally syndicated op-ed, he said it was constructed "on a base of lethal poisons" and was being recklessly "boomed as the panacea and cure-all in man's war against insects." Bromfield urged extreme caution: DDT was "potentially dangerous" and "very little" was known of it. That the country would embrace it so heedlessly was typical of American "imbecility" when it came to ecological problems. Rather than studying their root causes, he said, we look only for the quick fix, the wonder drug. "The fundamental should be, not the frequently futile 'doctoring' of disease after its inception and development, but the prevention of the disease in the first place."

By 1951, Bromfield's case against DDT had hardened. He had read troubling academic articles and seen the consequences himself in the field, where birds and fish were "killed in almost wholesale fashion by consuming insects which have been sprayed by DDT." The science that the doctors and chemists squabbled over seemed to him crystal clear: "Put in the simplest terms," he told the congressmen, "what is poisonous to the organic structure of an insect must also be poisonous in sufficient immediate quantities or sufficient accumulated quantities to other life as well." Bromfield pointed to studies showing that DDT builds up in the fatty tissue of animals and humans, eventually making its way "into the liver and kidneys, with a highly destructive effect." He speculated that it might have "some bearing upon the increase in the incidence of such dreaded diseases as cancer." Despite all this, he said, DDT and other potentially harmful chemicals had been adopted by American farmers and gardeners with terrifying speed. Now there was "scarcely an article of food" available to consumers that had not been "treated with some poisonous spray."

As dangerous as these substances were in themselves, Bromfield also emphasized that their use upset the balance of nature, creating unforeseen problems—for which new and more powerful products were often needed. He used the ladybug as an example. "If you were to spray to death every lady bug in every garden, you would be eaten up by aphids," he told the committee. "You must remember that when you are spraying that you are not only destroying the pest, but you are destroying the birds, the fish and the beneficial insects as well . . . It is a short-cut which can become dangerous." Yet another problem was resistance. Take the case of spraying DDT to kill barn flies. "The first two years its action was miraculous, and all the flies disappeared, but in the third year you have more, and then by the fourth year they can drink DDT and it will have no effect upon them. That is a beautiful example of what happens under Darwin's law of the survival of the fittest, because flies produce so many generations in a single summer that resistance develops quickly." The result was an arms race between man and insect, where new poisons had to be constructed to overpower ever-more-resistant pests.

Bromfield called for a "thorough" government investigation not only to establish the definite danger of DDT and similar substances but also to address the reasons for their existence in the first place: the "greedy" and shortsighted agriculture that had robbed the soil of the organic materials plants use to naturally ward off disease and pests. Bromfield said he was "among a small but increasing group which has for some years been interested in the growing and production of food products, whether vegetable or animal, under conditions which lessen or make unnecessary the use of any poisons." He envisioned a future in which food companies would print a special "label" on their products to verify that their foods had not been touched by chemicals.

Bromfield's opinions on chemicals were greeted at the time with skepticism and hostility. A garden columnist told his readers to ignore him and not to worry about vegetables sprayed with DDT—"the gardener can escape harm" by just washing them off. A USDA entomologist said Bromfield was mistaken in his alarm. "There is simply no basis for such claims. If used as prescribed, DDT will not harm animals, or human beings." A professor in Ohio said his fellow academics "choke with rage" when they read of Bromfield's "*ex-cathedra* pronouncements." As for the ordinary farmers, the professor said, they are "more concerned with the ravages of the corn borer which last year cost Iowa farmers an estimated 177 million dollars than they are whether DDT, a hopeful ally in the relentless struggle against insect infestation, is a dangerous 'patent medicine' as Bromfield insists."

Time, of course, would prove Bromfield right. In 1972, two years after the Environmental Protection Agency was founded, a decade after Carson's book, and nearly thirty years since Bromfield's first warning— DDT was finally banned in the United States. But that did not keep the chemical industry from developing other, less obviously lethal "patent medicines," including the herbicide glyphosate, the main ingredient in Monsanto's popular weed killer Roundup—which despite recent efforts to ban the substance in Europe and Asia and mounting evidence linking it to cancer, Parkinson's, and other diseases—is still dumped on American croplands at a rate of 300 million pounds per year.

—·—

Bromfield worried not only about the danger of synthetic pesticides but also about a growing tendency among farmers to overuse chemical fertilizers, which he warned could turn "living soils into dead ones." Yet he was not exactly an "organic" farmer in the modern sense of that term. He looked at the "rabid feud" developing in the 1940s between the agriculturalists of the organic and industrial schools as ridiculous and counterproductive. While acknowledging that "the organic people have much more evidence on their side," Bromfield said that "neither wholly organic farming nor wholly chemical-fertilizer farming offers a whole answer." On the one hand, he believed that any attempt to farm without constantly replenishing organic materials to the soil was "agricultural suicide." As a rule, he did not use rotenone or DDT or "any other poison" on his fields. He followed the spirit, if not the letter, of Albert Howard's *An Agricultural Testament*, and used an adapted form of his composting methods at Malabar. On the other hand, Bromfield knew that it was economically unfeasible to restore the huge tracts of eroded lands in post-Depression America with organic fertilizers alone. "Very often lime and chemical fertilizer are necessary in the beginning in order to secure the growth of green manures without which any farming becomes not only hopeless but actually destructive." Those who denied this fact, the organic purists, he dismissed as "extremists" and "cranks."

The main proponent of the organic purist school in America was Jerome Irving Rodale, an entrepreneur, health guru, and Howard disciple who had begun an organic farm in Emmaus, Pennsylvania, in 1942 and soon after started publishing *Organic Farming and Gardening* magazine, dropping the word "farming" from its title shortly thereafter when it failed to pick up readers. Rodale was inspired in part by the success of Malabar, according to his son Robert. "He was quite envious, I think[,] of Louis Bromfield who made a tremendous reputation as a novelist" and then "suddenly overnight" became "a great expert on agriculture in the U.S." J. I. Rodale also spoke at the Delaney hearings on chemicals in food, although many congressmen ignored his testimony because of his "shaky credentials" and outlandish claims (among them, that eating organic prevents colds and headaches). Bromfield had earlier supported Rodale, saying his 1945 book *Pay Dirt* was "excellent and very important." But he was wary of the organic school's taste for pseudoscience and its vilification of *all* chemicals, even in small quantities. Eventually, he broke with Rodale, calling him a "cultist."

These ancient disputes between industrial and organic farmers heavily influenced the way Americans eat today. Rodale's magazine struggled until the 1960s, when it was co-opted by the hippie counterculture and became a wild success. By the 1970s, its circulation had shot up to nearly 1 million, and organic farms and food co-ops entered the vernacular. Rodale's son Robert kept fighting for organics after his father's death in 1971, and his advocacy work helped pave the way for the USDA to eventually recognize and certify organic food, launching a modern industry that, in 2018 alone, generated sales in excess of $50 billion.

But instead of reforming American agriculture at large, organics have mostly thrived in isolation from it—like an elite "magnet school" in a broken school system. Today our food is divided into two classes: a gigantic, cheap, industrial system that is over-reliant on chemical inputs; and a tiny, expensive organic system, haloed in romance and difficult-to-prove health benefits. Despite massive growth in the organic industry, less than 1 percent of America's arable land is now organically cultivated. The compromise Bromfield suggested back in the 1940s and '50s, whereby a small amount of chemicals would be used judiciously, organic material would be conserved at all costs, and the long-term health of the soil would remain paramount—seems in retrospect like a very pragmatic middle ground.

Bromfield's contribution to postwar agriculture did not come only in the form of commentary. By the late 1940s, he thought he had discovered the best modern way to farm hill country, and that was by turning Malabar into a "grass factory." Drake had been right: the dream of the general farm was a fantasy. "The Plan" had failed. "The old-fashioned farm, with diversified crops and day-long, back-bending hours is disappearing," Bromfield said in 1947. "The general farm can't compete in the Machine Age with big operators. The future belongs to the specialist." Bromfield understood at last that his yearning for a general farm was rooted in Jeffersonian nostalgia and romance for a kind of European peasant self-sufficiency—neither of which had any basis in modern, industrializing America. He had learned this the hard way. Even with infusions from his writing income, he could barely afford to keep Malabar in business.

The turkeys that he believed would live off the farm "in a half-wild state" could not figure out how to feed themselves. The hay harvest was too big to manage by hand but not big enough to support the cost of a hay baler. It was the same story with corn and a corn picker, grain and a combine. To stay in business, they either had to acquire more land, use chemicals to raise their production per acre, or rent machines at a premium. The two hundred apple trees presented another problem: to be competitive they would need specialized equipment, sprays, more labor—but all this made their apples cost more to produce than they were worth. Maybe they could raise apples at a profit with five thousand trees, but not two hundred. Same with eggs. It did not matter how many records their hens set, there were only fourteen hundred of them, putting Bromfield "neither *in* nor *out* of the egg business."

He reduced the flock to just enough to supply his farm with eggs and poultry and turned most of his orchards into pasture. Rather than raising hogs from birth, he bought weanlings. He stopped growing most row crops, including wheat and corn, which mystified his neighbors. His new plan was streamlined and specialized, its chief product grass in the form of pasture, hay, and silage. The livestock became machines that processed the yields of the field, turning grass into milk, meat, eggs, and butter. He focused on growing protein-rich grasses and deep-rooted legumes like alfalfa, Kentucky fescue, and orchard grass that tapped into minerals in the subsoil, and used a system of rough tillage to conserve moisture and organic matter.

The advantages of "grass farming," as Bromfield called it, were enormous. With careful rotations, he was able to increase the carrying capacity from about 40 head of cattle to over 200 and gross more per acre while reducing the costs of labor and gasoline. His cattle were healthier.

He no longer needed to buy feeds or protein supplements. The legumes and manure eliminated the need for nitrogen fertilizer. Best of all, each year, he was increasing his capital by investing in the fertility of his land, improving the soil's organic content rather than tearing it down with row crops. "All of this money which we do not spend simply shows up on the profit side of the ledger." Bromfield's philosophy was sound, but these "profits" he spoke of were only theoretical.

——⋅——

In his books, Bromfield made himself out to be a shrewd businessman, emphasizing his personal wealth and the prosperity of his farm. The reality was that he always had trouble making ends meet. In his letters, he liked to say that he had inherited only relatives; he had no savings to fall back on and often had to bail out family and friends when they were hard up. His expensive lifestyle had been offset in the early days of Malabar by movie contracts and book deals. But even then he lived beyond his means, constantly entertaining, traveling, and donating to charity and political campaigns. His hang-ups about money were a vestige of his childhood. His parents had raised him to be ashamed of their position on the bottom rung of the middle class, to pretend "to the world that they were better off than they really were." The "horror" of being poor never left Bromfield, but when he became successful he tried to shake it by spending his money as though it meant nothing to him. The result was "a terrible self-consciousness," he wrote in *The Farm*, "which made it impossible for him to bargain, so that he always came out worst in every deal he ever undertook, and could never ask for the payment of a loan he had made. Even to talk about money was painful for him."

Despite Bromfield's sermons about self-sufficiency, his farm—even as a streamlined "grass factory"—never even covered its costs. His tax return for 1953 was typical. That year, Malabar grossed a respectable $23,249, but its expenses—mostly in the form of labor and machinery—

were $37,890, resulting in a net loss of nearly $15,000. Some expenses could be chalked up to Bromfield's constant "experiments," his desire always to invest in new methods. In any event, Bromfield wanted the farm losses deducted from his overall income on his taxes. His lawyer said that would be tricky, citing the tax code: "A person cultivating or operating a farm for recreation or pleasure, the result of which is a continual loss from year to year, is not regarded as a farmer." Bromfield listed both professional activities on his taxes—writer and farmer—but as Malabar continually failed to show a profit, his lawyer fretted. "If the farm always runs at a loss the time will come when the government will take the position that the farm is not really a business enterprise."

The failure of the farm to turn a profit was complicated by the fact that Bromfield's other sources of income were disappearing. The major movie deals had died with Hawkins, and the agricultural books did not sell nearly as strongly as his earlier novels. Bromfield thought one way to grow Malabar's revenue base—and spread its message of conservation—was by expansion. In 1949, he and the Chamber of Commerce of Wichita Falls, Texas, began an offshoot of Malabar, a 400-acre cattle ranch meant to showcase the grass-farming ideas he was pioneering in Ohio. He liked thinking of himself as a cattle rancher and began to dress the part. Gone were the days when he farmed in jodhpurs and four-buckle overshoes. Now he wore cowboy boots, blue jeans, and sometimes even sported a wide-brimmed hat over his buzz-cut, graying head. He had gained more weight, and when he smiled revealed black gums and rotten teeth from a lifetime of chain smoking. It all gave him a rugged, sawed-off look, like the town drunk in an old western.

By 1953, Texas Malabar had collapsed and the Wichita Falls Chamber of Commerce sued Bromfield, claiming he had mismanaged the ranch. He countersued. One local farmer said the only things that grew there were sunflowers and weeds. Around this time, Bromfield also tried to launch a wholesale business, selling jars of jams and preserves from fruit grown in Malabar's organic gardens. He got his packaging

In the early 1950s, Bromfield began dressing like a cattle
rancher as he pioneered "grass farming" techniques at Malabar
and at its short-lived Texas offshoot in Wichita Falls.

from The J. M. Smucker Company and sold a big batch to the New
York department store B. Altman. A year later the "slow-moving" jars of
musky grape jelly and peach butter found their way into the clearance
bin, and plans for a new line of Malabar products (including a nutritious
whole-grain bread) were shelved.

The Malabar name may not have been worth much to retail shop-
pers, but Bromfield saw that his own name still had some value. He
began to endorse a range of products from two-ply thermal underwear
to plant food to beer: "Ballantine Ale," he wrote in one ad, "is a breeze-

tossed field of barley . . . a fusion of light and air and taste." The literary lapses, the loudmouth punditry, and the disorganized business schemes all took a toll on his reputation. When he criticized a Democratic candidate running for a senate seat in Ohio, the man knocked back: "I'll tell you about this refugee from the Paris night clubs. He became sour because two presidents have refused to name him secretary of agriculture. He's a lemon."

15

Breeding

MALABAR FARM, 1952

Farmers, like kings, need plans of succession to ensure that their realm passes smoothly from one generation to the next. Bromfield never had such a plan for Malabar. His two younger daughters, Hope and Ellen, both wanted to be part of Malabar's future, and both married men who intended to be farmers. But these men clashed with Bromfield. In Hope's case, the conflict was agricultural in nature, about how best to run a farm. Ellen's case was more complicated. For one thing, Bromfield disapproved of her husband's "background," which was a nicer way of saying that he disapproved of the fact that her husband was a Jew.

Before the war, just like Wharton, Fitzgerald, and many other writers, Bromfield created Jewish characters who look today more like anti-Semitic caricatures. In the first pages of *The Green Bay Tree* (1924), he referred to a greedy lawyer as a "fat perspiring Jew" emitting an "offensive smell." By the time he wrote *The Farm* (1933), however, he was describing Jewish characters with affection and a tinge of exoticism. Now Mansfield's Jewish families were the followers of a "colorful, sensual tradition" that stood out against the meager Midwestern townscape. "When one went to play in a Jewish house one found it filled to overflowing with warmth and kindliness. One never left without receiving a gift, sometimes a worn toy to which you had taken a fancy, sometimes a bouquet of flowers for your mother, sometimes a piece of *apfelstrudel*, still warm from the oven and rich-scented with spices."

Less than a decade had passed between these books, yet Bromfield had changed. He had made friends with Jewish writers like Gertrude Stein and Edna Ferber. Living in Europe, he had watched at close range the rise of Hitler and his imitators, whose anti-Semitism struck him as so virulent—and dangerous—that it made the casual variety of earlier years impossible. And he had fallen under the spell of a set of British conservative politicians, including his friend Victor Cazalet, who had begun to call for a Jewish state in Palestine.

By the outbreak of World War II, Bromfield was not merely sensitive to the plight of the Jews but among their most ardent Gentile defenders. Upon returning to America, he had allied himself with a shadowy, charismatic figure he knew as Peter Bergson. The Lithuanian-born Jew's real name was Hillel Kook. He was a secret agent, sent to the United States from Palestine by the Zionist paramilitary group, the Irgun. In 1943, Kook formed the Emergency Committee to Save the Jewish People of Europe, one of several controversial groups in which Bromfield served as national co-chairman. They raised money to buy provocative full-page advertisements in major newspapers like the *New York Times*, which in some cases had buried the news of the camps. The ads bore slogans written to shock and outrage Americans, most of whom were ignorant of the Holocaust as it was happening:

HELP Prevent 4,000,000 People from Becoming Ghosts

ACTION—NOT PITY—CAN SAVE MILLIONS NOW
Already 2,000,000 of the Jews in Germany and Occupied
Europe have been murdered. The evidence is in the files
of our own State department.

In addition to the PR campaign, the Bergsonites appealed directly to American power centers. In June of 1943, Bromfield sent an impassioned telegram to his friend Eleanor Roosevelt at the White House.

THE NAZIS ARE RAPIDLY CARRYING OUT THE THREAT TO ANNIHILATE THE JEWISH PEOPLE OF EUROPE AS REPRISAL AGAINST APPROACHING DOOM. THERE IS REAL DANGER THAT UNLESS IMMEDIATE AND VIGOROUS ACTION IS UNDERTAKEN TO HALT THIS UNPARALLELED BUTCHERY THE SLAUGHTER OF INNOCENT CIVILIANS WILL BE EXTENDED TO OTHER PEOPLE OF EUROPE AND THE VICTORIOUS INVADING ARMIES OF THE UNITED NATIONS WILL FIND EUROPE NOT A CONTINENT BUT A CEMETERY. IT IS SURPRISING HOW LITTLE THE WORLD FORCES OF DEMOCRACY HAVE BEEN MOBILIZED FOR THIS URGENT TASK.

Eleanor, possibly stewing over the food fight that Bromfield had picked with the FDR administration that same year, replied coldly: "I have your telegram and can not see what can be done until we win the war." This was the typical line—not only of those in the White House but also of many powerful, assimilated American Jews, including some Hollywood executives and newspaper publishers, who feared making the patriotic, all-American war effort—which enjoyed broad popular support—into a campaign to save European Jews, whom many Christian Americans distrusted. Historians have since challenged Eleanor Roosevelt's claim that nothing could have been done until Hitler was defeated. And indeed Bergson's campaign to stoke outrage—aided not only by Bromfield but also by the playwright Ben Hecht and many other prominent Americans—eventually pressured the FDR administration, in 1944, to create the War Refugee Board, which is credited with having saved the lives of tens of thousands of Jews and other European civilians.

Immediately after the war, Bromfield and the other Bergsonites shifted their priorities to the establishment of a Jewish state, by whatever means necessary. They raised money for the Palestine Resistance Committee and other Irgun front groups, which helped to transport European Jews in displaced persons camps to Palestine and to build up a Zionist army (which critics said funded terrorism against Arabs and the British). Bromfield even took a turn as the narrator of a splashy play to support the cause of Israeli statehood, *A Flag Is Born*, written by Hecht with music by Kurt Weill and starring a young Sidney Lumet as a Jewish freedom fighter.

As devoted as he was to the Jews, Bromfield acted like a heartless bigot toward the Arab residents of Palestine, whom he described in a nationally syndicated 1946 op-ed as a "handful of backward, miserable uncivilized people" standing in the way of a righteous cause. "The way should be made clear, by force if necessary, for the agriculture, the horticulture and the civilization which the Jews have already brought into that sterile, barren, barbaric part of the earth . . . They have made the barren land desolated by the Arabs flower and bear fruit like the Garden of Eden." The Arab Foreign Office in Washington, DC, was outraged by this "venomous" column: "If anyone had written about the Jewish people one-tenth of what Mr. Bromfield has written about the Arabs, there would have been an outcry against him throughout the country as an anti-Semite, a fascist and a racial hate monger."

A few years after Israeli statehood, at an Ohio synagogue, the new nation presented Bromfield with an honorary scroll for his "unbending efforts" on their behalf. When Menachem Begin, the former Irgun leader and future Israeli prime minister, visited America in the fall of 1951, he gave Bromfield an inscribed copy of his memoir, *The Revolt:* "To the great, famous Louis Bromfield, who didn't hesitate, for Freedom's cause, to stand by and help hunted rebels, maligned by almost everybody, appreciated by you, assisted by almost nobody, this book is dedicated with gratitude and admiration."

By then Bromfield smugly thought of himself as above all petty squabbles related to race and creed, and he offered a simple recipe to correct them. "The cure for all of these racial differences and ills is at base equal economic opportunity, education ([which includes] better diet and better soil upon which that diet is grown), better ethics and finally the annihilation of ideas about the superiority of one race over another," he wrote in *Malabar Farm*. "Some day all races will commonly intermarry and when that day comes many of the problems plaguing us will have disappeared."

Intermarriage had always appealed to Bromfield as a way of fighting anti-Semitism. At a symposium on the eve of World War II, he said it was among the many things Jews could do to assimilate more fully into American culture. "I should ask the Jew to be less clannish, less orthodox. I should ask him not to huddle together with his fellows in certain quarters of Town. I should ask him not to teach his children that Jews are God's chosen people. I should ask him even to marry with Gentiles."

So long as the Gentile in question, Bromfield forgot to add, was not his own daughter.

—·—

Carson Zachary Geld was born in 1929 and, from a very young age, nursed dreams of becoming a farmer. This was not a typical path for a Jewish boy from Flatbush, Brooklyn, but Carson's father, Harry, was a fruit buyer who had taken his son on trips to orchards and farms upstate that made a lasting impression. When Carson was twelve, Harry died of a stroke. To help his mother pay the bills, Carson got a job stocking shelves at the neighborhood A&P and worked for tips as a delivery boy on Church Avenue. He was too young to be drafted when the war came, but he volunteered for a farm labor program and was sent to Cooperstown, New York, where he was assigned to work as a field hand for the Clark family, heirs to the Singer sewing-machine fortune. They ran an old-fashioned farm, with plows pulled by Percheron horses and grain harvested by scythe. Carson loved it. After the war, he went to junior college and eventually to Cornell, where he studied agriculture. To make tuition, he worked odd jobs, including one as the coat-check attendant in the student union, where in the fall of 1949 he met a seventeen-year-old honey-blond freshman named Ellen Bromfield. That summer, Ellen arranged for her new college sweetheart to get some practical farming experience at Malabar.

Carson was an energetic, opinionated boy, five-foot-nine, with bright hazel eyes and a wry smile. Bromfield disliked him almost immediately. He was too confident, too calculating, too clumsy. One summer evening, backing Bromfield's new station wagon out of the garage, Carson failed to notice that the passenger-side door was open. "With a grinding of steel and crumbling of mortar," Ellen recalled, "he managed in one efficient action to remove both the car door and a post whose primary function was to support the room above it." On another occasion, Bromfield was mowing the lower pastures when he looked up to see his future son-in-law drive his Willys jeep into the back of a stationary wagon loaded with hay. "Jesus Christ!" Bromfield said. "It's a psychopathic urge to destroy." Ellen said her father's distrust of Carson grew and "fed on itself like a disease." He would approach Carson by "circling him cautiously the way one does the irresponsible hind legs of a horse." Bromfield thought that this city boy could never be made into a real farmer, that he was only interested in agriculture because he believed there was "some easy trick to it."

And there was something in the boy's naked ambition, in the way he marketed himself, that Bromfield found distasteful. These reservations were not based on prejudice, he insisted in a long letter to Ellen. "Probably no *goy* in the world knows the Jewish people better than I do or has worked harder for them or has so many real and lasting friendships among them," he wrote. If anything, he had "a predilection for Jewish people." But this fact did not make him "blind to the differences of background and upbringing and tradition."

I do not know how Carson feels toward me and that has been one of the flies in the ointment since the very beginning . . . the question of where sincerity begins and calculation ends. I have seen him go to work on people visiting here for some calculated reason and the spectacle was not pretty and very harmful to Carson's own interest. It is here that one of the great differences in background come in . . . that such methods are conventional and perhaps even necessary in the hard competitive world in which Carson was brought up (I am full of sympathy for him in this respect) but they are very damaging in the larger world . . . and I wish I could persuade him of that.

By the fall of 1950, Bromfield's fatherly attentions had shifted from Ellen to his stylish middle daughter, Hope, who had moved to New York City and fallen in love with Robert T. Stevens Jr., whom Ellen described as a "tall, gentle, strongly determined New Englander." His father was the chairman of the giant textile company J. P. Stevens and would go on to serve as Secretary of the Army under President Eisenhower. Bob, as the young scion was known, had been educated at Phillips Andover and Yale but then went to Rutgers to do graduate work in agriculture. Now he was looking to strike out on his own and raise cattle. Bromfield heartily approved of their engagement—he called it "the marriage of two great worlds." After an avalanche of wedding gifts arrived at the Big House, Bromfield grabbed the face of one of his boxer dogs who had been playing in the wrapping paper. "It's a hell of a thing, old boy," he said with an exaggerated sigh. "But that's what comes of being famous and knowing so many people."

He planned the wedding at Malabar himself, picking the food, the wine, making all the flower arrangements, which included garlands of yew and hemlock and wreaths of evergreens. Hope wore a white lace gown with a fitted bodice and full skirt, a pearl cap holding her tulle veil in place. The affair was touched "with the kind of elegance, wealth and grandeur of which our father had always unadmittedly dreamed," Ellen said. "He had never quite gotten over his boyhood wonder at great and fashionable people . . . it excited him to be ranked among them."

A few days after Hope's wedding on December 23, Bromfield learned that Ellen was pregnant with Carson's child. Despite his reservations, he and Mary moved quickly to arrange another wedding, this time in New York City. On January 6, 1951, Ellen and Carson exchanged vows at the Little Church Around the Corner on Twenty-Ninth Street, with an Episcopalian minister performing the rites. A *New York Times* photograph shows them: Carson smiling broadly, Ellen with an impish grin, wearing a high-waisted dress that concealed her belly. The family hosted a breakfast reception before the ceremony at a Fifth Avenue hotel and a party afterward at a socialite friend's place on Park Avenue. It was not as grand as Hope's wedding, but it was not city hall, either, and a few days later Carson wrote Bromfield to thank him. "It would have been very easy for you to have just sent us down to New York and had us married by a Justice of the Peace and let it go at that, but you chose to do it as if nothing had happened and in doing so made the occasion a happy one for everyone concerned. Mr. B, I don't want to sound flowery but it was still wonderful of you and we will never forget it."

—†—

By 1952, Ellen and Carson had left Cornell. She and their infant son, Stevie, moved into the Big House at Malabar. Carson, now in the army, visited on furloughs. Meanwhile, Bob Stevens and the now-pregnant Hope bought an adjacent 267-acre farm, with plans to build a modern dairy and raise 180 head of cattle. The new pastures expanded the limits of Malabar, but Bromfield made clear he was taking Hope's husband on not as a partner but as a student. Stevens shyly and respectfully listened to his lectures, but inwardly he rebelled against his father-in-law's arrogance and his contemptuous attitude toward all those who questioned him. Bromfield overruled Stevens's plan to build a cattle trail and his decision to seed a hayfield with bluegrass, which he had earlier dismissed as a "noxious weed."

When Carson was discharged from the army, he returned to Malabar overflowing with new ideas. He and Ellen took over the farm's jam-making operations. They wanted to help out, to change things, to make Malabar something it never was: profitable. Bromfield fought them every step of the way. The truth is, Ellen wrote, "He didn't believe in us." He also didn't want to admit how much he needed their help. They had seen through his act. They knew that he was getting older, crankier, that the Hollywood royalties that had floated the farm for so long had dried up. They also knew that, despite his love of the hard work of plowing and milking, his genius for analyzing big-picture agricultural problems, he was hopeless when it came to the nitty-gritty business of farming: When to sell the hogs, how much to take for a used tractor. "Typical of his business transactions," said Ellen, "was the deal he made for the sale of an old silo by which he ended up paying the purchaser twice the selling price to haul it away."

Why could he not accept their help? He had achieved what every farmer hopes for. His daughters had married farmers and wanted to farm themselves. But just when this new generation seemed to make the continuation of Malabar a sure thing, Bromfield revolted, and now "a sense of doubt" hung over the future of the farm. Ellen thought that Malabar "was too precious to him, too much of an expression of himself, to risk its sharing." So she and Carson began secretly to look for their own land somewhere else in Pleasant Valley, but they could not raise the money. Bromfield and the children had terrible fights, and no one was left to play peacemaker. George was dead, Mary was too meek. Factions formed in the Big House. Ellen resented how close Bromfield had grown to the English gardener, David Rimmer, and his mother, the dutiful secretary Annie, to whom he dedicated his latest novel, the ungainly *Mr. Smith* (1951). Bromfield, meanwhile, felt threatened by Ellen's endless stream of ideas for the farm. "About El," Mary wrote to him, "I honestly think she doesn't want to push you out of Malabar."

A temporary solution was found. Ellen and Carson would move out of the Big House and into an outlying cottage, granting them a measure of autonomy. But they still wanted to be dealt into the adventure of Malabar. Carson tried, unsuccessfully, to explain that his intentions were benign. He did not see the farm "as an inheritance that might be mine some day." He just wanted a role to play. "I want to see some of my ideas in action and selfishly I want to take credit for some of the good ones."

By the early 1950s, Bromfield was spending long stretches of time traveling: South America, Europe, Jamaica, the western United States. The time away from the farm only increased his paranoia, his feeling that he was losing control. Sometimes he would send telegrams, demanding updates about morale. Unhappy to be away, he was also unable or unwilling to cut down on his workload, which now included writing farm books and a weekly newspaper column, hosting his own national radio show, and giving around 150 speeches on conservation a year. The work had driven all the fun out of him. His old friend Edna Ferber, who in the 1920s had marveled at his capacity for enjoying life, could find no trace of it when they met for lunch in New York. "I have thought of you often and often. For some reason, you seemed farther away at lunch that day at '21' than when you are in Ohio and I am in New York."

Mary could also see that something was wrong with her husband. She worried over his drinking, the stress of the travel, and her letters to him grew more frantic and pleading. "Are you taking care of yourself? *I don't trust you at all*," she wrote. It wasn't other women that concerned her; that kind of thing she had learned to live with. "I don't care how much fun you have or how naughty you are or *anything* else and I mean it—And you can divorce me and *remarry* if it's any help, but I don't want you to have a break up of any kind whatsoever or die. . . . Don't say 'I haven't time for a breakdown'—the bad, serious breakdowns catch up with you . . . Now I've lectured you and I mean every word of it—I happen to love you very much, and so do all of us as you may have gathered by now and we don't give a damn how poor ~~you~~ we are as long as you're well and happy."

Mary Bromfield in her bed decorated with the
titles of Bromfield's best-selling novels.

Mary had cause to worry about her husband, but by 1952 her own health
proved a more pressing issue. She was now sixty and had a rheumatic
heart condition that had grown worse with age, keeping her cooped up
inside the Big House and unable to participate in the strenuous life of
the farm. That illness brought out her reclusive nature; she retreated into
her room, which became a place of "peace touched with sadness." Everyone avoided her except Anne, the troubled eldest daughter, who spent
her days sitting by her mother's side "immersed in Greek mythology or
scribbling a poem or just staring at some inanimate object." If Mary ever

ventured beyond her room, she would roam aimlessly through the house, Ellen said, hoping but "not knowing how to become a part of our endless activity." When Bromfield inscribed a copy of one of his books to her, he wrote: "To Mary (still Alice in Wonderland)." As much as she loved Malabar, he meant, she was lost in it.

It was Anne who found her on the morning of September 14, 1952, in her bedroom next to Bromfield's office. She was sitting up in her bed, "as if death had come to her while reading." The headboard on the bed—inscribed with the title of Bromfield's novel *A Good Woman*—now served as a kind of epitaph. That was not exactly the one Mary had in mind. "When Louie and I pass on," she had told an interviewer four years earlier, "we're going to have twin stones. On his headpiece, which will be a tremendously imposing affair, will be listed all of his fine achievements. I'll lie at his feet, marked by a very small stone on which there will be this legend: 'Incidentally, This Is My Wife.'"

Bromfield had a different idea for a memorial. Shortly after her death, he sketched the plans to build an elaborate roadside vegetable stand by the large farm pond. Few things in his life would make him prouder. A wide pavilion built out of local sandstone, it displayed the bounty of Malabar's gardens in a series of wide troughs cooled by a cascade of running water that Bromfield diverted from a nearby spring. He sold Bibb lettuce, okra, beets, carrots, rhubarb, old-fashioned melons, baskets of premixed salads ("selling this way, we get about three times the price"), tiny red and yellow tomatoes, pearl onions, and watercress that grew in a green mat in the pond across the road. Bromfield took pride in charging more for his organic produce, attracting what he called "the class trade." "There is no point in the country roadside market attempting to compete with the chain stores on a basis of price," he said, anticipating a recipe upmarket grocers would soon perfect. "The chain store customer is quite frankly not the kind of customer we seek, but rather those who want freshness and high quality and are willing to pay for it."

Bromfield designed his farm stand to be "the roadside market to end all roadside markets," with native stone troughs through which spring water flowed to keep the vegetables fresh and crisp.

Bromfield put pots of petunias and geraniums around the stand. He trained trumpet vines over the roof and porcelain berries on the walls. And on one of the pillars he placed a bronze plaque that read: "To the memory of Mary Appleton Wood, who also loved this valley and found here peace, happiness and abundance." Perhaps this was not just wishful thinking. "I never saw such a beautiful light as this evening," Mary wrote to him in one of her last letters. "The hills and fields are even greener than when you left and the lakes are absolutely lovely. Sometimes I don't think this place is true."

Mary's death did not soften Bromfield or loosen his grip on Malabar. Soon after the funeral, Hope and Ellen both realized that their dream of sharing the farm with their father was hopeless. "More and more often," Ellen wrote, "as I sat alone at dusk, looking over the land I knew and loved perhaps more than any land before or after, I was struck with the sensation that I was saying goodbye. It was obvious that the boss, as long as he could walk, talk, think and act in his noisy expansive way, could never share his valley. Whatever the price of remaining alone and independent, he would gladly pay it."

She and Carson decided they needed a fresh start, a new life, and a new farm. They left on a boat from New Orleans in February 1953, heading for Brazil. They were being taken on by one of Bromfield's disciples, Manöel Carlos Arhaña, who had partnered with a team of conservation-minded businessmen to build a farm 50 miles northwest of São Paulo, to be named Malabar-do-Brasil. They had saved enough money for the passage by selling Malabar-branded jams and jellies. Bromfield was skeptical of their success. "When I think of you with your lack of experience and education, Christ, my blood runs cold." But he did not try to stop them. About a month later, Bob and Hope sold their land and bought themselves a new place in Leesburg, Virginia, taking Nanny White with them and leaving Bromfield alone with only Anne in the Big House. The brooding tyrant now watched over his kingdom from an empty castle.

16

Unto the Ground

Ophiostoma ulmi is a microscopic, caramel-colored fungus that can be fatal to elm trees. It most likely originated in Asia and is carried on the bodies of tiny bark beetles that latch onto the tips of the elm's branches and gnaw their way into its sap channels, scattering spores. The fungus multiplies with the beetles, invading the limbs and then the trunk of the tree, choking off the movement of water and nutrients. The disease arrived in Europe at the end of World War I, attacking French elms so dramatically that infected trees were confused with those that had been destroyed by artillery fire. It was the Dutch, whose canals are lined with elms, who first traced the problem to the beetle and then to the fungus, earning for their trouble an unfair association with the plague, which is still known today as Dutch elm disease.

A shipment of European lumber spread DED to the United States during the early years of the Depression. Despite federal quarantines and marauding trucks spraying fungicides, the disease advanced from port cities in the northeast to Canada and eventually across the continent, becoming one of the more devastating pandemics to strike American woodlands, killing by some estimates 100 million trees and turning Elm

Streets throughout the land into stumpy memorial grounds. Among the many victims were the glorious old elms on the sprawling central New Jersey estate of the tobacco heiress Doris Duke.

The blight was only one of many problems on the 2,700-acre property she had inherited from her father, which included formal gardens, nine lakes, heated stables, and an elaborate working farm with Jersey cattle, sheep, and pigs. Overwhelmed, she sought solutions in Bromfield's books, and then she sought out Bromfield himself.

Duke was six-foot-one, an inch shorter than Bromfield and sixteen years younger, with long legs, fine blond hair, a broad forehead, and a strong chin. She met him in the early 1930s, when she was already a tabloid curiosity, known as the "richest girl in the world." The following two decades were unkind to her: two marriages ended in divorce, and her only biological child died a day after she was born. When she and Bromfield were becoming close, in the early 1950s, he told her that they had each seen enough of life to dispense with pretense. "It is very difficult to think of any way of addressing you that does not seem either silly or false," he wrote in one of their first intimate letters. "So I will just call you Doris which is a nice shepherdess's name out of Greek poetry."

Bromfield's relationship with the reclusive billionaire is somewhat shrouded by the cloud of gossip that surrounds Duke, whose love affairs, eccentric companions, and rarefied tastes have always made her an object of public speculation. Hope Bromfield said that a romance was "possible" but that her father never spoke about it. "Daddy may have felt he didn't want us to know," she said. "Actually, he was lonely and I would have been glad." In 1996, Duke's nephew and godson, Pony, wrote a pulpy, unsourced biography filled with scurrilous rumors about her affair with the man from Malabar Farm: "She used to tell people that it was atop Mount Jeez where she and Louis first had sex and it was named after her echoing cries of 'Oh Jesus!' as she reached climax."

Duke's professional biographers, Stephanie Mansfield and Sallie Bingham, are much more circumspect about the relationship but they agree that Bromfield and Duke loved each other, even if the nature and extent of their bond remains a mystery. They spent time together in New York and made several trips to each other's farms. In the fall of 1955, Bromfield visited Hillsborough with his gardener David Rimmer and his friend Ralph Cobey. "We met everybody," said Cobey. "Cary Grant was there. She attracted a lot of people like that. So did Bromfield." They talked about conservation, what could be done with Duke Farms, whether the Friends of the Land should help manage the property and possibly use it as a test site and research station. Rimmer eventually would be hired by Duke as a park manager. But Bromfield's personal involvement with her farm was cut short, like so much else, by illness.

Bromfield always bragged about his "perfect health" and told Duke that he had "the heart and the constitution of an ox." But as early as 1950 a newspaper reporter noted that he was coughing vigorously. "Too many cigarettes," he said. In the winter of 1954, his rotten teeth had been replaced by dentures. A few weeks later he fell ill—a fever of 105, flulike symptoms. The doctors diagnosed pneumonia. He received a large dose of penicillin and spent several days recuperating in the hospital. He left looking haggard, his paunchy, sun-ripened body now emaciated. He claimed his illness had given him an attractive "hollowed-eyed adolescent look." While he was in the hospital, the doctors discovered other health problems: mild emphysema, a hiatal hernia. "I am not a bit surprised. You haven't stopped running for a long time," wrote Ellen. "I hope now that you will do as the doctors say, take it easy, less drinking and far less smoking and far less rushing about . . . you're as mortal as the rest of us."

Over the next year, his symptoms worsened. In January of 1956, he went to New York, where he could be seen by the eminent physicians at Doctors Hospital. He told reporters, lying through his fake teeth, that it was only a "routine" checkup. "The results show I'm in fine shape . . . couldn't be better." Actually, the doctors were pinpointing what was killing him: multiple myeloma, a type of bone-marrow cancer. Bromfield may not have known his case was terminal, and he used it as an excuse for further self-promotion, telling reporters he was suffering from a "trop-ical infection" contracted on a recent trip to Malabar-do-Brasil. "The whole medical profession of NYC," he told Duke, had taken an "intense" interest in his condition and were treating him like a "scientific guinea pig." "I'll tell you all about it the first moment we can be alone." He pro-posed a tête-à-tête at a quiet bistro in New York.

> My suggestion is this—I have to have a 9 p.m. injection of a whole new therapy. Once that is over there is no reason why I cannot join you for dinner at one of the nice quiet places (I am thinking of a small good place the Provencal), and perhaps, if it meets your approval, go back to the flat and talk and drink alone. We are both shy people and both of us have been hurt again and again. I think we need no longer be shy . . . And so my Greek shepherdess and good friend, let me know if this suits you . . . I am writing this in the middle of the night because I had to in all *sincerity* and with much love.

Bromfield passed this note to Duke via a certain "Dr. Taccata," because it was "the safest method of communication." He was concerned about the rumors already percolating about their romance. "There's noth-ing to it," he told a reporter. "We are only good and very old friends." He was discharged from the hospital on January 21 and went to Duke's palace in New Jersey, where he rested in "complete luxury." She put a chauffeur at his disposal, fed him "wonderful food," and personally injected him with his medicine three times a day. "Miss Duke has had hospital training," he said in a letter to his secretary. "My doctor tested her out and found her competent." He shuttled back and forth from Hillsborough to New York, receiving outpatient treatments and blood transfusions that made him, at least temporarily, feel like a "new person."

But these doses of vitality were short-lived. By the time he returned to Malabar, in February of 1956, Bromfield looked ghostly. A friend, a local Pontiac dealer, C. J. Solomon, had arranged to give him a new car as a late birthday gift. He was photographed receiving it and a reporter again asked him about rumors of a romance with Duke. This time, he admitted it. "We are very fond of each other. We may get married, but it won't be right away." Solomon, who had become close to Bromfield, had a few weeks earlier visited him at Duke Farms. Now Solomon took the bold step of writing to Duke directly, apparently without Bromfield's knowledge, to tell her how much she meant to his ailing friend. "If I am out of order or appear to you in being too personal, I apologize, because the following information is given with deep sincerity." Solomon said that Bromfield could not stop talking about Duke, about her "sincere love of nature"—but "confidentially," he added, he was not only interested "in your love of agriculture, but you." His illness had "weakened" him but also "opened his true heart." The other women over the years, the "continuous train of widows and divorcees that travel to his farm has never touched that part of him as you have . . . Believe me, Doris, he is as rattled as a teenager for some reason only he and you would know. For some reason you have given him the personal desire to live a long time."

Solomon seemed to be urging Duke and Bromfield to get married, but in his own letter to Duke from Malabar, Bromfield did not mention when, or whether, they would see each other again. He only thanked her for her generosity. "I can never be grateful enough to you for taking me in. I think it's the first time in my life I have ever had someone really take [care] of me like that—or perhaps permitted anyone to do so."

So much work awaited Bromfield when he got back to the farm. He was in debt, his cash reserves down to practically nothing. He had piles of farm letters, taxes, and bills to get through. Ellen was writing from Brazil, concerned about his health, imploring him to come down for a rest. "The yellow acacia tree is blooming in front of the house, which is usually a sign that you are already here. We miss you."

Bromfield was still writing his weekly op-ed column and even trying to venture into new art forms. Lincoln Kirstein, of the New York City Ballet Company, had asked him to write the libretto for an ill-fated George Balanchine ballet about Johnny Appleseed, one of Bromfield's *teched* heroes. "We are collaborating bar by bar, dance by dance. It looks better every day," he told Duke in his final letter to her, written in the middle of the night while he lay sick in bed listening to a "magnificent" recording of *Tosca* as the boxers snored. "I decided the other night that really there wasn't much difference between a ballet, a beautiful farm and music . . . They really all express the same thing."

He was too sick to work more than half days, but he needed money, so he reluctantly signed a contract to cut down some timber at Malabar, following the pattern of the cash-strapped farmers he long criticized.

Malabar Farm, circa 1953.

His health continued to deteriorate. A trickle of friends and relatives stopped by with food. His cousin Catherine McGinty came one day to find the Big House empty except for Bromfield, who was lying prostrate on the floor—"whether drunk or ill could not be determined." A doctor sent him to the university hospital in Columbus. He was admitted on February 28. He did not have enough money to pay the hospital bills, so he wired Harper for an advance. The doctors, suspecting another case of pneumonia, told the press that his condition was "satisfactory." Yet a week later, Hope was summoned to her father's bedside from her farm in Virginia. She told reporters that Bromfield was now "gravely ill," suffering from jaundice and growing weaker. His kidneys and liver were failing. Anne and Hope were by his side when he slipped into a coma on March 17; he died a day later, at 8:32 p.m. Hope sent a cable to Ellen, who had given birth to a second child in Brazil. "DO NOT COME. DADDY KNOWS YOU ARE THINKING OF HIM."

—·—

The news of Bromfield's death was carried by every paper in the land. The *New York Times* ran his obituary on the front page, below the fold. "A later generation," it wrote, "may decide whether Mr. Bromfield made a deeper impression with his novels or his experimental farming and farm theories. Either of the intertwined careers would have been enough to insure fame to the tall, loose-limbed, restless Ohioan." The *Chicago Tribune* wrote, "Few men of his time did more to improve agricultural practices, and no one exceeded his devotion to the earth from which all things grow." A friend, the columnist Inez Robb, remembered his generosity: "He gave of himself to everyone in need, whether the need was financial or for the comfort and strength that goes with a steady and understanding friendship . . . And now Louie has gone back to Malabar and the earth he loved so much, and those of us who loved him are infinitely poorer." These eulogies could not surpass the eloquence of a headline from a small newspaper in Dover, Ohio, which simply read: A GREAT FARMER DIES.

The funeral was held on March 22 in Mansfield, at the First Congregational Church, which was filled to capacity. The guests were prominent but hardly A-listers; neither Duke nor Bogart made the trip. A few old Senlis friends showed up, a sampling of New York literati and aging screen stars. Max Drake came; so did the state governor Frank Lausche, and Bromfield's editor, Cass Canfield. An organist played a Mendelssohn andante and some of his favorite poems were read: "The World Is Too Much with Us" and "I Wandered Lonely as a Cloud," both by William Wordsworth, as well as Psalm 23, an obvious choice for a committed pastoralist: "The lord is my shepherd; I shall not want/He maketh me to lie down in green pastures: he leadeth me beside the still waters."

In his will, Bromfield gave what little cash he had to his cook and household employees. The rest of his estate—the property (valued at $140,000) and the rights to his books—was left in trust to his three children. He had asked to be cremated. A few weeks later, Hope scattered his ashes in the small cemetery at Malabar beside Mary's grave and those of his parents, who had both died in the 1940s. It was the same graveyard used by generations of farmers in Pleasant Valley, its old tombstones now overgrown with moss and wild roses. A newspaper report noted that the small service was conducted "against a steady zooming noise in the background created by hundreds of bees left homeless when a threshing machine upset a number of bee hives near the burial ground."

It took several days for the telegram to reach Ellen on her farm in the countryside north of São Paulo. Inside Malabar-do-Brasil, she took a seat at her typewriter and tapped out a remembrance, published April 1 in the *Mansfield News Journal*. The piece has a staccato rhythm, full of ellipses—one imagines her typing it quickly, with tears streaming down her cheeks. She pictures the ancient house in Senlis, the garden on the edge of a river, her father bending over a bed of carnations. She remembers riding on his shoulders down the middle of Switzer's Creek, the taste of the food he cooked on Sunday nights—morels sautéed in butter, onion soup. She sees him in a station wagon loaded with "arrogant and comical" boxer dogs and then on a hay mower racing across a field of alfalfa before the summer rain pours down. She ends the piece abruptly, with just this line: "Such a being does not simply cease to exist."

Epilogue

The White Room

ITATIBA, SÃO PAULO STATE, BRAZIL, 1954

In the large sense, every one of us is a farmer,
for the keeping of the earth is given to the human race.
—LIBERTY HYDE BAILEY

Bromfield was wrong about Ellen and Carson. They struggled to create Malabar-do-Brasil—against floods, drought, plant disease, and killing frosts—but in less than two years the new farm began to thrive. It had grown out of a ruined plantation, or fazenda, in the valley of the Atibaia River, 50 miles north of São Paulo. This was hill country, like Pleasant Valley, and its rolling farms had once been rich and fertile. But a history of single-crop agriculture—in this case coffee—had robbed the soil of its vitality. When Carson and Ellen arrived, early in 1953, the fields were a mess of brushwood and St. John's wort, the hills were gullied, the tung trees ravaged by ants. Carson spent the first several months just trying to clear the weeds. They had little experience to draw on, even less money, but, Ellen said, "We had tremendous pride and love for that run-down *fazenda.*" They lived in a crumbling, clay-walled, tile-roofed house by the river that was shaded by two enormous kapok trees and covered in flowering vines.

Bromfield had only a minority stake in this 1,700-acre farm. His Brazilian partners had installed Ellen and Carson as managers "virtually against [his] wishes." When he was their age, he would have seized such an opportunity for himself, but experience had turned him from "an adventurer into a conservative" and now he feared the job was far more than two novice farmers with a baby could handle. Ellen's letters suggested otherwise. Within a few months, she and Carson had renovated the farmhouse. They picked up the language, not classical Portuguese but the local *caboclo* slang of the village. For help, they hired Brazilians of all races and recently arrived immigrants from Italy and Japan. Carson spent his days herding half-wild cattle among termite hills and dreaming up business plans. Ellen began every morning by making her *cafezinho* and then sitting at her typewriter before she went out to dig in the gardens. She soon became a wispy, Brazilianized version of her father: writing novels, spreading manure, filing weekly columns for the *O. Estado de S. Paulo,* the largest newspaper in Brazil. On weekends, she hosted artists, diplomats, and cattle ranchers for lunch, continuing the family tradition begun in Senlis.

When Bromfield arrived for his third—and final—trip to the farm in the winter of 1955, Malabar-do-Brasil looked "unrecognizable" from the scruffy old coffee plantation he found only two years earlier. The fields were now lush, fertile enough to support four harvests a year. They grew corn, soybeans, wheat, rye, rice, peanuts, potatoes, garlic, avocados, watermelon, mangoes, and a wealth of fragrant tropical fruits like jabuticaba and chuchu (or chayote). Bromfield loved the polyglot atmosphere of the fazenda, how the Japanese gardener presented his harvests in artful arrangements and the Italian field hands from the Po valley sang strains of Puccini as they dug in the fields. What most delighted him was seeing his grandson, Stevie, completely at home in this faraway place. "He is already indeed what his grandfather would like him to be—a citizen not of one country but of the world. Nothing is more comical than the sight of this four-year-old falling flat on his face, picking himself up and saying philosophically, '*Pusha la vida!*' "—a mix of baby talk and Portuguese that Bromfield took to mean: "What a life!"

He was now on Ellen's turf, and she and Carson proudly walked him over their fields, showing him all they had accomplished by themselves but also, Ellen said, showing "what an excellent teacher he had been." He made his usual forceful suggestions, explained what they were doing wrong: They should mulch the orchards instead of cultivating them, they should get hardy chickens like Rhode Island reds to better control insects. But he was impressed, even a bit deferential. Ellen felt the "terrible shyness and suspicion" that had long separated father and daughter melt away. "Now we saw one another simply as friends."

—·—

He was already sick then; he might have even known that he didn't have much time left. Ellen showed him to his room at the back of the rambling old farmhouse. It was a large, simple room but something about it made him feel immediately at peace. The clay walls were whitewashed. The wood furniture—a wardrobe, a small bed, a worktable and chair—was also painted white. The ceiling sloped down toward the veranda, and there was a big window through which he could see trees full of canaries and tropical fruits and hear tractors, bawling cows, healthy children at play. He called it "the White Room," and here he wrote his final book, *From My Experience*. It is a memoir about agriculture, part of the series of hurriedly written volumes that began with *Pleasant Valley*—and that are still treated as instruction manuals and prayer books by organic farmers around the world. The chapters are full of discussions on growing tomatoes, irrigation methods, the importance of trace elements in soil. But at the end—following a disquisition on the ideal moisture content of a hay bale—Bromfield added a coda, which he titled "The White Room" and subtitled: "A Somewhat Serious and Personal Chapter."

He began it by taking stock. He still did not understand what strange force had propelled an Ohio farm boy with a "Protestant-Puritan, Anglo-Saxon middle-class American background" to this white room in Brazil "by way of France and India and the whole world." Yet he thought that, if his life had a theme, it had something to do with escape, with the desire to eliminate "nonessentials and creeds and doctrines and Protestant brooding and materialism" in favor of what he now called "direct living." Twice he had tried to make a great escape. He fled America to build a life in France devoted to beauty and pleasure, to fine furniture and flowers and fancy friends. And then he fled Europe and went home, building not just a new house but a new landscape and, "without quite knowing it, a whole new career and a whole new life." That life pushed him deep into agriculture, conservation, politics.

But he could never entirely lose himself in these missions, however urgent they felt. All along he was dogged by "gloomy doubts," driven by "a force" he did not understand. His material possessions had "come to bore [him] and to constitute a burden." He sought enlightenment, some belief system built around the affinity he felt toward nature, that sense of being *teched*. He never believed the Lord was his shepherd, that there was some God-father mulling over the "puny ambitions" of humankind. But at certain moments he did feel part of some "gigantic scheme of creation," and even had intimations of a kind of immortality—one "that had nothing to do with plaster saints and tawdry heavens" but with something "more profound" and "richer in dignity." For a time he tried to practice a version of animism, worshipping "God" in the form of trees and rocks and springs and small animals of the field. But the cynic in him felt there was something hopelessly detached in this philosophy, which failed to deal with the material facts of the world as it was.

Among the many books he brought with him to Brazil was a memoir, Albert Schweitzer's *Out of My Life and Thought*. Originally written in the 1930s, the book became an international bestseller after its author won the Nobel Peace Prize in 1952. Schweitzer is not very well known today but at midcentury he was widely regarded as an intellectual saint, a mix of Mother Teresa and Søren Kierkegaard. His life story contained even more transformations than Bromfield's. Born in 1875, Schweitzer grew up in an Alsatian village, the son of a Lutheran minister. A musical prodigy and boy genius, by age thirty he had mastered the church organ, written three landmark books, and was considered one of the greatest living experts on Bach, Kant, and biblical history. Yet his pursuit of these high-minded subjects collapsed one day, in 1905, when rereading the Gospels (in the original Greek), he came across the lines in which Jesus instructs his followers to "heal the Sick" and "cleanse the lepers"—"Freely you have received; freely give."

That was enough for Schweitzer to drop everything, enroll in medical school, and then move to Lambaréné, in French Equatorial Africa, where he spent the rest of his life living in a makeshift hut, running a hospital, and treating thousands of cases of leprosy, dysentery, elephantiasis, and yellow fever. As he struggled to save lives, he watched two wars ravage Europe and the rise of nuclear weapons that could reduce the whole planet to dust. He sought a kind of modern ethics that looked this terrible new world straight in the face. His readings in philosophy, Eastern and Western, had left him "dangling in midair." The notions of "Good" they offered were "all so lifeless, so unelemental, so narrow, and so lacking in content." Earlier ethics had seemed only concerned with "the relations of man to man." But Schweitzer believed that our concept of good had to be broader, to encompass "the universe and all that it supports."

He believed that people could only be ethical when all life—plants, animals, as well as other people—was sacred to them. It did not matter that nature seemed full of examples in which one form of life preyed on another. Because humans were endowed with the ability to sympathize with other life forms, it was their duty to escape as much as possible the contradiction between the will to live and the need to exploit other living things. Schweitzer called his ethical creed "Reverence for Life," and believed it assigned responsibility to everyone. "It does not permit the artist," he said, "to exist only for his art; even if it gives the inspiration to many by its means. It refuses to let the businessman imagine that he fulfills all legitimate demands in the course of his business activity. It demands from all that they should sacrifice a portion of their own lives for others."

Today the message of "Reverence for Life" may seem like the kind of vague ethical exhortation one finds printed on the wall of a yoga studio. Yet Schweitzer's philosophy—which emphasized the interdependence of all living things—had a profound impact on the first generation of environmentalists. Rachel Carson dedicated *Silent Spring* to Schweitzer, beginning her book by quoting from one of his letters, written to a French beekeeper whose hives were destroyed because of the use of pesticides on nearby farms. "Man has lost the capacity to foresee and to forestall. He will end by destroying the Earth."

Bromfield described the experience of discovering Schweitzer's philosophy in his white room in Brazil as the greatest epiphany he ever had. It was like watching "the bursting of a rocket high in the darkness of the night air." It seemed to explain, for the first time, why he had treated his cattle so well, why he could not punish the thieving raccoons, why the sight of a clear-cut forest or a gullied field made him almost physically sick. He wrote that, even if he did not understand it clearly, the principle of Reverence for Life was practiced by every good farmer—"for he lives close enough to life to hear the very pulsations of the heart."

After Bromfield's death, his family began to drift apart. Nanny died in the early 1960s. Hope and Bob Stevens sold their cattle ranch in Virginia, and moved to Montana with their two daughters. Bob made his fortune there, in the travel business, and eventually his family settled on a 1,600-acre ranch outside of Helena, which is now a wildlife preserve. Anne Bromfield, unable to care for herself, spent much of her adult life in an assisted living facility near them, in Bozeman. She died in 2001. Bob died in 2014 and Hope two years later.

Ellen and Carson left Malabar-do-Brasil in the late 1950s and eventually bought their own farm, Fazenda Pau d'Alho, 80 miles east, where they raised five children. Right up until her death in October 2019 at the age of eighty-seven, Ellen remained a sprightly presence on the farm—still gardening, still writing, still making sure all her guests had something to drink. Carson, now ninety-one, suffered a stroke a few years ago. Though he uses a wheelchair to get around and has trouble speaking, his mind is sharp. A home health attendant helps him mount his horse twice a week to inspect the cattle. After decades of disuse, Malabar-do-Brasil (now known as Fazenda Malabar) was recently taken over by a team of idealistic young eco-entrepreneurs who farm the land without chemicals and are pioneering a sustainable meal delivery service, called DuLocal, to bring healthy organic food to office workers in São Paulo.

As for Malabar itself, after Bromfield's death in 1956, the farm was nearly lost—one prospective buyer wanted to make it a country club, another to carve it up into a suburban-style housing development. The Friends of the Land, with the financial help of Doris Duke, the movie star James Cagney, and a collection of Ohio businessmen, raised $140,000 to buy the farm from Bromfield's estate and ensure a measure of financial security for his daughter Anne. Bromfield had once dreamed that Malabar would become a research center devoted to the study of "man's relation to his environment" that looked at everything from economics to nutrition to wildlife preservation to flood control. "Someday this country and the world will be forced to wake up and undertake some ecologic pattern which emphasizes all of the interlocking factors," he wrote in 1952. "When this is done, there will be an immense conservation of money [and] energy . . . and infinitely more solid advances toward feeding the world, bettering the general lot of mankind and establishing a full foundation for world peace."

Malabar never became a research center. After the Friends of the Land faded in the late 1950s, the farm was taken over by a foundation plagued by internal conflict and financial troubles. Ownership eventually passed to the state of Ohio, which turned Malabar into a state park. Today, Malabar is visited by tens of thousands of people each year, but fewer and fewer of them have heard of the writer and agricultural visionary who built the place. They come for car shows or barn dances. They hike through the Doris Duke Woods, buy syrup made from the farm's maple grove, take pictures by a log cabin (the site of the opening scene of the 1994 film *The Shawshank Redemption*). A few visitors stay for tours of the Big House, which is preserved with all its furniture. They step inside Bromfield's office, see the bed where Bogie and Bacall spent their wedding night, peek into George Hawkins's wood-clad bachelor's pad, open the doors covered in scratch marks made by the boxers. They listen with polite interest as the volunteer tour guide sketches the life of an unknown man who, half a century earlier, would have needed no introduction.

Malabar is still a working farm, but it is a far cry from the agrarian paradise that Bromfield imagined and briefly brought to life. The dairy is in cobwebs. The herd has been reduced to a few dozen beef cattle, which are fed a mixture of grass, hay, and grain. The barn—with its little pens for rabbits, goats, and sheep—looks more like a petting zoo for visiting children. The fields are still planted along Bromfield's original contours, but all that is grown are corn and soybeans in rotation, the same monocultures that cover millions of acres in the American Midwest.

Although it may be difficult to detect in the fields, Malabar's original spirit can still be found by the spring pond, where a bed of watercress planted by Bromfield grows just like it did along the banks of the Nonette. The pond is ringed by flourishing broad-leafed butterbur plants that he brought to Ohio from his journeys in India. Across the street, spring water still flows through the empty vegetable stand, which bears the plaque memorializing Mary. Next-door is an old inn, which, until it shut down last year, housed the Malabar Farm restaurant. At this writing, the Park Service is still looking for another tenant.

However diminished, Malabar Farm is one of the very few places where Bromfield's legacy remains visible. Generations of literary scholars have ignored his novels, dismissing the early ones as derivative and the later ones as trashy. Lefty environmentalists declined to champion his work because of his conservative politics, Hollywood connections, and shameless self-promotion. Organic purists disapproved of the relatively moderate stance he took toward chemicals and his insistence on an agriculture that could scale. Even his local reputation is thorny. Many in Pleasant Valley curse Bromfield's name to this day for his advocacy, in the early 1950s, of the multiflora rose as a natural way to divide pastures, fight soil erosion, and shelter game birds. Bromfield did not know that this "living fence" was actually an aggressive invasive species that has since occupied Pleasant Valley, crowding out some native plants and tormenting generations of backyard gardeners.

So who does that leave? Only the farmers—thousands of them, who read Bromfield and started dreaming. His books were like seeds, sown far and wide, some of which failed to germinate. The ex-navy aviator George Herbert Walker Bush and his young wife, Barbara, both read *The Farm* when they were in their twenties and fantasized about tending their own land. "This is for me," Barbara said after finishing the book. But she and her husband wanted to become economically self-sufficient, and they realized that agriculture, unlike oil exploration, was never going to make them rich. "No matter how we looked at it," the future president wrote, "George and Barbara Farms came off as a high-risk, low-yield investment."

Other seeds sprouted. There was A. P. Thomson, a chemistry major who grew up on a failed Virginia dirt farm in the Depression and thought he wanted to be a doctor until, as a navy man posted to Pearl Harbor during World War II, he found a copy of *Pleasant Valley* in the PX. "Well, sir, that little book really lit a spark in me," he said. "After reading it, I understood *why* my father's fields had eroded so badly and *why* our family's farm had suffered from low productivity for years." He went on to create Golden Acres Orchard in the foothills of the Shenandoahs, which became one of the country's first and best-known organic apple orchards, where Thomson taught a whole generation of farmers how to grow fruit without chemicals on healthy soil.

After reading Bromfield, J. David Bamberger gave up his position as chief executive of Church's Chicken to invest his fortune into rehabilitating 5,500 acres of the worst, most overgrazed Texas hill country, creating the Arcadia known as Selah Ranch, a model of land use and environmental stewardship. After reading Bromfield, Davis Bynum quit his career as a newspaper reporter to grow organic Pinot Noir in Sonoma

County, California, establishing the Russian River valley as a premier wine region. Joel Salatin of Polyface Farm in Swoope, Virginia, who today enjoys Bromfield's old title of "America's most famous farmer," took a simple message from books like *Malabar Farm* and *Out of the Earth:* "I can do this." Salatin called Bromfield "an idea marketer and storyteller, hopelessly romantic and poetic, but that is what drew people to him. You don't attract people by telling them it's overly hard and probably won't work and most will fail."

Perhaps his most important disciple is Wendell Berry. The Kentucky poet-farmer found Bromfield's books in the 1960s. He learned from them how to make environmental issues into urgent moral and political problems, how to celebrate traditional farming culture while exposing all that is wrong with the way we feed ourselves. "I am still grateful for the confirmation and encouragement I received from those books," Berry said. "At a time when farming, as a vocation and an art, was going out of favor, Bromfield genuinely and unabashedly loved it. He was not one of those bad pastoral writers whose love for farming is distant, sentimental, and condescending. Bromfield clearly loved it familiarly and in detail; he loved the work and the people who did it well." A decade ago, Berry was presented with the Louis Bromfield Society Award during a ceremony at Malabar. He said in his acceptance speech that a time was coming when Americans would realize that the kind of love Bromfield had for the land was not some "quaint souvenir of an outdated past" but an "economic necessity," essential for a livable future.

Organic, sustainable, regenerative, permanent: Whatever you call the farming movement that Bromfield and his allies inspired in the first half of the twentieth century, it is still with us today—larger, more sophisticated, but also facing larger and more sophisticated problems. For every encouraging anecdote about the growth of the organic industry or the rise of community-supported agriculture and other sustainable initiatives, there are frightening statistics about increasing rates of soil erosion and the catastrophic effects of industrial farming on the environment and public health.

It is striking to consider just how many agricultural problems Bromfield identified that have only gotten worse since his day. He advocated for the humane, almost sacred, treatment of livestock and wrestled with the ethics of eating animals, once writing, "It is very hard to dine upon a friend." Yet today the majority of American farm animals spend their lives caged, crowded, and drugged in an industrial system that produces a superabundance of meat whose cheap price does not factor in its enormous nutritional and ecological costs. He railed against farm subsidies, which he called a form of "bribery" that encouraged the "worst element of our agriculture—the inefficient, the ignorant, the speculators and the single-crop farmers." Yet today American taxpayers still spend over $20 billion a year on subsidies, most of which prop up the cultivation of commodity crops that fuel the feedlots or are made into processed foods and ethanol. Such subsidies, Bromfield said, are "the best system I know for maintaining rural poverty and continuing to destroy, through erosion and depletion, the most valuable of all our natural resources—the good earth of this country."

Of all the subsidized crops, Bromfield singled out corn as a particularly "vicious and destructive tyrant," saying that the cost of growing it—measured in energy, fertilizer, and wasted soil fertility—made it "the most expensive feed a farmer can employ." Yet today corn and other commodity grains still dominate our agriculture, covering two-thirds of American croplands. (Fruits and vegetables, by comparison, now take up less than 3 percent.) Finally, Bromfield warned about the dangers of becoming addicted to chemical fertilizer, yet each year we use more and more of it, which runs off fields into waterways, poisoning marine life and creating algae blooms and oxygen-sucking dead zones like the 7,000-square-mile one measured in the Gulf of Mexico in the summer of 2019.

Bromfield himself had no idea what would become of his crusade. In his later years, he looked back with embarrassment on the naïveté of the Plan, the fantasy that Malabar would create a "new race of pioneers" to heal the Earth. Such idealism now seemed "ludicrous and a little pathetic." But in the space between what he imagined the farm could be and what it actually was, he found something like a destiny. Malabar, he wrote, "always existed for me in two manifestations, partly in a dreamlike fashion, partly on a plane of hard reality and struggle. Perhaps those two manifestations represent the sum total of a satisfactory life. I do not know."

Acknowledgments

I should start by thanking the shepherds who led me to this story: John and Sukey Jamison, sustainable sheep farmers in the Laurel Highlands of Pennsylvania, who introduced me to Bromfield one fall day in 2015 over a delicious bowl of lamb soup.

My first visit to Malabar brought me in touch with Tom Bachelder of the Malabar Farm Foundation and Timothy Brian McKee, both of them self-taught scholars who were enormously helpful in reconstructing Bromfield's story. Shortly after, I met David Wiesenberg, whose Wooster Book Company is the only reason works like *Pleasant Valley* remain in print. David is a romantic and a skeptic; he taught me where Bromfield "fit" in the story of American ecology and also to not always take the squire of Malabar at his word. One David led to another, David Greer, who knows more about midcentury farming than anyone this side of the Mississippi; he got me out of the Big House and into the soil.

In France, I am grateful to the Société d'Histoire et d'Archéologie de Senlis and in particular to its vice president, Jean-Marc Popineau, who helped me understand the life of that medieval town in the interwar period. Thanks also to Gabrielle Montarnal and to Jean-Marc Vasseur of the Abbaye Royale de Chaalis—Musée Jacquemart-André.

After I found the story, I had to write a book proposal. Laura Mamelok and Russell Galen's suggestions were helpful in revising early versions. Elaine Sciolino, my one-time Paris neighbor, was a savvy guide and great source of encouragement. She connected me to Amy and Peter Bernstein, my tireless agents, who believed in this project from the start and helped me refine the proposal: Bless them both. I am most grateful to Alane Salierno Mason, my brilliant editor, who took a chance on this book and who understood far better than I what final shape it should take. Her support and that of all her talented colleagues at W. W. Norton—Mo Crist, Sarah Daniels, Rachelle Mandik, Will Scarlett—was more than any first-time author could ask for.

Thank you to Wes Jackson, David W. Orr, Jeff Moyer, Chad Montrie, and R. Douglas Hurt—all deep thinkers who schooled me in the complexities of America's agricultural and environmental history. It has been almost fifteen years since I've sat in his classroom, but Mark Feeney is still teaching me things. His interventions in some early chapters of this book felt like major surgery: painful, possibly lifesaving. I'm also grateful for some face-saving suggestions from Justin Spring, one of very few people who could be called an expert on both the literary and horticultural sides of this story.

A shout-out is in order for the small clutch of academics (Jayne Waterman, David Seamon, Randal S. Beeman, Daniel Bratton, and especially the late David D. Anderson and Ivan Scott) who, against fashion, have carefully studied Bromfield's books. I drew on their scholarship time and again. Thank you to all librarians everywhere but, above all, to Rebecca Jewett and her team of crack assistants at the Ohio State University's Thompson Special Collections.

I would not have been able to complete this project without fellowships from the National Endowment of the Humanities Public Scholar Program and the Leon Levy Center for Biography (which is generously funded by Shelby White). At the Levy Center, my thanks to Kai Bird and Thad Ziolkowski and to my fellow Fellows (Rebecca Donner, Jennifer Homans, Samanth Subramanian) for all their helpful suggestions and biographical solidarity.

My friends and family made this book better: Thanks to Julia Felsenthal, Lauren Shields, David Kennedy Jones, Matt McCann, Bryan Maygers, Dina Litovsky, Todd Heyman, and especially to my chief psychologist (a.k.a. my sister, Jessie Heyman) and to my greatest cheerleader (a.k.a. my mom, Maddy Heyman).

Finally, my deepest thanks go to Bromfield's family—to Melanie Read for sharing with me Hope's side of the story; to Liz Geld, for telling me to "find the White Room"; to Kenneth and Sara Geld and their children for an unforgettable welcome to Brazil; to the indomitable Carson Geld; and especially to Ellen Bromfield Geld, who through a lifetime of writing and farming became the best custodian of her father's extraordinary legacy.

Notes

A Note on Sources

In the following pages, I have tried to provide citations for all facts and quotations taken from books, letters, interviews, or unpublished manuscripts. Newspaper and magazine archives were also essential sources—especially the Paris edition of the *New York Herald Tribune* (which chronicled Bromfield's expatriate years) and the *Mansfield News Journal* (which tracked the rise and fall of Malabar). Yet space constraints made it impossible to cite individually all the newspaper and magazine articles quoted in this book. A comprehensive list of references (as well as suggestions for further reading) is available at theplanterofmodernlife.com.

In several cases, particularly with botanical names, I have for the sake of clarity corrected the spelling and capitalization used in original letters.

For the epigraph that opens this book, I consulted Jonathan Mayne and P. E. Charvet's translations of "The Painter of Modern Life" before rendering my own version of the quotation from Baudelaire's essay.

The portraits of each season at Malabar in Chapter 13 were drawn not only from Bromfield's own farm journals, many of which were never published, but also from Ellen Bromfield Geld's "Malabar Notebook," a regular newspaper column that ran in the *News Journal* between 1951 and 1953.

The books by and about Bromfield that I quote most often are referred to using the abbreviations that appear below in bold.

Farm	*The Farm* (New York: Harper, 1933)
FME	*From My Experience* (Harper, 1955)
GBT	*The Green Bay Tree* (New York: Frederick A. Stokes, 1924)
MF	*Malabar Farm* (Harper, 1948)
PV	*Pleasant Valley* (Harper, 1945)
TRC	*The Rains Came: A Novel of Modern India* (Harper, 1937)

Forgotten	Ivan Scott, *Louis Bromfield, Novelist and Agrarian Reformer: The Forgotten Author* (Lewiston, NY: Edwin Mellen, 1998)
Heritage	Ellen Bromfield Geld, *The Heritage: A Daughter's Memories of Louis Bromfield* (Athens: Ohio University Press, 1999)
Yrs, Ever	*Yrs, Ever Affly: The Correspondence of Edith Wharton and Louis Bromfield,* ed. Daniel Bratton (East Lansing: Michigan State University Press, 2000)

I quote from the following archives most frequently, and in these source notes, they are referred to using the abbreviations below in bold.

Duke	David M. Rubenstein Rare Book & Manuscript Library, Duke University
MF Papers	Bromfield papers and ephemera archived at Malabar Farm State Park, Richland County, Ohio
NYPL	Manuscripts and Archives, New York Public Library
OSU	Louis Bromfield collection, Rare Books and Manuscript Library, the Ohio State University
UVA	Albert and Shirley Small Special Collections Library, University of Virginia
Yale	Beinecke Rare Book & Manuscript Library, Yale University

In these source notes I use the abbreviations below to make reference to the following people and publications.

DD	Doris Duke
EBG	Ellen Bromfield Geld
EH	Ernest Hemingway
ER	Eleanor Roosevelt

EW   Edith Wharton
FSF   F. Scott Fitzgerald
GS   Gertrude Stein
LB   Louis Bromfield
LL   Louis André Lamoreux
MB   Mary Bromfield

NYER   *The New Yorker*
NYT   *New York Times*
NYHT   *New York Herald Tribune*
MNJ   *Mansfield News,* renamed the *Mansfield News Journal*
          after 1932

Introduction

1 **Vogue photographed the interiors:** MB, "Settling in Senlis," *Vogue,*
   November 1, 1931, 62–63.
2 **"old-fashioned French":** Janet Flanner, untitled typescript, c. 1941, OSU,
   Box 123.
2 **"genius for living":** *Forgotten,* 257.
4 **"Most of our citizens":** LB, "A Primer of Conservation," pamphlet, Garden Club of America (1942), OSU, Box 42.
5 **"foolish idea" and "new race of pioneers":** *PV,* 48.
5 **one of the best-selling nonfiction books of 1945:** Alice Payne Hackett,
   60 Years of Bestsellers, 1895–1955 (New York: R. R. Bowker, 1956), 182.
6 **"nightclubs and manure piles":** LB, "A Piece of Land," *The Land Letter*
   1, no. 3 (1941): 20.
6 **"It is possible that to some":** *FME,* "Apologia," vii.

1: Foreign Soil

9 À LA DEMI LUNE, **"rat cheese," and "gastronomic memories":** LB, unpublished memoir, "Before It's Too Late," OSU, Box 3.
10 **151 pounds and "hard and wiry":** LB's army service record, National
   Archives and Records Administration, St. Louis, MO. He was assigned
   to Section 577 of the US Army Ambulance Corps.

10   "the gayest of the gay": *The Annual of the Mansfield High School*, 1914, OSU, Box 124.

10   homespun clothes: *Farm*, 176–77.

10   sixteen days at sea: LB left New York on December 26, 1917, on the *Pastores*, a United Fruit Company banana boat converted by the navy into a troop carrier. "Synopsis of Voyage 5, December 26, 1917, through February 8, 1918, of the USS PASTORES," Record Group 45, Records of the Naval Library Subject File, 1911–1917, Entry 520, *US Naval Vessels*, National Archives, Washington, DC.

10   born on December 27, 1896: LB's birth certificate, Richland County Public Health Office.

10   "strange, new vitality": LB, untitled typescript ("He was born during a violent thunderstorm"), OSU, Box 53.

11   "The country is zig-zagged" and "more than any of the apparatuses": Arlen J. Hansen, *Gentlemen Volunteers: The Story of the American Ambulance Drivers in the First World War August 1914–September 1918* (New York: Arcade, 1996), 92.

11   "The trees were green" and "The sky was a special and ineffable blue": Malcolm Cowley, *Exile's Return: A Literary Odyssey of the 1920s* (New York: Penguin, 1976), 42.

11   "I can't let a show like this go on": Carlos Baker, *Ernest Hemingway: A Life Story* (New York: Scribner, 1969), 60.

11   "It is better to be killed": *Farm*, 344.

11   "college extension": Cowley, *Exile's Return*, 38.

12   "the great generalissima," "unimaginable," and "just one long senseless slaughter": Hermione Lee, *Edith Wharton* (New York: Knopf, 2007), 454, 493.

12   "Auntie" and "behaved admirably in emergencies": GS, *The Autobiography of Alice B. Toklas* (New York: Harcourt, Brace, 1933), 212.

12   Michelin Guide: James Mellow, *Charmed Circle: Gertrude Stein & Company* (New York: Avon, 1976), 277.

12   "with delicacy and distinction" and "an artist": Alice B. Toklas, *The Alice B. Toklas Cook Book* (New York: Harper, 2010), 57–59.

13   lied about his age: LB's army enlistment paper, June 6, 1917, LB's army service record, National Archives.

13   minimum age: "Men younger than 21 must have the written consent of

their parents or guardians." American Ambulance Field Service recruitment notice (c. 1916), Samuel V. Chamberlain Papers, Phillips Library, Peabody Essex Museum.

13 **Rue de la Paix:** James McGrath Morris, *The Ambulance Drivers: Hemingway, Dos Passos, and a Friendship Made and Lost in War* (Boston: Da Capo, 2017), 23.

13 **"incredible assortment of men":** "Before It's Too Late," OSU.

13 **Mrs. Gibbons, "Madame Foch," and "Marquis de Paltz":** *Forgotten*, 48.

14 **"I have a chance to gain":** LB to Edith Braun, December 28, 1917, UVA. This letter was likely written at sea and sent upon his arrival in France.

14 **"How much more worth knowing":** LB to Braun, October 15, 1918, UVA.

15 **the ambulance could fit:** Hansen, *Gentlemen*, 110.

15 **a raspberry:** "Before It's Too Late," OSU.

15 **"I can't tell you the genuine affection":** LB to Braun, August 8, 1918, UVA.

15 *singe*: Hansen, *Gentlemen*, 84.

15 **"possessed no subtle bouquet" and "heartening":** Samuel Chamberlain, *Etched in Sunlight: Fifty Years in the Graphic Arts* (Boston Public Library, 1968), 7.

15 **"Those who envied [us]":** Larry Barretto, *Horses in the Sky* (New York: John Day, 1929), 109–10. Barretto served with LB and dedicated this autobiographical novel: "For Louis Bromfield, who shares with me memories of 1918 and the Aisne."

16 **"the dead literally piled":** *Forgotten*, 49.

16 **thirteen of the twenty cars:** John R. Smucker, "The History of the United States Army Ambulance Service," Appendix C, SSU 577. Accessed May 25, 2019, http://www.ourstory.info/library/2-ww1/Smucker/usaac08.html.

16 **"I've been so tired and nerve-worn":** LB to Braun, August 8, 1918.

16 **"decaying leaf mold"** . . . **"they turned out very well":** *FME*, 145–67.

17 **"Fritz captured all my clothes":** photograph dated July 1918, MF papers.

17 **"The Germans had been"** . . . **"in a neat row":** LB to family, June 8, 1918, in MNJ, July 20, 1918.

17 **"nervous state of expectation"** . . . **"spread out before our eyes":** LB to family, August 31, 1918, in MNJ, September 25, 1918, 7.

18 **"a great explosion"** . . . **"simply dust":** LB to Braun, August 8, 1918.

19   "They cry out": LB to family, August 31, 1918.

19   "so long as the men were not left lying": Barretto, *Horses*, 175.

19   "The innumerable nationalities": LB to family, August 31, 18.

19   "blue evening light": LB, *The Man Who Had Everything* (New York: Harper, 1935), 129.

20   "This is really a letter from the front": LB to family, June 27, 1918, in *Mansfield Shield*, August 16, 1918, 2.

2: Invasive Species

21   "Every man of talent": Honoré de Balzac, "La Muse du Département," *Œuvres complètes de H. de Balzac*, Volume 6 (Paris: Houssiaux, 1855), 377, quoted in *Paris and Its People: An Illustrated History*, ed. Robert Laffont (New York: Doubleday, 1958), 180.

21   "Ladies' Home Urinal" and "Vanity Puke": Ezra Pound, *The Selected Letters of Ezra Pound* (New York: New Directions, 1971), 186.

21   The dollar had recently doubled: Frederick J. Hoffman, *The Twenties: American Writing in the Postwar Decade* (New York: Viking, 1955), 27. The dollar bought 16 francs in July 1923 and 36 francs in July 1926.

21   "Neanderthals": Harvey Levenstein, *Seductive Journey: American Tourists in France from Jefferson to the Jazz Age* (Chicago: University of Chicago Press, 1998), 240.

22   "distinguished Roman empress": LB, "Ford Madox Ford," OSU, Box 17.

22   small oil stove: MB, "A la Recherche du Temps Perdu," *Town and Country*, January 1943, 28, 58–61.

22   fancy liqueurs and French brandies: Jimmie Charters, *This Must Be the Place: Memoirs of Jimmie, the Barman as Told to Morrill Cody* (New York: Lee Furman, 1937), 66.

22   "My Melancholy Baby": Herbert Gorman, "Ford Madox Ford: The Personal Side," *Princeton University Library Chronicle*, April 1948, 119.

22   "the materialism of America": LB, "The Last of Montparnasse," *Cosmopolitan*, June 1948, 104.

23   "hearty alcoholic laughter": George Slocombe, *The Tumult and the Shouting* (New York: Macmillan, 1936), 226.

23   "seething with literary impulse": Hoffman, *Twenties*, 30.

23   "wafted him away": Alice B. Toklas, *What Is Remembered* (New York: Holt, Rinehart and Winston, 1963), 114.

23 "Young man," he said: GS, *The Autobiography of Alice B. Toklas* (New York: Harcourt, Brace, 1933), 270.

24 discharged from the army: LB's army discharge papers, OSU, Box 124.

24 "white collar slave," "glowing in the gutters," and "heaped up in the pier sheds": *Forgotten*, 63, 68.

24 "Sit in the corner of any club": LB, "Indifference in College," *The New York Times*, August 29, 1920, sec. 2.

25 "He was moving fast": Frieda Inescort, "Louis Bromfield of Mansfield," *Saturday Review of Literature*, April 14, 1934, 629.

26 "We fancy that": LB, "The New Yorker," *The Bookman*, July 1925, 581–82.

26 "Jazz will eventually become": "Jazz Will Eventually Be United States Folk Music," *Central New Jersey Home News*, November 14, 1929, 1.

26 "should give satisfaction": LB, "The New Yorker," *The Bookman*, August 1925, 685.

26 "clever but empty": LB, "The New Yorker," *The Bookman*, March 1925, 77.

26 "on a / Log": LB, "The New Yorker," *The Bookman*, April 1925, 209.

26 "He had time for everything": Inescort, "Louis Bromfield."

27 "On fair mornings": Gladys Brooks, *Boston and Return* (New York: Atheneum, 1962), 225.

27 undecorated: LB's army service record, National Archives; *Forgotten*, 76.

28 "We have added a new fixed star": *Forgotten*, 86.

28 unconventional heroines: LB, "My Favorite Character in Fiction," *The Bookman*, May 1926, 324.

28 "I couldn't give up all my life to a man": *GBT*, 157.

29 Appletons and the Mathers: *Forgotten*, 66.

29 "either boastfully, to our shame" . . . "Once again": MB, "Happy New Year," *Vogue*, December 21, 1929, 53.

30 "She had been sheltered": *Heritage*, 26.

30 "the story of the Divine creation": Hoffman, *Twenties*, 275. Clarence Darrow, the famous attorney who defended Scopes in the trial, wrote to the magazine *Forum* after Bromfield's short story "Justice" appeared in December 1925. The courtroom drama was "done so well and is altogether so idealistic, that I cannot refrain from writing you about it. It must be that Mr. Bromfield has been a juror. He has stated the psychology of jurors in a remarkable way. . . . [His story] might have the effect of making readers somewhat more kindly to their fellow men."

30 **"moral gown,"** Ku Klux Klan, and **"America"**: Roderick Nash, *Nervous Generation: American Thought 1917–1930* (Chicago: Rand McNally, 1970), 143–46.

30 *Melting-Pot Mistake* and **"a hybrid race"**: Ibid., 72–77.

31 **Sylvia Beach:** Noël Riley Fitch, *Sylvia Beach and the Lost Generation: A History of Literary Paris in the Twenties and Thirties* (New York: Norton, 1985), 84.

31 **"the lunatic fringe"**: LB, "The New Yorker," *The Bookman*, August 1925, 683.

31 **"to the size of an orange"**: Henry James, "The Story-Teller at Large: Mr. Henry Harland," in *The Fortnightly,* Volume 69: January to June 1898 (New York: Leonard Scott, 1898), 650.

31 **a Champagne cocktail at the Ritz:** 10 francs, cited in Arlen J. Hansen, *Expatriate Paris: A Cultural and Literary Guide to Paris of the 1920s* (New York: Arcade, 2012), Kindle edition, chapter 1 "The Grand Hotels."

31 **A picturesque Left Bank apartment:** 250 francs, cited in Jacqueline Tavernier-Courbin, *Ernest Hemingway's A Moveable Feast: The Making of a Myth* (Boston: Northeastern University Press, 1991), 227. Present-day prices were calculated by converting to dollars using the 1926 exchange rate cited earlier ($1 = 36 francs) and then by adjusting for inflation.

31 **"fell softly in feathering whirls"**: LB, unpublished memoir, "Before It's Too Late," OSU, Box 3.

32 **"a typical French maid"** . . . **"And what"**: Henry Albert Phillips, "In Defense of Our Literary Expatriates," *The Bookman*, June 1927, 412.

32 **"better than anywhere else in the world"** and **"inexhaustible"**: Introduction to *Nicole's Guide to Paris* (Paris: Amiot Dumont, 1951), 10–11.

32 **"permanent"** . . . **"Shop windows tempt you"**: MB, "Paris When One Lives There," *Vogue*, 37–38, 96–106.

34 **"At least"**: *Heritage*, 99.

34 **"informal, arranged almost at the spur"**: MB, "Paris When One Lives There."

34 **"Is Gatsby dead?"**: FSF to Maxwell Perkins, c. December 1925, *The Letters of F. Scott Fitzgerald*, ed. Andrew Turnbull (New York: Scribner, 1963), 193.

34 **"characterless and almost sordid"** . . . **"I have the idea"**: LB to Arthur Mizener, c. December 1950, Princeton University Library.

36 "Bloomfield's next book is about a preacher": EH to FSF, March 31, 1927, in *The Letters of Ernest Hemingway*, vol. 3: 1926–1929, eds. Rena Sanderson et al. (Cambridge: Cambridge University Press, 2015), 221.

36 "wild to see" and "She doesn't believe": EH to LB, c. March 1926, *Ernest Hemingway Selected Letters 1917–1961*, ed. Carlos Baker (New York: Simon & Schuster, 2003), 194–96.

36 "I went out there to dinner": EH to FSF, March 31, 1927.

36 "We shall try": EH to FSF (quoting LB's letter to EH), December 31, 1925, *The Letters of Ernest Hemingway*, Volume 2: 1923–1925, eds. Sandra Spanier et al. (Cambridge: Cambridge University Press, 2013), 459–60.

37 "You and Ford" . . . "seeing a lot of you both": EH to LB, c. March 1926.

37 "a hollow or bitter satire": EH to Maxwell Perkins, November 19, 1926, in *Letters of Ernest Hemingway*, Volume 3, 158.

38 "Jesus Christ": LB to EH, c. December 1926, Ernest Hemingway Collection, JFK Library.

38 "What rubbish people write": MB to EH, December 8, 1926, Ibid.

38 "Maybe you would come too": EH to Perkins, November 24, 1927, *Letters of Letters of Ernest Hemingway*, Volume 3, 221.

39 "gargling French" . . . "my cook Yvonne": LB, "The Real French," *The Boulevardier*, September 1927, 6, 50.

40 "I spent the European war in Spain": EH, "The Real Spaniard," *The Boulevardier*, October 1927, 6, 50.

40 "Did you see how Fanny Butcher": EH to FSF, c. September 15, 1927, *Letters of Ernest Hemingway*, Volume 3, 291.

40 "lost all sense of taste": EH to Perkins, July 26, 1933, *Ernest Hemingway Selected Letters 1917–1961*, 395.

40 "Secretariat of Agriculture": *Conversations with Ernest Hemingway*, ed. Matthew J. Bruccoli (Jackson: University Press of Mississippi, 1986), 52.

41 Geneveva de Momus . . . "Well, what nationality are these people?": FSF, *Tender Is the Night* (New York: Scribner, 1996), 31.

41 "Côte d'Ordure": LB, *The World We Live In: Stories* (New York: Harper, 1944), 55.

41 "the lower level of the Grand Central": LB to Marian Hall, n.d., UVA.

42 "Very poor sport": *Forgotten*, 102.

42 "in the open air" . . . "the latest little *cocotte à la mode*": MB, "St-Jean de Luz," *Vogue*, September 14, 1929, 170.

42 "capacity for enjoying life" . . . "You're coming to our house": Edna Ferber, *A Peculiar Treasure* (New York: Doubleday, Doran, 1933), 333–34.

42 "the power of an immense and wealthy nation": LB, "Expatriate—
Vintage 1927," *Saturday Review of Literature*, March 19, 1927, 1.

44 "some kind of anti-American plot": Levenstein, *Seductive Journey*,
257–69.

44 "French Spoken Here": William G. Bailey, *Americans in Paris, 1900–
1930: A Selected, Annotated Bibliography* (New York: Greenwood Press,
1989), 41.

44 "It was a beautiful night": LB to Henry Fuller, c. June 1927, Newberry
Library.

45 "easily, pleasantly" . . . "you do not belong": MB, "Paris When One
Lives There."

3: Hothouse

46 "Let's go to Senlis": EH, *The Sun Also Rises* (New York: Scribner, 2014),
6.

46 the Marché Saint-Pierre: Samuel Chamberlain, *Clémentine in the Kitchen*
(New York: Modern Library, 2001), 13–15.

47 "This old town": *Michelin Guide to the Battlefields of the World War*, Volume I (Milltown, NJ: Michelin, 1919), 73.

48 Gerald and Sara Murphy: Amanda Vaill, *Everybody Was So Young: Gerald and Sara Murphy: A Lost Generation Love Story* (Boston: Houghton
Mifflin, 1998), 140, 160.

48 "like a mother about her baby": Alice B. Toklas, *The Alice B. Toklas Cook
Book* (New York: Harper, 2010), 266.

48 Harry and Caresse Crosby: Linda Hamalian, *The Cramoisy Queen: A Life
of Caresse Crosby* (Carbondale: Southern Illinois University Press, 2009),
54–56.

48 Other expatriates moved to Chantilly: Russell Page, *The Education of a
Gardener* (London: Collins, 1983), 22–23.

48 October 29, 1929: William K. Klingaman, *1929: The Year of the Great
Crash* (New York: Harper & Row, 1989), 278–97.

49 it was small: "Senlis," 1931 population, accessed May 26, 2019, http://
cassini.ehess.fr/cassini/fr/html/fiche.php?select_resultat=35988.

49   ten minutes from the main line: MB, "Settling in Senlis," *Vogue*, November 1, 1931.

49   a pupil of Escoffier: Samuel Chamberlain, *Bouquet de France* (New York: Gourmet, 1951), 481.

49   "the finest flower garden": "Except," she added, "Mrs. Edith Wharton," whose garden is discussed in the next chapter. Janet Flanner, *Paris Was Yesterday: 1925–1939*, ed. Irving Drutman (New York: Harvest, 1988), xvi.

49   "a ripe and rich Monet": Francis Rose, *Saying Life* (London: Cassell, 1961), 380.

49   "It was the only garden in France": Page, *Education*, 23.

50   "manoirs," "*très coquette*," and "If you want a good cook": MB, "Settling in Senlis," 63, 90.

50   "I wanted that particular house": LB, "Les Demoiselles," NYER, May 26, 1945, 22.

51   a shabby, undistinguished pile of limestone: MB, "Settling in Senlis"; Jean-Marc Popineau, vice president of the Société d'Histoire et d'Archéologie de Senlis, interview with the Author, April 2017.

51   "What would we do with the money?": LB, "Les Demoiselles," 23.

53   "French abuse" and the interior of the Presbytère: MB, "Settling in Senlis," 90.

54   *Twenty-Four Hours*: The novel was serialized as "Shattered Glass" in 8 parts (beginning March 1930). In a letter to EW, LB claimed the magazine was paying him "upwards of $20,000" for the serial rights (a bit over $300,000 in today's money), which he described as "solid although not extravagant."

55   weekly salary of $2,500: *Heritage*, 7.

55   "Why did you hire me?": LB often told different versions of this story, which were repeated in gossip columns through the 1940s. See Sheilah Graham, *The Garden of Allah* (New York: Crown, 1970), 218.

55   "Holed up in his room" and "I'm perfectly capable": *Heritage*, 7–9.

56   "his friends" and "lead a life apart": *PV*, 69.

56   "boils and rickets": *Heritage*, 3.

58   "spare, sickly, ill-tended," "frontier agriculture," and "No one talked about": LB, unpublished manuscript "Gardens," OSU, Box 19.

58   "But Bosquet liked artichokes": LB, "The Happiest Man I Have Ever Known," *Reader's Digest*, April 1944, 12–14.

60   "I've reached my second childhood": LB to Harry Hansen, c. October 1931, Newberry Library.

60   *"contre la grippe"*: *Heritage*, 58.

60   "He was not very bright": *PV*, 203.

60   "ripened like wine" and "He felt no qualms": *Heritage*, 54–59.

61   Bromfield chose to plant: LB, "Gardens."

62   "voracious" . . . "It is really indescribably": LB to GS, u.d. letter, Yale.

63   "gape in ecstasy": Chamberlain, *Etched in Sunlight*, 63–64.

63   "chi-chi and whoopee": LB, "Please Don't Disturb," *Vogue*, May 15, 1939, 39.

63   "exciting" and "something will happen": GS to LB, u.d. letter, OSU, Box 1 (correspondence collection). Stein's letters to LB are reproduced with helpful annotations in Kathryn Smeller, *Some Letters from Gertrude Stein to Louis Bromfield*, master's thesis, Ohio State University, 1975.

63   "make no effort at being host": LB to Edward Marsh, u.d. letter (c. 1932), Henry W. and Albert A. Berg Collection of English and American Literature, NYPL.

64   "perfect imitations": Flanner, *Yesterday*, xvi.

64   Mainbocher was so impressed: Flanner, *An American in Paris: Profile of an Interlude Between Two Wars* (New York: Simon & Schuster, 1940), 249.

64   "startling in its variety": LB to Edward Marsh, u.d. letter (c. 1932).

64   "He liked to mix people": Interview with Hope Bromfield Stevens, in *The Man Who Had Everything*. Directed by Brent Greene. Columbus, Ohio: WOSU-TV, 1999.

64   There were fiercely intellectual writers: Scrapbooks, OSU, Boxes 65–67.

66   "such funny stories": Harry Salpeter, "The Boswell of New York," *The Bookman*, July 1930, 384.

66   "For godsakes, Louis": *Bons Mots, Wisecracks and Gags: The Wit of Robert Benchley, Dorothy Parker, and the Algonquin Round Table*, ed. Robert E. Drennan (New York: Skyhorse, 2012), 153.

66   "Because he knows all about gardens": GS, *The Autobiography of Alice B. Toklas* (New York: Harcourt, Brace, 1933), 248.

66   "a tramp and a Don Juan": *PV*, 203–4.

67 "never seen anything like a poodle before": MB, "A la Recherche du Temps Perdu," *Town and Country*, January 1943, 58.

67 "his beautiful marcelled white coat": *PV*, 203–4.

68 "nursed and comforted for the remainder of the day": MB, "A la Recherche du Temps Perdu."

68 "Basket didn't suffer": LB to GS, postmarked December 29, 1931, Yale.

68 "We are going to plant morning glories": GS to LB, u.d. letter, OSU, Box 1 (correspondence collection).

68 "Alice": GS to LB, summer 1932, OSU, Box 1 (correspondence collection).

4: *"Teched"*

69 "rocks and trees and hay": GS to LB, summer 1938, OSU, Box 1 (correspondence collection).

69 "I at heart am only 1/3 gardener": GS to LB, summer 1933, OSU, Box 1 (correspondence collection).

69 "We seldom discussed": LB, "A Tribute to Edith Wharton" in *Yrs, Ever*, 110.

69 "found another literary gardener": LB to EW, u.d. letter (circa October–November 1931), in ibid., 2.

71 "turgid welter of schoolboy pornography": Hermione Lee, *Edith Wharton* (New York: Knopf, 2007), 610.

71 "Perceiving that everyone": EW to LB, September 18, 1933, in *Yrs, Ever*, 52.

71 "I've been at the Crillon": EW to LB, June 12, 1933, in ibid., 46.

72 "Horrible": Lee, *Wharton*, 622.

72 "as close in many senses"... "For her a drouth": "A Tribute," in *Yrs, Ever*, 110.

73 "black as a crow's wing": *PV*, 85.

74 "the subject, like an etching" . . . "an air of immense dignity": Ibid., 84–86.

76 "thrusting shoots of wisteria" . . . "He laughed": Ibid., 85–88.

77 "boy who could talk with the birds" . . . "a unifying magic": EW, *A Backward Glance* (1934), quoted in Allan R. Ruff, *An Author and a Gardener: The Gardens and Friendship of Edith Wharton and Lawrence Johnston* (Oxford: Windgather Press, 2014), Kindle edition, chapter 1, under "The Jones Family of New York."

78 severe splendor: EW, "Gardening in France" in *Yrs, Ever*, 135–39; Lee, *Wharton*, 531–33.

78   "her gardens were better than her books": Lee, *Wharton*, 563.

79   "Wherever you first caught sight": Percy Lubbock, *Portrait of Edith Wharton* (New York: D. Appleton, 1947), 140.

80   "When are you coming north?": LB to EW, c. March 1932, in *Yrs, Ever*, 10–11.

80   "You make me envious": EW to LB, May 2, 1932, in ibid.

81   "Come & see my Primulinuses!!": EW to LB, August 8, 1933, in ibid., 50–51.

81   "If you cd see my peonies": EW to LB, April 13, 1934, in ibid., 63.

81   "I want to swank": EW to LB, July 30, 1932, in ibid., 28–29.

81   "the best insurance agent": LB to EW, c. fall 1931, in ibid., 3.

81   "Nature continues to take no notice": LB to EW, c. May 1936, in ibid., 84.

81   "Yes; the garden is": EW to LB, June 12, 1933, in ibid., 49.

82   to revive the spirit of Lesbos: Suzanne Rodriguez, *Wild Heart: Natalie Clifford Barney and the Decadence of Literary Paris* (New York: Harper-Collins, 2007), Kindle edition, Chapter 8: "The Salonist."

83   "one met lesbians" and "high collars and monocles": Diana Souhami, *Wild Girls: Paris, Sappho, and Art: The Lives and Loves of Natalie Barney and Romaine Brooks* (New York: St. Martin's, 2004), 2.

83   "with high cheekbones," "careless, flamboyant Amazone," and "nervous the way": Brenda Wineapple, *Genêt: A Biography of Janet Flanner* (New York: Ticknor & Fields, 1989), 116–18.

83   She grew herbs: Ibid., 121.

84   "Outside of a man and a woman": Amanda Vaill, *Everybody Was So Young: Gerald and Sara Murphy: A Lost Generation Love Story* (Boston: Houghton Mifflin, 1998), 272.

84   "an intangible mist" and "transparent like sugar flowers": FSF, *Tender Is the Night* (New York: Scribner, 1996), 38–39

85   "The well-being which came to him": *Heritage*, 55.

5: Tangled Roots

86   "Some day, there will come a reckoning": *Farm*, 342.

86   "It is as though every grain of dust": Michael Fanning, *France and Sherwood Anderson: Paris Notebook, 1921* (Baton Rouge: Louisiana State University Press, 1976), 28.

86   "to its utmost clod" . . . "mated with poetry": EW, *A Motor-Flight Through France* (New York: Scribner, 1909), 5.

87   "plowing and grazing are the two breasts": Stéphane Hénaut and Jeni Mitchell, *A Bite-Sized History of France* (New York: New Press, 2018), Kindle edition, chap. 23.

87   "It is the rural people" and "the holy work of France": James R. Lehning, *Peasant and French: Cultural Contact in Rural France During the Nineteenth Century* (Cambridge: Cambridge University Press, 1995), 12, 18.

87   "potatoes in a sack" and "more through exchange with nature": Karl Marx, *A Karl Marx Reader*, ed. Jon Elster (Cambridge: Cambridge University Press, 1999), 254.

88   "money was almost unknown": Eugen Weber, *Peasants into Frenchmen: The Modernization of Rural France, 1870–1914* (Stanford, CA: Stanford University Press, 1976), 35.

88   "Any French peasant": *PV*, 7.

88   jobless numbers: James R. Green, *The World of the Worker: Labor in Twentieth-Century America* (Urbana: University of Illinois Press, 1998), 135.

88   city-dwellers fainted . . . burned their worthless wheat: *PV*, 236.

89   "we can buy an acre": Thomas Jefferson to George Washington, June 28, 1793, in *The Papers of Thomas Jefferson*, vol. 26 (May 11–August 31, 1793), ed. John Catanzariti (Princeton: Princeton University Press, 1995), 396–98.

89   "We ruin the lands": "Marked While Reading," *The Land* 1, no. 1 (1941): 60.

89   "rampant erosion, sour soils, mounting floods": Paul Conkin, *A Revolution Down on the Farm: The Transformation of American Agriculture since 1929* (Lexington: University of Kentucky, 2008), 187.

89   40 percent of the population: Ibid., 3.

89   the price of farm commodities: Michael E. Parrish, *Anxious Decades: America In Prosperity and Depression, 1920–1941* (New York: W. W. Norton, 1994), 82.

90   "the most terrible toboggan slide": Frederick Lewis Allen, *Only Yesterday: An Informal History of the 1920s* (New York: Harper, 1931), 161.

90   the failing market: Parrish, *Anxious*, 82–83.

90   bank failures tripled, and nearly a million farmers: Nathan Miller, *New World Coming: The 1920s and the Making of Modern America* (New York: Scribner, 2003), 87.

91   corn fell . . . hog prices: Jane Ziegelman and Andrew Coe, *A Square Meal: A Culinary History of the Great Depression* (New York: Harper, 2016), 86.

91   "There is a feeling," Oscar Ameringer, and "the paradox of want amid plenty": Ibid., 116.

91   1 million acres: Ibid., 86.

91   "dust pneumonia" and "America is doomed agriculturally": Randal S. Beeman and James A. Pritchard, *A Green and Permanent Land: Ecology and Agriculture in the Twentieth Century* (Lawrence: University Press of Kansas, 2001), 12.

92   "blatantly represented" . . . "one long query": *Forgotten*, 195.

93   "'The Farm' is the story of a way of living": *Farm*, v–vi.

94   "Let Bromfield feed their chaotic minds": Zelda Fitzgerald to FSF, c. April 1934, in *Dear Scott, Dearest Zelda: The Love Letters of F. Scott and Zelda Fitzgerald*, eds. Jackson R. Bryer and Cathy W. Barks (New York: St. Martin's, 2003), 189.

95   "Fat rumps" . . . "coffee and sausages": *Farm*, 1.

96   Bromfield's real great-grandfather, Jacob Barr: Alan Wigton, *The Richland County Historical Society Member Update* 6, no. 3 (March 2016): 1–5.

97   "not once but many times": *Farm,* 37.

97   "He went, like all the others" . . . "Jamie, in the mere necessity": Ibid., 40–55.

98   "Each farm was in itself" . . . "wheezing of the wood-burning locomotives": Ibid., 67–69.

99   "in the vast difference": Ibid., 214.

99   "ferocious black mustachios" and "They were the first peasants": Ibid., 117.

99   "atmosphere of soot and carbon dioxide": Ibid., 153.

99   "which had an air of belonging" and "boastful houses": Ibid., 120.

99   "pictures bought" . . . "no core": Ibid., 175.

99   the Coulter family farm: *PV,* 57–58.

100   three daughters and five sons: "Lifelong resident," MNJ, July 27, 1917.

100   a daughter, Marie: Marie Brumfield birth certificate, August 13, 1886, Richland County Public Health Office.

101   "waste your life on a farm": *PV,* 49.

101 "with a strange tenacity": *Farm*, 71.

101 "Always, it seemed": Ibid., 91.

101 Charles Jr., born in 1899: Charles (Chas.) Brumfield Jr. birth certificate, December 22, 1899, Richland County Public Health Office.

101 "You went to sleep" and "thick toothsome candy": *Farm*, 80–81.

102 "there was a whole procession": Ibid., 73–74.

102 "straight bare fences" . . . "crimson and gold": Ibid., 76.

103 "that their bloom should not be" . . . "When he had finished": Ibid., 255, 257.

104 "Brumfield's Bargains": MNJ, November 7, 1911.

104 "romantic farms hidden away" . . . "economic disaster": *Farm*, 267.

105 two Russian émigrés: LB, unpublished memoir "The Day I Met Pavlova," OSU, Box 12.

105 "This is the life" . . ."Just think": *Forgotten*, 19–21.

105 "It was either that or the farm": Ibid., 23.

106 "revolting": *Farm*, 296.

106 "Cholera might wipe out": Ibid., 297.

106 "in the last remaining fragment": Ibid., 312.

106 "keen pleasure" . . . "What good was it": Ibid., 328–31.

107 as if "on a treadmill": Ibid., 342.

107 "rather more like a factory" . . . "machines which never": Ibid., 313.

107 "chocking and creaking" . . . "She was silent": Ibid., 343–44.

108 "shiny motor" . . . "like the arrowheads": Ibid., 345–46.

108 "Speaking technically" . . . "The important thing": GS to LB, summer 1933, OSU, Box 1 (correspondence collection).

109 "I adore our being bestsellers together": GS to LB, fall 1933, OSU, Box 1 (correspondence collection).

109 "What a thunderbolt!": EW to LB, September 28, 1933, in *Yrs, Ever*, 54.

6: Blight

110 "I'm an incorrigible life-lover": EW to Mary Berenson, October 11, 1936, in *The Letters of Edith Wharton*, eds. R.W.B. Lewis and Nancy Lewis (New York: Scribner, 1988), 598.

110 "strange, wild character," Hureau standing proudly, and "scarlet wonder": "A Tribute," in *Yrs, Ever*, 110–11.

111 "not in a dull doctrinaire" . . . "it is always thus": Ibid., 111–12.

113 "I look": Ibid., 114.

113 "seeing a ghost" . . . "on that day": Ibid., 109–13.

113 "You can't imagine": Hermione Lee, *Edith Wharton* (New York: Knopf, 2007), 750–51.

114 "a simple funeral" and "friends and flowers": Allan R. Ruff, *An Author and a Gardener: The Gardens and Friendship of Edith Wharton and Lawrence Johnston* (Oxford: Windgather Press, 2014), Kindle edition, "Introduction."

114 he'd rather be a living German . . . "I don't want to go to war": Alan Riding, *And the Show Went On: Cultural Life in Nazi-Occupied Paris* (New York, Knopf: 2010), 11, 21.

116 "I think no intelligent American": *PV*, 4–5.

116 "It was as if all the while my spirit": Ibid.

117 "they had no leaders" . . . "I wished them": LB, untitled typescript ("It was the Christmas before the end of the world . . ."), OSU, Box 52.

117 Alcide: LB, "Les Demoiselles," NYER, May 26, 1945, 26.

118 "We were received by dozens": MB, "A la Recherche du Temps Perdu," *Town and Country*, January 1943, 60–61.

119 Elsie de Wolfe's "Circus Ball": "Fête at Versailles," August 15, 1938, *Vogue*, 89, 165, 171; Charlie Scheips, *Elsie de Wolfe's Paris: Frivolity Before the Storm* (New York: Abrams, 2014) 51–77.

120 "living upon borrowed time": *PV*, 62.

121 In open letters: "Americans in Need," *Washington Post*, June 23, 1938, sec. X; "American Wounded: Those Arriving in France from Spain Need Help," NYHT, June 25, 1938.

122 more than 1,000 Lincoln Brigadiers: Carey Longmire, "America's Good Samaritan," *Los Angeles Times*, April 30, 1939, sec. I.

122 Legion of Honor: "France Confers Highest Honors upon Bromfield," MNJ, April 4, 1939.

122 "When Mr. Chamberlain debased the dignity": *PV*, 5.

122 "a clique of compromising": LB, *England, Dying Oligarchy* (New York: Harper, 1933), 33.

123 The mayor of Senlis issued a proclamation: "Mairie de Senlis: À la Population," town poster, September 24, 1938, MF Papers.

123 "never met a man with greater charm": LB to EW, February 1932, in *Yrs, Ever*, 7.

124   "a big irresistible child": *Forgotten*, 286–87.

124   "And as we walked about the great park": *PV*, 6.

125   "a faint sickness" and "dead now": Ibid.

125   he died in Paris in 1943: LB's portrayal of Gillet as a paragon of French humanism overlooks the scholar's far-right political connections in the run-up to World War II. See Adrien Le Bihan, *James Joyce travesti par trois clercs parisiens: essai* (Paris: Cherche-bruit, 2011), 98–100.

125   "the medieval fortress-manor": *FME*, 6.

126   "not the loss of the intellectual life" . . . "The thing I should miss most": *PV*, 7–8.

127   "Et tu brute": GS to LB, u.d. letter, in *Forgotten*, 304.

127   "It is a bright white Sunday": GS to LB, winter 1938, OSU, Box 1 (correspondence collection).

7: The Rains Came

129   "with a carriage so superb": MB, unpublished India memoir, OSU, Box 121.

130   "a rugged individualist" . . . "The smell alarmed me": LB, unpublished memoir "The Last Queen," OSU, Box, 26.

130   "Oriental dirt" . . . "Nothing was mattering": MB, India memoir.

131   "a vast middle western county jail," "Klondike saloon," and *chotapegs*: LB, *Night in Bombay* (New York: Harper, 1940), 51–55.

131   "any eventuality" and "either of fertility or plenty": MB, India memoir.

132   "It was as if they said" and "Here they *believed*": *TRC*, 10.

133   "I don't want to go north": Paul Fussell, *Abroad: British Literary Traveling Between the Wars* (Oxford University Press, 1982), 132.

135   "chemical manures": Thomas Hager, *Alchemy of Air: A Jewish Genius, a Doomed Tycoon, and the Scientific Discovery That Fed the World but Fueled the Rise of Hitler* (New York: Broadway, 2008), 7–8, 33–59, 78–79.

135   two divergent ways and Haber-Bosch process: Michael Pollan, *The Omnivore's Dilemma* (New York: Penguin, 2007), 42–47, 145–51; Philip Conford, *The Origins of the Organic Movement* (Edinburgh: Floris, 2001), 26–46.

136   "deeper essences" . . . "peasant wit": Suzanne Peters, *The Land in Trust: A Social History of the Organic Farming Movement*, PhD diss., McGill University, 1979, 24–27.

136　a nine-month tour of the Far East and "which, with fortitude and rare wisdom": Gregory A. Barton, *The Global History of Organic Farming* (Oxford University Press, 2018), 83–84.

136　"mineral fertilizers" . . . "be continued indefinitely": Franklin Hiram King, *Farmers of Forty Centuries* (Madison, WI: Mrs. F. H. King, 1911), 1.

137　"quality as well as on the yield": Barton, *Global History*, 74.

138　"my professors": Ibid., 88–91. In his book (based on the discovery of Howard's missing papers), Barton rejects the long-held idea that the Indore Process repackaged "indigenous peasant knowledge for a modern scientific world." Rather, he argues, Howard's discovery was the result of rigorous scientific experimentation and owed practically nothing to the methods of peasant farmers whom he only later held up as "my professors." Barton argues that Howard started writing about the "wisdom of the East" years after he left India in the 1940s, when he sought to capitalize on the emergent organic movement's interest in traditional farming cultures. Barton also points out that, in his earlier work, Howard expressed no dogmatic "aversion to artificial fertilizers or to pesticides"— a fact that would scandalize many of his disciples today.

138　"Mother earth never attempts to farm": Sir Albert Howard, *An Agricultural Testament* (Oxford University Press, 1940), 4.

138　"the best book I know on soil": *PV*, 148

138　"perhaps the ideal fertilizer," "prodigious results," and cheap labor: Ibid., 197–98.

139　2.2 million people: Stanley Rice, *Life of Sayaji Rao III, Maharaja of Baroda*, Volume 1 (Oxford University Press, 1931), viii.

139　"a nightmare," "choking the air," and "sacred monkeys": MB, India memoir.

140　outlawed child marriage: Fatesinhrao Gaekwad, *Sayajirao of Baroda, the Prince and the Man* (Bombay: Popular Prakashan, 1989), viii–ix.

140　modern water system: Rice, *Maharaja*, 58–59.

140　the monsoon of July 1927 and initial reports suggested: Gaekwad, *Prince*, 355–56.

140　"a most successful method of irrigation": MB, India memoir.

141　"no faith and very little good news": *Forgotten*, 208

141　a dinner given in their honor and "the most attractive woman": MB, India memoir.

142 "everyone from old ladies": LB to EW, c. February 1933, in *Yrs, Ever*, 34.

142 a bachelors' trip: *Forgotten*, 268–69; "India" scrapbooks, OSU, Box 67.

142 "delicate pink nose" . . . "She had tiny brown paws": *PV*, 206–7.

143 "than I had ever been in my life": LB to GS, u.d., Yale.

144 had begun it in Cooch Behar . . . half a dozen drafts: *TRC*, 597; OSU, Boxes 43–44.

144 "a useless liberal in a sick world": *TRC*, 105.

144 "writhe and thrust" . . . "vegetable ecstasy": Ibid., 187

144 "The dam had been in a way a kind of symbol": Ibid., 314.

145 "the *accouplement* of two *pie* dogs": Ibid., 157.

145 sixty-eight weeks on the bestseller list: "The Rains Came" publication history, researched by Vandna Gill, "20th Century Bestsellers," accessed June 9, 2019, https://bestsellers.lib.virginia.edu/submissions/230.

145 "accomplished something of a miracle": Pearl S. Buck, u.d. typescript ("for Cosmopolitan Magazine"), Manuscripts Division, Princeton University Library.

145 "You know how sensitive we Indians": Krishnalal Shridharani to LB, June 4, 1938, OSU, Box 93.

146 identical telegrams: Lynn Kear and John Rossman, *The Complete Key Francis Career Record* (Jefferson, NC: McFarland, 2016), 223.

147 fifth highest-grossing film of 1939: "Top Grossing Movies of 1939" (by actual domestic box office), accessed May 29, 2019, http://www.ultimatemovierankings.com/top-grossing-movies-of-1939.

147 He chose to name his place "Malabar": The name was inspired not only by Malabar Hill in Bombay but also by the Malabar Coast of southwestern India, which Bromfield visited in 1936 and called "one of the most beautiful parts of the earth." *PV*, 64.

8: Seeding

151 "Don't put off till tomorrow": Hesiod, *Works and Days*, trans. A. E. Stallings (New York: Penguin, 2018), Kindle edition, lines 410–11.

151 "enrich the soil as much as dung": Cuthbert W. Johnson, *The Farmer's Encyclopedia and Dictionary of Rural Affairs* (Philadelphia: Carey and Hart, 1848), 783.

151 "Of all the occupations": Cicero, "On Duties," in *Delphi Complete Works of Cicero* (Hastings, East Sussex, UK: Delphi Classics, 2014) Kindle edition, quoted in Doug Metzger, "Then Came Hard Iron," podcast audio, May 4, 2018, https://literatureandhistory.com.

151 "fierce of feature": Virgil, *Georgics: A Poem of the Land*, trans. Kimberly Johnson (New York, Penguin, 2010), Kindle edition, Book 3, line 53.

151 "I want death to find me": Michel de Montaigne, "That to philosophize is to learn to die," in *The Complete Essays of Michel de Montaigne* (Stanford, CA: Stanford University Press, 1976), 62.

152 a whole progressive agrarian estate and "To have cultivated a field": S. G. Tellentyre, *The Life of Voltaire* (New York: G. P. Putnam's Sons, 1907), 338, 454.

152 "simple cultivator" . . . "What should we American farmers": J. Hector St. John De Crèvecoeur, *Letters from an American Farmer* (New York: Duffield, 1904), xxxi, 27.

152 "those Trojans" and "What shall I learn": Henry D. Thoreau, *Walden: Or, a Life in the Woods* (Boston: Houghton Mifflin, 1899), 241–51.

153 "Didn't I once meet you": Ford Madox Ford, *It Was The Nightingale* (Philadelphia: J. B. Lippincott, 1933), 161.

153 literary peers who experimented: Ferber: Treasure Hill (Connecticut); MacLeish: Uphill Farm (Massachusetts); Dos Passos: Spence's Point (Virginia), White's farm (Maine), Parker: Fox Farm (Pennsylvania).

154 "the maze of a vaguely remembered dream": *PV*, 1.

154 "Be careful!": LB, u.d. journal entry ("Outside the snow is falling"), OSU, Box 53.

154 Cartier wristwatch: November 1939 A. J. Reynolds insurance policy, OSU, Box 99.

155 "Beautiful" . . . "tinted with the last pink light": *PV*, 10–11.

155 "luminous like the unreal": *FME*, 5.

155 "snugness" and "not of wild and overpowering": MB, "The Bromfields Live in Ohio," *Vogue*, September 15, 1941, 75.

155 "knocking at the door" and "the perfumes of Araby": *FME*, 2, 5.

156 "warm like the nest": *PV*, 37. Bromfield referred to the Herring family in this and other books by the pseudonym "Anson," likely to protect their privacy.

156 sell the place for $20,000: The payment is recorded on January 30, 1939, to the Farmers Savings and Trust Company of Mansfield. OSU, Box 125.

156 **a bank loan for $34,000:** Jane Williams, "Bromfield Finds His Dream Farm," MNJ, January 11, 1939.

157 **"as if it belonged there":** *PV,* 70.

157 **"I might not have been the *most* informed"** . . . **"utter disregard":** LL, "An Architect's Story of Louis Bromfield's Big House at Malabar," *Cleveland Plain Dealer Pictorial Magazine* (published in two parts), March 3 and March 10, 1957.

157 ***"big* people" and "a big rambling room":** *PV,* 68–69.

158 **"It would have been more economical":** LL, "Architect's Story."

159 **Months passed, hundreds of sketches:** Ibid.; I. T. Frary, "Malabar Farm," *American Antiques Journal,* January 1947; *PV,* 78–79.

159 **"was a kind of museum":** MB, "The Bromfields Live in Ohio."

159 **"I am not a gadgeter"** . . . **"tell them all to go to hell":** LL, "Architect's Story."

160 **"All the pressure in Mansfield"** . . . **"I won't know until July":** LB to LL, April 14, 1939, OSU, Box 138.

161 **a benefit for Jewish refugees:** LB to Hamilton Fish Armstrong, November 30, 1938, Mudd Manuscript Library, Princeton.

162 **officials at the State Department and politico Jim Farley:** *Forgotten,* 314.

162 **"gutless" and "Jew-baiting":** LB, "Behind the Investigation of the Movies," *The Washington Post,* September 16, 1941.

162 **"Here is a man":** ER, "My Day, February 13, 1939," The Eleanor Roosevelt Papers Digital Edition (2017), accessed May 31, 2019, https://www2.gwu.edu/~erpapers/myday/displaydoc.cfm?_y=1939&_f=md055188.

162 **"delightful":** ER, "My Day, June 26, 1942," The Eleanor Roosevelt Papers Digital Edition (2017), accessed May 31, 2019, https://www2.gwu.edu/~erpapers/myday/displaydoc.cfm?_y=1942&_f=md056222.

162 **"He was traveling constantly," Eleanor Harris, and Millicent Rogers:** LL, "Architect's Story."

163 **"Here's the story I told the family":** LL to LB, March 8, 1940, OSU, Box 138.

163 **"I possess, unfortunately":** *PV,* 76.

164 **"All of us, family, architect, carpenters":** Ibid., 77

164 **"more than anything in the house"**. . . **"I'm afraid it's going to be":** LL, "Architect's Story."

166 **"The effect was such" and "fanatic hatred":** *Heritage,* 88–90.

168 **"of the painter Veronese":** *PV,* 81.

168 **"There is no parlor":** Ibid., 82.

9: Germination

169 he got ten cows, two old draft horses: "Closes Deal," MNJ, January 14, 1939; *Heritage*, 76–77.

171 "rabid theorists" . . . too "sot" in their ways: *PV*, 51.

171 "by ignorance, by greed": *FME*, 6.

171 definition of a "good farmer": *PV*, 51–53.

172 "a darkly handsome young man": *Heritage*, 81.

172 "I got through a couple chapters" . . . a boozy lunch: "Max Drake Remembers Bromfield," *Return to Pleasant Valley*, ed. George DeVault (Chillicothe, IL: American Botanist, 1996), 160–62.

173 "a small kingdom" . . . "the terrible economic insecurity": *PV*, 53–59.

173 a newspaper in Germany and banks close in France: "Farm Problems I," *Country Life*, February 1942, 15–16.

173 "thrifty island of security": *Heritage*, 81–84.

175 The Plan called for: "Farm Problems I," 45–46.

175 birds and the raccoons and "We accepted its principles": *PV*, 59–61.

175 "above average" and "low": *Forgotten*, 332.

175 "the adventure" . . . "*pro rata*": *PV*, 61

177 "I spend my days working hard": LB to LL, u.d. letter, OSU, Box 138.

179 "*Of course* I don't want to go out" . . . "I wish I could describe": MB to LB, u.d. letters (c. summer 1939), OSU, Box 106.

179 pictures that sometimes upset young children: unpublished Malabar memoir (2001), Jeanine Collins Malarsky, Mansfield Public Library, Sherman Reading Room.

179 "Wednesday was my birthday": MB to LB, u.d. letter, OSU, Box 106.

180 "I wish I'd gotten into the house by mistake" . . . "your old shoe": MB to LB, ibid.

180 "Louis, I love this place" . . . "You will find the place entirely changed": Ibid.

181 5 cents a bird: Max Drake to LB, June 25, 1939, OSU, Box 107.

181 "Things are growing well": Ibid.

181 "the wastage of soil and moisture resources": Soil Conservation Act, April 27, 1935, "74th Congress, Chapter 85," accessed June 1, 2019, https://www.loc.gov/law/help/statutes-at-large/74th-congress/session-1/c74s1ch85.pdf.

182 survey of Malabar: Soil Conservation Service Land Use Map and Cooperative Agreement (c. 1939–1940), OSU, Box 92.

182   "The gullies were big enough": "Max Drake Remembers Bromfield," 161.

182   "Well, I'm supposed to be in charge" . . . "everything was changed": Ibid.

182   "What the hell has been going on here?": *Forgotten*, 380.

182   So Drake told him the outlines of the plan: LB, "A Piece of Land," *The Land* 1, no. 3 (1941): 204–6.

183   "It is marvelous the quickness": Ibid., 205.

184   "faint crackling sound": *PV*, 280.

185   "My travel, my experience": LB, "A Piece of Land," 206.

10: Victory Garden

186   "He is the greatest patriot": "Marked While Reading," *The Land* 1, no. 1 (1941): 60.

187   "a revolution": LB, "Revolution in Agriculture," *Country Book* 4, no. 2 (1944): 1.

188   "It was a truly terrifying strike" and "a sense of shame": Russell Lord, *The Care of the Earth: A History of Husbandry* (New York: Thomas Nelson & Sons, 1962), 277. Lord's book is dedicated "To Louis Bromfield."

188   "To have to destroy a growing crop": John C. Culver and John Hyde, *American Dreamer: A Life of Henry A. Wallace* (New York: W. W. Norton, 2001), 123. While the AAA's crop-reduction program benefited landowners—who had property to remove from production and could use the government money to invest in machinery or convert their holdings—it devastated many poor sharecroppers in the South and other tenant farmers who, in many cases, were driven off the land and forced on relief. See R. Douglas Hurt, *Problems of Plenty: The American Farmer in the Twentieth Century* (Chicago: Ivan R. Dee, 2002), 68–80.

189   "When it arrived": Lord, *Forever the Land: A Country Chronicle and Anthology* (New York: Harper, 1950), 101.

189   the first federal agency : Between those years, Woodrow Wilson did create the National Parks Service, in 1916, whose mission included conserving "the scenery" and the "wild life" of the nation's parklands.

189   just like long-extinct civilizations: Paul B. Sears, *Deserts on the March* (Norman: University of Oklahoma, 1935), 22–24.

189   Aldo Leopold and Coon Valley: Curt D. Meine, *Aldo Leopold: His Life and Work* (Madison: University of Wisconsin Press), 313.

189 soon be called "organic": The term was coined by Lord Northbourne in his 1940 book *Look to the Land*. John Paull, "Lord Northbourne, the Man Who Invented Organic Farming: A Biography," *Journal of Organic Systems* 9, no. 1 (2014): 31–53.

189 three thousand independent cinemas and 8 million people: Drew Pearson and Robert S. Allen, "The Washington Merry-Go-Round, *Pittsburgh Press*, October 29, 1937.

190 100 million acres: "SOS—Save Our Soil," *The Austin American*, January 25, 1936. For detailed information about soil erosion in the United States in the 1930s, see B. W. Patch, "Soil Conservation and Agricultural Adjustment," *Editorial Research Reports 1936*, Volume 1 (Washington, DC: CQ Press, 1936). Accessed June 1, 2019, http://library.cqpress.com/cqresearcher/cqresrre1936012700.

190 the outlines of the new society: Margaret L. Eppig, "Russell Lord and the Permanent Agriculture Movement: An Environmental Biography," PhD diss., Antioch University, 2017, http://aura.antioch.edu/etds/365. 162–64.

191 "Any land is all of one body": Lord, *Forever*, 44.

191 "We are creatures" and "Do we first start a magazine": Ibid., 64, 67.

192 "a meeting of extremely long-range visionaries" and "One hundred days after its founding": Ibid., 53, 72.

192 "small-fry": Eppig, "Lord," 173.

192 "I think that had we had him with us": Lord, *Forever*, 70.

192 "the spontaneous co-operation": *PV*, 263–64.

193 "For three centuries" and "We can never think again": Stuart Chase, "The New Patriotism," *The Land* 1, no. 3 (1941): 183–85.

193 a picnic that Bromfield was giving: *PV*, 260–61.

194 "extravagant lawn" . . . "We have sought merely": Ibid., 290–96.

194 "evangelists, some very nearly fanatics": Ibid., 266.

194 at least sixty speeches: Lord, *Forever*, 182.

195 "It wasn't General Sherman": Ibid., 264–65.

195 thick, black silt: *PV*, 262.

195 "Every time he pulled a fact" and "Max," he said: Interview with Max Drake, in *The Man Who Had Everything*. Directed by Brent Greene. Columbus, Ohio: WOSU-TV, 1999.

196 *"The Land"*: *The Land* 1, no. 2 (1941): inside cover.

196 "folly" to publish it: *Forgotten*, 399.

196 **selling 340,000 copies:** Charles B. Shaw, "University of Oklahoma Press," *Southwest Review 31*, no. 1 (1945): 65.

196 **Bromfield's promotion of it in *Reader's Digest:*** LB, "The Evangelist of 'Plowman's Folly,'" *Reader's Digest,* December 1943, 35–39.

196 **"It is a tremendous joy" and 100,000 copies:** *Forgotten*, 385.

197 **full-dress opening:** Lord, *Care of the Earth*, 287

197 **"*The Land* seems to me the most important documentary":** LB, "Beauty, Danger, and Terror," *The Land* 1, no. 3 (1941): ii.

197 **"When soil fails" and "A change has come over":** *The Land*. Directed by Robert J. Flaherty. Washington, DC: US Department of Agriculture, 1942.

198 **"I beg the indulgence" and "The French can't":** Lord, *Forever*, 205.

198 **"In his platform demeanor":** Ibid., 114.

11: Food Fight

200 **"parlor pink":** H. L. Mencken, "Louis Bromfield," typescript, September 6, 1940, H. L. Mencken Papers, NYPL.

201 **odd article to the *Sunday Worker*:** LB, "A Spectacle of Heroism," January 8, 1939, *Progressive Weekly Sunday Worker*.

201 **In a confidential memo:** Memorandum, Special Agent J. C. Buckle to Mr. Kramer, August 2, 1941, LB's FBI File (100-HQ-30238).

201 **"will go to those who are fighting":** *Spécialités de La Maison* (New York: Collins Design, 2010). The book was originally published in 1940 by the Friends of France.

201 **De Gaulle sent a telegram:** "De Gaulle Thanks Bromfield," NYHT, August 11, 1942.

201 **hidden under the floor boards:** *Forgotten*, 303.

202 **"I would appreciate if you saw Louis Bromfield":** "Letter Smuggled Out of Starving France" (dated August 15, 1942), *Boston Globe*, January 10, 1943.

203 **"unorganized and inarticulate":** LB, "It's a Farmer's War, Too," *Collier's,* June 12, 1943, 11.

203 **"largest production in the history":** R. Douglas Hurt, *The Great Plains During World War II* (Lincoln: University of Nebraska, 2008), 157.

204 **an open letter to Secretary Wickard:** "A Letter to Secretary Wickard" (dated December 26, 1941), *Farm Journal and Farmer's Wife*, February 1942, 14.

204   "We need more of your kind of plain talking": Mrs. H. L. (Lucile) Stevens to LB, January 23, 1942, OSU, Box 107.

204   "MORE POWER TO YOU": Raymond G. Nelson to LB, January 23, 1942, OSU, Box 107.

204   "We appreciate very much": G. A. Dustman to LB, January 13, 1942, OSU, Box 107.

204   planting "Victory Gardens": "Garden Club Hears Louis Bromfield," MNJ, April 11, 1942.

204   22 million of which were planted: "Victory Gardens," *Encyclopedia of War & American Society*, ed. Peter Karsten (New York: MTM, 2005), 874.

205   "had not been harvested" and were now "lost": LB to Henry Wallace, December 6, 1942, Henry A. Wallace Papers, University of Iowa Libraries.

205   "frozen by some bureau in Washington": Maury Klein, *A Call to Arms: Mobilizing America for World War II* (New York: Bloomsbury, 2013), 579–80.

205   intense four-page, typewritten letter: LB to Wallace, December 6, 1942.

206   "very thought-provoking" and "I am halfway minded": Wallace to LB, December 21, 1942, Iowa.

206   "She was inclined to laugh if off": LB to Henry Wallace, December 26, 1942, OSU, Box 108.

206   machinery had been cut by 80 percent . . . 1.5 million farmhands had been drafted: Klein, *Call to Arms*, 578.

206   "incompetent," "absurdities," and "From a Democrat": LB, "Food Situation Called Grim," NYT, February 11, 1943.

206   "My Children and I": ER, "My Day," March 20, 1942, The Eleanor Roosevelt Papers Digital Edition (2017), accessed June 3, 2019, https://www2.gwu.edu/~erpapers/myday/displaydoc.cfm?_y=1942&_f=md056138.

207   "Louie, whom I believe you know quite well": Eugene Casey to ER, October 20, 1943, Eleanor Roosevelt Papers, Box 1208, FDR Presidential Library.

207   "at any price" and "Not even a tramp": LB, "Results of U.S. Muddling Shown at Malabar Farm," *Akron Beacon Journal*, February 19, 1943.

208   conditions on the home front: Klein, *Call to Arms*, 581–91.

209   "starvation rations" . . . "By December this year": LB, "It's a Farmer's War, Too."

209 "We are already rationed": LB, "We Aren't Going to Have Enough to Eat," *Reader's Digest*, August 1943, 111.

210 dairy farmers were setting new highs . . . hogs were going to market: Klein, *Call to Arms*, 592.

210 "strong-arm methods": LB, "Bromfield Raps 'Bungling' of Food Situation in U.S. By Roosevelt Government," *Cincinnati Enquirer*, August 20, 1944.

211 "phonies" and "wonderful guys": Gerald Duchovnay, *Humphrey Bogart: A Bio-bibliography* (Westport, CT: Greenwood Press, 1999), 96.

212 "One of my mother's favorite Venetian lamps": *Heritage*, 107.

212 "There was no way Bogie and I": Lauren Bacall, *By Myself* (New York: Knopf, 1978), 129.

212 "Dear Father Bromberg": A. M. Sperber and Eric Lax, *Bogart* (New York: William Morrow, 1997), 301.

213 "a very tall man" . . . "Malabar was more beautiful": Bacall, *By Myself*, 139, 147–48.

214 "buying himself out of the marriage": Sperber and Lax, *Bogart*, 302.

214 "Great" . . . "Cameras were whipped out": Bacall, *By Myself*, 153–57.

216 "Every photographer in the world was there": Sperber and Lax, *Bogart*, 306.

217 "The picture was always complete": Bacall, *By Myself*, 148.

12: Erosion

218 "The trouble with the animals on this farm": *PV*, 229.

219 "the happiest of men": Ibid., 146.

219 "A farm is always in some kind of tizzy": E. B. White, "Malabar Farm," *NYER*, May 8, 1948, 104.

220 "lots of money" and "translated into every language": *PV*, 50.

220 "literary tragedy": Sinclair Lewis, "The Boxers of M. Voltaire," *Esquire*, October 1945, 78–79.

221 "trashy stuff": H. L. Mencken, "Louis Bromfield," typescript, NYPL.

221 wrote to Bromfield in advance: Ross to LB, April 3, 1944, *New Yorker* Papers, NYPL.

221 "Don't worry about Eddie": LB to Ross, April 11, 1944, ibid.

221 cut Bromfield to the quick: EBG, interview with the author, January 2019.

221   "simply a way of making a living": *FME*, 4.

222   "Here's your humus, mucus, retch and vetch" and "dreadful, hogwash-preaching": *Heritage*, 153–54.

223   "You, Mr. B.": Lord, *Forever the Land: A Country Chronicle and Anthology* (New York: Harper, 1950), 196.

223   "To pry into the privacy" and dead of a heart attack: *Heritage*, 157–58.

223   One of the owners of the "21" club: Mac Kriendler to LB, April 19, 1948, OSU, Box 106.

224   "Your telegram late last night": Hugh Bennett to LB, April 12, 1948, ibid.

225   "They keep him alive": MB to LB, u.d. letter, ibid.

225   "incomprehensible" . . . "You have no idea": *Heritage*, 159.

225   graduated from an agricultural institute in Wales: 2003 interview with David Rimmer by Joseph M. Ciccone, Doris Duke Oral History Collection, Duke.

226   "All the shrubbery": LB to EBG, u.d. letter, OSU, Box 105.

13: Four Seasons at Malabar

227   "people and bustle and sociability": *MF,* 102.

228   "We're not interested in pedigrees": Ibid., 28.

228   "they only nuzzle the hay": Ibid., 92.

230   tree frogs crying out : LB, *Animals and Other People* (New York: Harper, 1955), 189.

230   "The question of whether there will be a killing frost": u.d. journal entry ("Easter Sunday"), OSU, Box 124.

230   "When this happens": *MF,* 166.

232   "kind of kindergarten" and Blondy: Ibid., 34, 200.

232   "as delicate as a Cellini bird": LB, u.d. journal entry ("October fifth"), OSU, Box 52.

232   "gaudily painted miniature planes": *MF*, 82.

233   the Ferguson Place: Ibid., 16–17.

233   "Sometimes they brushed my head": LB, *Animals and Other People*, 165.

234   "Them that works, eats" and "glorified tomato juice": *Heritage*, 105.

234   Twenty thousand people visit: "Louis Bromfield," *Chicago Tribune,* March 20, 1956.

234 summer is the busiest season: LB, u.d. journal entry ("August 8"), OSU, Box 124.

234 "quick look around" and "faithful tribe": *Heritage*, 130–31.

234 Mount Jeez is not only for sermonizing: LB, u.d. journal entry ("August first"), OSU, Box 124.

235 "A violation" . . . "diverse selection": *MF*, 13.

235 "scarcely loud enough" and "the natural clown": Ibid., 12.

236 "deft at catching cray fish": LB, u.d. journal entry ("Last year we found . . .), OSU, Box 52.

237 "fresh, young": *MF*, 16.

237 "I am sure the Lord understands": Ibid., 35.

238 "People came to say" : Ibid., 173–75.

14: On the Hill

239 Some of the first serious congressional hearings: The House Select Committee to Investigate the Use of Chemicals in Food Products examined the risks of pesticides and chemical food additives during forty-six days of hearings in Washington and other cities in 1950 and 1951 that produced over 2,700 pages of testimony. Christopher J. Bosso, *Pesticides and Politics* (Pittsburgh: University of Pittsburgh Press, 1987), 75.

239 birds falling from the sky: "DDT Found to Harm Birds," *Tampa Tribune*, June 11, 1949.

239 poisoned fish: "Farm and AAA News from the County Agent," *Fort Payne Journal* (Alabama), September 12, 1945.

239 a rosarian with intestinal hemorrhaging: Malcolm O. Herzog to LB, August 1, 1951, OSU, Box 108.

239 young turkeys: *Chemicals in Food Products: Hearings Before the House Select Committee to Investigate the Use of Chemicals in Food Products* (Washington, DC: US Government Printing Office, 1951), 256.

240 the same substance in meat: Ibid., 251.

240 "I am not interested in rats": Rep. Arthur L. Miller said this on a May 10 hearing to L. E. Harris, a professor at the Utah State Agricultural College. Ibid., 252.

240 33 to 106 million pounds: *Federal Pesticide Control Act of 1971: Hearings Before the Committee on Agriculture, House of Representatives, Ninety-*

Second Congress (Washington, DC: US Government Printing Office, 1971), 845.

240   **"Mr. Bromfield, will you come forward":** *Chemicals*, 289.

241   **"on a base of lethal poisons" and "boomed as the panacea":** LB, "Preventative Medicine Need of Industry, Writer Says," *Cincinnati Enquirer*, September 30, 1945. Bromfield was hardly the only one in America who issued stark warnings about DDT long before *Silent Spring*. See Elena Conis, "Beyond Silent Spring: An Alternate History of DDT," *Distillations*, February 14, 2017, accessed August 13, 2019, https://www.sciencehistory.org/distillations/beyond-silent-spring-an-alternate-history-of-ddt.

241   **"Put in the simplest terms" and a special "label":** *Chemicals*, 291–301.

243   **"choke with rage" and "*ex-cathedra* pronouncements":** Clayton S. Ellsworth, "Ceres and the American Men of Letters since 1929," *Agricultural History* 24, no. 4 (1950): 181.

243   **cancer, Parkinson's, and other diseases:** Katarina Zimmer, "How Toxic Is the World's Most Popular Weedkiller Roundup?," *TheScientist.com*, February 7, 2018, accessed June 5, 2019, https://www.the-scientist.com/news-opinion/how-toxic-is-the-worlds-most-popular-herbicide-roundup-30308. Debate continues on the health risks of glyphosate. In 2015, a scientific body of the World Health Organization concluded that it is "probably carcinogenic" (adding it to the same category as red meat); other recent studies have found links to Parkinson's and shortened pregnancy lengths.

243   **300 million pounds per year:** Shahid Parvez et al., "Glyphosate Exposure in Pregnancy and Shortened Gestational Length: A Prospective Indiana Birth Cohort Study," *Environmental Health* 17, no. 1 (2018): 23.

243   **"living soils into dead ones":** LB, *Out of the Earth*, 65.

243   **"the organic people have much more evidence":** LB, "Foundation for Life," NYT, January 19, 1947, Book Review.

244   **"any other poison":** *MF*, 245.

244   **adapted form of his composting methods:** *FME*, 326. LB was not in the purist "organic school," but Albert Howard's widow, Louise, among other important figures in the British organic farming group the Soil Association, saw him as an ally. "No one has done more for the things we stand for," Louise told him. L. Howard to LB, September 30, 1950, OSU, Box 93.

244   **economically unfeasible:** The influential "beyond organic" farmer Joel Salatin believes that Bromfield only resorted to chemical fertilizer because large-scale organic methods were expensive and impractical in his time.

"If he were alive today, I do not doubt that he would become more pure with regards to chemicals." Salatin, interview with the author, April 2019.

244 **"Very often lime and chemical fertilizer":** LB, "Foundation for Life."

244 **dropping the word "farming":** Andrew N. Case, *The Organic Profit: Rodale and the Making of Marketplace Environmentalism* (Seattle: University of Washington Press, 2018), 39.

244 **"He was quite envious":** Ibid., 34.

244 **"shaky credentials" and "excellent and very important":** Ibid., 19, 37–41.

244 **"cultist":** Carlton Jackson, *J. I. Rodale: Apostle of Nonconformity* (New York: Pyramid, 1974), 76.

245 **nearly 1 million:** Gregory A. Barton, *The Global History of Organic Farming* (Oxford University Press, 2018), 171.

246 **Maybe they could raise apples and "neither *in* nor *out*":** *MF*, 47–48.

246 **The advantages of "grass farming":** Bromfield called grass "the great healer" and was among the first to popularize "grass farming" in the United States (*MF*, 107–58). The method, formalized by the French agronomist André Voisin, has been promoted more recently by Allan Nation and Salatin, among others (Michael Pollan, *The Omnivore's Dilemma* [New York: Penguin, 2007], 187–91). In addition to the health benefits of grass-fed milk and meat, grass farming, when done properly, conserves soil and sequesters carbon.

247 **"All of this money":** LB, *Out of the Earth*, 171.

247 **The "horror" of being poor:** *Farm*, 182.

248 **a net loss of nearly $15,000:** Dick Moser to LB (Schedule of Farm Income and Expenses 1953), May 14, 1954, OSU, Box 100.

248 **"A person cultivating":** Chauncey Belknap to LB, October 17, 1939, OSU, Box 100.

248 **"If the farm always runs at a loss":** Belknap to George Hawkins, May 10, 1945, OSU, Box 100. This letter lists farm losses for the first six years of Malabar: 1939 ($9,014.10); 1940 ($9,087.65); 1941 ($6,495.57); 1942 ($3,579.29); 1943 ($10,163.91); and 1944 ($11,569.31).

15: Breeding

251 **"fat perspiring Jew" . . . "offensive smell":** *GBT*, 5.

251 **"When one went to play":** *Farm*, 158.

252 **"HELP Prevent 4,000,000 People":** Advertisement, NYT, November 5, 1943.

252 "ACTION—NOT PITY": Advertisement, NYT, February 8, 1943.

253 "THE NAZIS ARE RAPIDLY": Telegram, LB to ER, June 21, 1943, Eleanor Roosevelt Papers, Box 852, FDR Presidential Library.

253 "I have your telegram": ER to LB, June 25, 1943, Ibid.

254 War Refugee Board and Bergsonites shifted their priorities: Kai Bird, *Crossing the Mandelbaum Gate: Coming of Age Between the Arabs and Israelis 1956–1978* (New York: Scribner, 2010), 356–62.

254 "handful of backward, miserable, uncivilized people": LB, "Oil Seen Behind Palestine Muddle," *Cincinnati Enquirer*, December 1, 1946.

254 "To the great, famous": Menachem Begin inscription to *The Revolt* (1950), MF Papers.

255 "The cure for all of these racial differences": *MF*, 405.

255 Carson Zachary Geld: EBG, unpublished essay (provided to the author); Kenneth Geld, interview with the author, May 2019.

256 "With a grinding of steel" . . . "circling him cautiously": *Heritage*, 168–69.

256 "Probably no *goy* in the world" . . . "I do not know": LB to EBG, u.d. letter, OSU, Box 105.

257 "tall, gentle, strongly determined" and "It's a hell of a thing": *Heritage*, 167.

257 He planned the wedding: LB, "Christmas Wedding in the Country," typescript, OSU, Box 9.

257 "with the kind of elegance": *Heritage*, 167.

258 "It would have been very easy": Carson Geld to LB, u.d. letter ("Wednesday"), OSU, Box 105.

259 "noxious weed" . . . "Typical of his business": *Heritage*, 170–73.

259 "About El": MB to LB, March 3 [1952], OSU, Box 106.

260 "as an inheritance that might be": *Forgotten*, 550.

260 "I have thought of you": Edna Ferber to LB, November 29, 1951, OSU, Box 107.

260 "Are you taking care of yourself?": MB to LB, u.d. letter, OSU, Box 106.

261 "peace touched with sadness" . . . "not knowing how": *Heritage*, 179–80.

262 "To Mary (still Alice in Wonderland)": Handwritten dedication to *The Wild Country* (1948), MF Papers.

262 "selling this way": LB to EBG, u.d. letter, OSU, Box 105.

262 "There is no point": *FME*, 314–15.

264 "More and more often": *Heritage*, 182–83.

264 "When I think of you": Ibid., 182–83, 188.

16: Unto the Ground

266 **formal gardens, nine lakes, heated stables:** Stephanie Mansfield, *The Richest Girl in the World: The Extravagant Life and Fast Times of Doris Duke* (New York: G. P. Putnam's Sons, 1992), 19–21.

266 **"It is very difficult to think":** LB to DD, u.d. letter, Duke.

266 **"Daddy may have felt":** Mansfield, *Richest*, 217.

266 **"She used to tell people":** Pony Duke and Jason Thomas, *Too Rich: The Family Secrets of Doris Duke* (New York: HarperCollins, 1996), 144.

267 **the nature and extent of their bond:** Mansfield, *Richest*, 216–17; interview with Sallie Bingham (author of the 2020 biography of DD, *The Silver Swan*), February 2019.

267 **"We met everybody":** Mansfield, *Richest*, 217.

267 **Rimmer eventually would be hired:** 2003 interview with David Rimmer by Joseph M. Ciccone, Doris Duke Oral History Collection, Duke. Rimmer worked for Duke from 1958 to 1967.

267 **"perfect health":** LB, "Louis Bromfield," NYHT, October 7, 1951, sec. E.

267 **"the heart and constitution of an ox":** LB to DD, postmarked February 1956, Duke.

267 **A few weeks later he fell ill . . . "hollowed-eyed":** *Forgotten*, 603–4.

267 **"I am not a bit surprised":** EBG to LB, u.d. letter, OSU, Box 105.

268 **"The whole medical profession" . . . "My suggestion is this":** LB to DD, u.d. letter, Duke.

268 **"Miss Duke has had hospital training":** LB to Mrs. Annie Rimmer, u.d. letter (c. December 1955), Mansfield Public Library, Sherman Reading Room.

269 **"If I am out of order":** C. J. Solomon to DD, January 18, 1956, Duke.

269 **"I can never be grateful enough":** LB to DD, February 1956, ibid.

270 **"The yellow acacia tree":** EBG to LB, u.d. letter (c. February 1956), OSU, Box 105.

270 **an ill-fated George Balanchine ballet:** LB once sketched his vision of the Johnny Appleseed ballet in a letter. This "American folk-tale" would climax with the death of Johnny "in springtime under a flowering apple tree." The Indians should be "garbed as they were in the absurd plays of Voltaire with ostrich plume headdresses" and Johnny's "steady companion" should be "a very chic black and white lady skunk (done by Bergdorf

Goodman)." LB to Lincoln Kirstein, u.d letter (c. 1955), NYPL for the Performing Arts.

270   "We are collaborating bar by bar": LB to DD, February 1956, Duke.

270   cut down some timber: Duke later donated money to preserve the trees, which is why a section of forest at Malabar Farm State Park is today called the Doris Duke Woods.

271   "whether drunk or ill": *Forgotten*, 631.

271   wired Harper for an advance: Telegram, LB to Ramona Herdman, Harper & Bros, March 5, 1956, OSU, Box 107.

271   "DO NOT COME": Telegram, Hope Bromfield Stevens to EBG, March 21, 1956, OSU, Box 107.

272   left in trust to his three children: LB's last will and testament, August 9, 1955, Richland County Courthouse.

Epilogue: The White Room

274   "In the large sense": Liberty Hyde Bailey, *Universal Service* (Ithaca, NY: Comstock, 1919), 145.

274   Malabar-do-Brasil and "We had tremendous pride": *Heritage*, 185–87.

275   1,700-acre farm, "virtually against [his] wishes," "*'Pusha la vida!'*": *FME*, 112–13, 142.

276   "Now we saw one another": EBG, *Heritage*, 189.

277   "A Somewhat Serious" . . . "direct living": *FME*, 336–41.

277   "gigantic scheme" and "that had nothing to do with": LB, *Animals and Other People*, 64.

278   "dangling in midair" . . . "the universe and all": Albert Schweitzer, *Out of My Life and Thought* (New York: Henry Holt, 2014), 154–57.

279   "the bursting of a rocket" . . . "for he lives": *FME*, 345–49.

280   Nanny died in the early 1960s . . . Bob died in 2014 and Hope two years later: Melanie Read (Hope Bromfield Stevens's daughter), interview with the author, May 2019.

280   Ellen and Carson left Malabar-do-Brasil: Kenneth Geld, interview with the author, May 2019.

281   Fazenda Malabar and DuLocal: Felipe Gasko, interview with the author, January 2019.

281   raised $140,000 to buy the farm: Anneliese Abbott, "Historic Soil Con-

servation at Malabar Farm, 1939–1972," Honors thesis, Ohio State University, 2016. Retrieved from http://hdl.handle.net/1811/76518. This excellent history covers the murky period between Bromfield's death and Ohio's acquisition of Malabar in 1972.

281   **the study of "man's relation to his environment":** Ibid., 62, 106.

282   **Malabar is still a working farm:** Brian Miller, Ohio State Department of Natural Resources, interview with the author, April 2019.

283   **"This is for me":** Roman Popadiuk, *The Leadership of George Bush: An Insider's View of the Forty-First President* (College Station: Texas A&M University, 2013), 10.

283   **"No matter how we looked at it":** Ellie LeBlond Sosa and Kelly Anne Chase, *George & Barbara Bush: A Great American Love Story* (Camden, ME: Down East Books, 2018), 95.

283   **"Well, sir, that little book":** "Organic Apples: The A. P. Thomson Interview," *Mother Earth News*, January/February 1981, accessed June 7, 2019, https://www.motherearthnews.com/homesteading-and-livestock/organic-apples-zmaz81jfzraw.

283   **J. David Bamberger gave up his position:** Interview with the author, April 2019.

283   **Davis Bynum quit his career as a newspaper reporter:** Peg Melnik, "Visionary Sonoma County Viticulturalist Davis Bynum Dies at 92," *Press Democrat* (Santa Rosa, CA), December 3, 2017, accessed June 7, 2019, https://www.pressdemocrat.com/news/7718891-181/visionary-sonoma-county-viticulturalist-davis.

284   **"I can do this":** Salatin, interview with the author.

284   **"I am still grateful"** . . . **"economic necessity":** Wendell Berry, "For the Love of Farming," *Farming*, Summer 2009, 58.

285   **"worst element of our agriculture":** LB, "Misleading Figure," *San Bernardino County Sun*, January 22, 1956.

285   **"the best system I know":** LB, "The Great Corn Illusion Robs Taxpayer and Farmer and the Soil," *Decatur Herald*, October 1, 1949.

285   **"vicious and destructive tyrant":** Ibid.

285   **"the most expensive feed":** LB, *Out of the Earth* (New York: Harper, 1950), 182.

285   **less than 3 percent:** "The Healthy Farmland Diet: How Growing Less Corn Would Improve our Health and Help America's Heartland," 2013

report, Union of Concerned Scientists, accessed August 12, 2019, https://
www.ucsusa.org/sites/default/files/legacy/assets/documents/food_and_
agriculture/healthy-farmland-diet.pdf.

285 **each year we use more and more of it:** "World Trends and Fertilizer
Outlook to 2020: Summary Report," Food and Agriculture Organization
of the United Nations, 2017, accessed August 13, 2019, http://www.fao
.org/3/a-i6895e.pdf, 2–3.

286 **"ludicrous and a little pathetic":** *FME*, 6.

286 **"always existed for me in two manifestations":** *PV*, 2.

Credits

Index